Dedication

This book is dedicated to the Certified LSM Eagle Teachers (Level I and Level II) who have chosen to study this information in a training setting so as to teach it to others. They are now out there in the trenches of the world, helping others to understand the value of the Keys of the Kingdom—binding and loosing. These keys of prayer make it possible to stop allowing the past to argue with your life today. Winston Churchill once said, "When you allow your past to argue with your present, you lose your future." Together, these teachers and I are laboring to let the body of Christ know that there are keys to unlocking the past's hold on all of our lives. We have a glorious future with Christ, and part of that future is going to happen right here on earth. I have special gratitude to those LSM Eagle Teachers who have contributed to this book in unique ways. In particular, I would like to thank:

Linda Cady of Sacramento, California, Level II Teacher, for her courageous work on new understanding on the strong man.

Carla Clark of Atlanta, Georgia, Level II Teacher, for her brilliant ideas on teaching children how to understand their own unsurrendered souls and how to pray with the Keys of the Kingdom.

Robert Little of Vacaville, California, Level II Teacher, and Nancy Rankin of Corpus Christi, Texas, Level II Teacher, who introduced me to Dr. Soul Care and who also helped me with several other ideas in this book.

Dawn Veldman, Ontario, Canada, Level I Teacher, whose contributions are greatly appreciated.

The
Unsurrendered
SOUL

Liberty Savard

Bridge-Logos

Orlando, Florida 32822

Bridge-Logos
Orlando, FL 32822 USA

The Unsurrendered Soul
by Liberty Savard

Printed in the United States of America.

Library of Congress Catalog Card Number: 2006931486
International Standard Book Number 0-88270-880-5

G163.318x.MB.m607.35230

Contents

Introduction vii

1 Things Are Not Always What They Seem 1

2 Diagnosis: Born-Again, Unsurrendered, and Earthen 19

3 X-Ray of the Soul's Distress 41

4 Façades and Wrong Behaviors 69

5 Fine-Tuned Prayer Principles that Mend and Heal 93

6 Mother in a Mine Field 117

7 Woman with a Mission 145

8 Obedience and Surrender 171

9 Power Leadership—Surrendered Souls with
   Servant Attitudes 203

10 Agree with God and Just Do It! 235

Appendix 1: Teaching Others About the Keys 249

Appendix 2: Teaching Kids About the Keys 273

Glossary 303

Introduction

Do you really feel excited every minute about God? Are you filled with anticipation of what God will ask of you next, or do you fear it instead? Do you feel put upon and duped by scriptural promises that have never manifested answers or blessings in your life? Do you feel overwhelmed and overworked by what you think God wants from you?

Here are the words Apostle Paul wrote to the Galatian Christians (and to you and me) two thousand years ago. God knew that you would need to understand this today:

"Something crazy has happened, for it's obvious that you no longer have the crucified Jesus in clear focus in your lives. His sacrifice on the Cross was certainly set before you clearly enough. Let me put this question to you: How did your new life begin? Was it by working your heads off to please God? Or was it by responding to God's Message to you? Are you going to continue this craziness? For only crazy people would think they could complete by their own efforts what was begun by God. If you weren't smart enough or strong enough to begin it, how do you suppose you could perfect it? Did you go through this whole painful learning process for nothing?

"It is not yet a total loss, but it certainly will be if you keep this up! Answer this question: Does the God who lavishly provides you with his own presence, his Holy Spirit, working things in your lives you could never do for yourselves, does he do these things because of your strenuous moral striving or because you trust him to do them in you?" (Galatians 3:1-5, The Message)

"Anyone who tries to live by his own effort, independent of God, is doomed to failure. Scripture backs this up: 'Utterly cursed is every person who fails to carry out every detail written in the Book of the law.' The obvious impossibility of carrying out such a moral program should make it plain that no one can sustain a relationship with God that way. The person who lives in right relationship with God does it by embracing what God arranges for him. Doing things for God is the opposite of entering into what God does for you .... Rule keeping does not naturally evolve into living by faith, but only perpetuates itself in more and more rule keeping, a fact observed in Scripture: 'The one who does these things (rule keeping) continues to live by them'" (Galatians 3:10-12, *The Message*).

"I tried keeping rules and working my head off to please God, and it didn't work. So I quit being a 'law man' so that I could be God's man. Christ's life showed me how and enabled me to do it. I identified myself completely with him. Indeed, I have been crucified with Christ. My ego is no longer central" (Galatians 2:17-21 *The Message*).

The Apostle Paul was quite frustrated that these early day Christians were forgetting their freedom in Christ and falling back into the old ways of religiosity. Here we are, two thousand years later, believers doing exactly the same thing today. As Solomon said, *"There is nothing new under the sun."*

The early Christians' unsurrendered souls pulled them away from the knowledge of freedom in Christ, encouraging them to work for their salvation. Today, unsurrendered souls of believers are still working Christians to death doing things for the church, chaperoning youth trips, serving on committees for the Men's Group, and making pies for the Missionary Bake Sale. And that was just on last Friday! Am I saying these things are wrong? Absolutely not. While these "works" are good and increase your value to your church, they will never make you more valuable to God.

The truth is that after you are born again, no amount of hard work in your church or outside of it can make God love you more.

The incredible flip side of that truth is that no amount of failure in your church or outside of it can make Him love you any less! You are one of the beloved kids of the almighty, omnipotent, omniscient, omnipresent God of everything—one of His kids right here on earth. He loves you regardless of the struggles your unsurrendered soul keeps having. You just need to know what to do to get your soul off the throne of your life before that rascal works you to death trying to self-validate itself.

The Plan

The inner workings of the unsurrendered soul are the cause of the Christian's daily conflict over obeying God. The treatment for that is to make your soul surrender! In Matthew 5:3, Jesus said, *"Blessed are the poor in spirit, for theirs is the kingdom of heaven."* If we used the original Greek word meanings here, this verse would read, "Blessed are those who are willing to choose to give up all of their souls' personal agendas and wrong beliefs, for theirs is the kingdom of heaven." Jesus Christ left us the Keys of the Kingdom to help us to demolish and break up those very self-agendas.

In Matthew 16:19, Jesus said, *"I will give you the keys of the kingdom of heaven; whatever you bind on earth will be bound in heaven; and whatever you loose on earth will be loosed in heaven"* (*NIV*).

In 1985, the Lord began speak to me of an exciting new revelation regarding binding and loosing. I did not have any internet access in 1985, or much access to spiritual resource books, and I had almost no human support. In fact, my pastor told me he was very concerned about how I was praying because he was afraid I was going to get hurt. I have always tended to attack new understanding like a brakeless Zamboni on a frozen lake—in full-slide mode!

I eagerly began binding my will to the will of God, binding my mind to the mind of Christ, and binding myself to the whole truth of the Word. Then I started using the loosing key in my prayers and things began to shake! I found that loosing was a magnificent prayer word!

It was the key of binding that held me steady and stabilized me as the shaking began. As presented in all of my other books, using the key of binding in prayer means that you are:

- Stabilizing yourself,
- Steadying your walk,
- Seat belts are fastened, and your
- Safety harness is in place!

This is good. All too often radical change in our lives causes instability and rockiness that startles us. That is why you need His safety harness and seat belt—to hold you steady until things settle. These principles of prayer ARE GUARANTEED to bring radical life change for the better.

When you pray using the loosing key, you enact a powerful spiritual action that results in:

- Shattering strongholds,
- Smashing and slashing deception,
- Self-surgery, and
- Spiritual warfare!

My other books, particularly the Keys of the Kingdom Trilogy, have extensive Greek and Hebrew definitions of the binding and loosing words from the Bible's original languages. For here, I would like to include just a quick list so that you have some idea of the power of the principles you are reading about and getting ready to use.

TO BIND means to undergird, heal, hold, persuade, steady, cause fragmented pieces to come back into one whole, put oneself under obligation, and cling to. I have also found several other words used in our English translations of the Scriptures that mean bind. For instance, Paul said, *"For I am persuaded, that neither death, nor life, nor angels, nor principalities, nor powers, nor things present, nor things to come, nor height, nor depth, nor any other creature, shall be able to separate us from the love of God, which is in Christ Jesus our Lord"* (Romans 8:38-39, *KJV*). The word "persuaded" as used here comes from the Greek word *peitho* (pi'-tho), which means to bind to, to be allied with, to rely upon. Paul so knew this to be true, he was bound to the truth of it.

TO LOOSE means untie, break up, destroy, dissolve, melt, put off, wreck, crack to sunder by separation of the parts, shatter into minute fragments, disrupt, lacerate, convulse with spasms, break forth, burst, rend, and tear up. Now that's powerful! To loose also means to set at liberty. As you pray with this key, you can begin to dissolve the roots of any bitterness in your soul, you can thoroughly disrupt the recycling of negative thoughts in your mind, you can burst open the deception and half-truths your soul clings to, and you can tear up your soul's garbage-collecting habits.

The only small problem I have seen with the loosing prayers is that some people become so enamored with the powerful process of loosing these things, they just keep loosing and loosing. They fail to recognize that they have been set free. This is like the dog that has always been chained with a twelve-foot chain. When he is older, the chain can be removed and the dog will never voluntarily go beyond twelve feet from the stake that held the chain. If you pick the dog up and take him outside of that twelve-foot radius, he gets nervous. More than once I have had to insist that some people just need to step out of their old residue and fallen walls, get past the length of their former "chains," and get on with their destinies!

The Apostle John said in 1 John 3:8 that "... *the reason the Son of God appeared was to destroy the devil's work*" (*NIV*). The word "destroy" in this verse is the same Greek word (*luo*) used in Matthew 16:19 to mean loose. Jesus Christ appeared to the world to loose, crush, smash, and destroy the bondage of Satan's darkness from mankind. Now, you and I are to go and do likewise with the Keys of the Kingdom that He has given to us! We are to do it in both our own lives and the lives of others. An important thing to remember as you read the Bible or this book are these words:

- Knowledge is knowing what the facts are.
- Wisdom is knowing what to do with those facts.
- Integrity is DOING IT and following through!

So get ready to just do it! Using these keys to bring freedom is definitely doable.

Some people ask if there are any examples in the Bible of Jesus using the binding and loosing keys in prayer. I believe the purpose of these keys (as it appears that J. B. Phillips did as well, according to his introduction written for the *Interlinear KJV-NIV Parallel New Testament in Greek and English* by Alfred Marshall) is that these keys allow us to pray in agreement with God's already established will in heaven. Since Jesus was always in agreement with the will of His Father, He didn't need to do any slashing, cutting, and shattering in His soul to make it surrender. The keys were really just for us. Jesus said, *"I will give YOU the keys of the kingdom ...."*

The Gap

Unfortunately, the biggest gap in the world often stands between what we should do and what we actually do. If we all did what we should do, we'd all be walking in great abundance, joy, peace, and power. One non-believer said that if we did what we should do, we'd all be rich, skinny, and happy!

- This book contains keys to doing what you need to do.
- This book helps you begin doing what you should do.
- This book shows you how to surrender your unsurrendered soul.
- This book shows you how to help others to do the same thing.

Once your soul is surrendered, you won't need anyone to tell you what to do anymore. You will know that you know that the Answer to every question and situation resides in your born-again spirit and is longing to reside in your surrendered soul as well. Once you understand how to surrender everything about yourself to His loving will and His good ways, you will become united—body, soul, and spirit—with His plans and purposes. You will become the recipient of all that God has for you.

"As it is written: 'Eye has not seen, nor ear heard, nor have entered into the heart of man the things which God has prepared for those who love Him'" (1 Corinthians 2:8-9, NKJV).

There is nothing we can think of that we would like to have from God that comes anywhere close to what He actually wants to give us. We can't even imagine what He wants us to have—it is so new, so fresh, so big, and so incredible! So, what are you waiting for? Let's get ourselves ready to enjoy our God and the glorious future He has always planned for us to walk out.

one

Things Are Not Always
What They Seem

C an you imagine anything sweeter than being in perfect agreement with whatever God wants for you, from you, and through you? If we know this would be so good, why do so many Christians find themselves in constant conflict over doing so? Because they are still stuck in the first stage of transitioning out of their old creatures' past into their new creatures' life. Our "old" creatures seem to exist in a "virtual reality" time warp of our pasts. Our "now" creatures struggle to keep from stumbling all over themselves and falling off the path while trying to learn how to do this "walking in the Spirit" thing we're all supposed to do. And our "new" creatures' lifes often seems beyond reach out there somewhere in a fuzzy, out-of-focus future. Yet the Word of God says, *"Therefore, if anyone is in Christ, he is a new creation; old things have passed away; behold, all things have become new"* (Corinthians 5:17, *NKJV*).

Many Christians realize that there is a transition from the old creature to the new creature that needs to happen and that a doable process of change probably exists. But less of them than you would think understand how to successfully interact with that process. The struggle with this old-to-new transition is not a new problem of these times; it has always been so since the fall of man in the Garden of Eden. The Apostle Paul struggled mightily with this very same conflict of moving out of the old into the new. Paul, already faithfully serving

1

God with signs and wonders following him, made himself very transparent when he admitted his struggles:

> *"What I don't understand about myself is that I decide one way, but then I act another, doing things I absolutely despise. I obviously need help! I realize that I don't have what it takes. I can will it, but I can't do it. I decide to do good, but I don't really do it; I decide not to do bad, but then I do it anyway. My decisions, such as they are, don't result in actions … I truly delight in God's commands, but it's pretty obvious that not all of me joins in that delight. Parts of me covertly rebel, and just when I least expect it, they take charge"* (Romans 7:15-24, *The Message*).

While this battle was distressing Paul greatly, he did not do what too many seem to do today when they feel defeated. He did not become discouraged and disheartened; he did not try to justify and rationalize his problem, nor did he seek sympathy and agreement with it. Paul knew that Jesus Christ was the answer to this dilemma, so he just kept pressing towards knowing Him better to end his dilemma.

GOOD NEWS: Jesus is THE answer.

NOT-SO-GOOD NEWS: We have to overcome our souls' self-declared civil war to get them lined up with our born-again spirits' knowledge of that fact!

Paul said to the Philippian *believers*: *"Wherefore, my beloved, as ye have always obeyed, not as in my presence only, but now much more in my absence, work out your own salvation with fear and trembling"* (Philippians 2:12, *KJV*). Paul was admonishing believers here, people whose spirits were already saved—people who had been born again. Paul told them there still was a working-out needed and it was a serious thing—it was to be done with fear and trembling. It was the salvation of their unsurrendered souls.

How About a Spiritual Coup d'etat?

Your unsurrendered soul believes it is the Ruler of Your Life, while actually giving a good impersonation of doing just that. This is not good at all, so might I suggest a revolution, a throwing out of the present ruling party? If your unsurrendered soul is not challenged and made to surrender, it will end up attracting unwanted allies in its war against your born-again spirit. Unless squashed, this civil war conflict within you can give the devil access to toss spiritual pipe bombs and Molotov cocktails through your soul's open doorways to ratchet up your anxiety and fear levels. Soulish rebellion and resistance from within and demonic harassment from without. Is it any wonder that we feel overwhelmed sometimes? The Word of God proclaims (through Paul's encouragement and instructions to the Roman Christians) that there is a freedom promised we can trust—we simply need to speak in agreement with it.

"The word is near you; it is in your mouth and in your heart, that is, the word of faith we are proclaiming: That if you confess ① *with your mouth, 'Jesus is Lord,' and believe in your heart that God raised him from the dead, you will be saved. For it is with your heart that you believe and are justified, and it is with your mouth that you confess and are saved. As the Scripture says, 'Anyone who trusts in him will never be put to shame'"* (Romans 10:8-11, NIV).

Victory comes through ① Proclaiming it ② Believing it. You must have both!

If you have confessed this, then your Lord—not that tiny sweet baby in a manger on your Christmas cards—but YOUR LORD, the KING OF KINGS, the MIGHTY WARRIOR, is ready to live His life through you! He is ready to flood His love and peace and victory and power through you. He comes knocking expectantly because your born-again spirit cried out its invitation to Him, but your unsurrendered soul growls, "Nobody home, go away." And your soul immediately begins raising all of its strongholds and walls of defense to keep Him out of its innermost parts. Your born-again spirit calls out, "That's not true, Jesus, we're here! We're in here."

Jesus just continues to stand at the door and knock. Someone has to be silenced here before He will come in and reign, and it is not your born-again spirit!

This book is designed to help you decrease your soul's control systems and make room within yourself so that Jesus can come in fully and flood your whole being—your body, soul, and spirit— increasing His life in you in every way. The Keys of the Kingdom, Matthew 16:19, will empower you to make it so with effective prayers of binding your soul to God's will and loosing all of its strongholds and barriers. Your part will be to choose to pray in such a way.

Understanding How We Got So Messed Up

Various Scriptures in Ephesians and Colossians tell us that we were born in pretty bad shape:

- Ephesians 2:1 (*NIV*) tells us we were dead in our transgressions and sin.
- Ephesians 2:12 (*NIV*) tells us we were separated from Christ, excluded from Israel, and without hope.
- Ephesians 4:18 (*NIV*) tells us we were darkened in our understanding and ignorant.
- Ephesians 5:8 (*NIV*) tells us we were once darkness.
- Colossians 1:21 (*NIV*) tells us we were alienated from God and enemies in our minds.

We came into this world like darkened little lumps of living clay with no shape or form. Think about the state of our dark little minds, the condition of our orphan spirits, and our inability to receive any guidance or understanding from God. Then think of those who molded and shaped our souls from the earliest moments, those who nurtured our ability to form ideas and draw conclusions. Our parents, authority figures, teachers, older siblings (many of whom had lived all their lives filled with darkened understanding and hopelessness) proceeded to help us the best they knew how to determine who we were, who others were, and who God was or was not.

We learned to draw all of our conclusions about ourselves, others, and God from these role models who were filled with darkened understanding themselves. Then we began to try to figure out other people who had darkened understanding and wrong ideas about themselves, us, and God. Can you see how some of your earliest basic beliefs and mindsets could be wrong? Who knows how much deception we were exposed to? Our unsurrendered souls can't tell us, because the very nature of deception is that it is always hidden from those who are deceived.

If a man was coerced into signing away his home and his life savings while he was coming out of heavy anesthesia in a hospital recovery room, no court in the world would hold him responsible for those documents. Nor are you held captive to the original darkened understanding and wrong beliefs that your soul has documented with such fierceness. Praying with the key of binding can position you to receive new information and truth, while praying with the key of loosing can weed out all of your old conclusions to ensure that you have room to receive that new information. You are going to get a brand new start on truth and goodness. Yahoo!

Heart and Soul

The word "heart" as used in the Bible almost always means the soul—the mind, will, and emotions. Psalms 86:11-12 tells us that David prayed, *"Teach me your way, O LORD, and I will walk in your truth; give me an undivided heart, that I may fear your name. I will praise you, O Lord my God, with all my heart; I will glorify your name forever" (NIV). Matthew Henry's Commentary on the Whole Bible* tells us this about these verses: "A hypocrite has a double heart; let mine (Author's note: *let my soul*) be single and entire for God, not divided between him and the world, not straggling from him. Our hearts (Author's note: *our souls*) are apt to wander and hang loose; their powers and faculties wander after a thousand foreign things; we have therefore need of God's grace to unite them, that we may serve God with all that is within us."

The real work of the surrender of the heart/soul becomes easier when we understand what it is up to. That nagging little feeling that all of us feel at times but cannot identify is often because our unsurrendered souls are in trouble and God is pushing us to accept His examination, testing, and healing. In Jeremiah 17:9-10, we read that God has said, *"The heart (soul) is deceitful above all things, and desperately wicked; who can know it? I, the LORD, search the heart (soul), I test the mind, even to give every man according to his ways, according to the fruit of his doings" (NKJV).*

The word "heart" in this verse means the mind, will, and emotions. The word "wicked" as used in this verse means frail, feeble, sick, and full of woe. Even the Old Testament prophets knew that the unsurrendered soul, the divided heart of unregenerated man, was weak, sick, and full of sadness. In its weakness and sickness, the desperate soul will resort to dangerous deception and trickery to get its way.

How Do You Discern Between Soul and Spirit?

All born-again believers have a surrendered, submitted, regenerated human spirit in communion with the Spirit of God. This is one issue that is settled and we can cling to it with certainty, no matter what else seems to be happening in our lives! Still, born-again believers often struggle with trying to force their human souls (minds, wills, emotions) to surrender their internal files of their traumatic memories, mindsets, wrong attitudes, and carnal understanding. We might realign our external behaviors and words to be thought acceptable by others, but we will never change until our perceptions, thought patterns, and understanding are surrendered to God's truth. It is very important to know when your unsurrendered soul is trying to deceive you by pretending to speak for your spirit. How can you tell whether you are being influenced by your unsurrendered soul (your old creature) or by your born-again spirit (your new creature) connected to the Spirit of the Father? Whenever you are feeling stressed, discouraged, upset, worried, frustrated, or angry—whether you are in denial or not—you are being influenced by your unsurrendered soul. These are the negative feelings of the unsurrendered soul's unhealed emotions.

When you are being influenced by your born-again spirit, you will always feel at least a tiny glimmer of hope, anticipation, and expectation of God showing up, regardless of the circumstances you are standing in the middle of. You can stand in a full-blown crisis and know that God will work everything out if—big IF—if you know how to shut out the negativity of your soul. The simplest way to do that is to stand still, forcing yourself to become as quiet as you can, and then pray and bind your mind to the mind of Christ and loose all wrong patterns of thinking that your soul is trying to run. You may need to do it more than once. If so, then repeat the steps above slowly and deliberately. These steps involve quieting the body (standing still), quieting the soul (loosing wrong patterns of thinking), and reaching out for Jesus' thoughts (binding your mind to His mind).

I have repeated these steps as many as three times which usually works for me. I would have no problem doing this more times, but three just works for me. Praying with these steps help you get your body, soul, and spirit into a position of quietness and listening for

Jesus' thoughts so you know what you should or should not do. Your soul has caused adrenaline to start pumping through your body while it has been chasing your mind, will, and emotions around and around like hens in a chicken coop with a fox in it, too.

Have you ever tried to round up spooked chickens? Achieving that goal can mean you have to take more than one swipe at them, sometimes making several passes at them, as chickens don't herd well in their best frame of mind. Your soul won't "herd" well either when it is in one of its worst frames of mind.

I want to address this next issue very carefully. Feeling "peace" is not always a sign that you are hearing from your born-again spirit. Some unsurrendered souls can learn how to deceive with false "peace." How often have you heard a Christian (who is clearly making a wrong choice) say, "I have the peace of God in my spirit about this."? False peace usually involves feeling "peaceful" about doing something the soul wants to do.

When the loving concern of others produces reactions of anger, hurt feelings, or agitation in the person making a questionable choice, then the person in question does not have the peace of God. When sincere and gentle questions are asked to try to clarify a person's thinking about a pending choice and are then resisted—the person becoming visibly upset (red flushing of the skin, averted eyes, increased breathing rate)—this person's "peace" about the pending choice would not be the peace of God.

Philippians 4:7 tells us, *"The peace of God, which transcends all understanding, will guard your hearts and your minds in Christ Jesus"* (NIV). James 3:17 tells us, *"The wisdom that is from above is first pure, then peaceable, gentle, willing to yield, full of mercy and good fruits, without partiality and without hypocrisy"* (NKJV).

Several years ago, I was very concerned about a choice one woman made to pursue a relationship with a backslidden Christian who was struggling with a drug addiction. The woman insisted that God had given her peace about this relationship. When I questioned her fairly closely about her choice and her "peace," she became very angry and accused me of trying to take her peace away from her. If your peace is truly from God, concerned questions cannot take it away from you. In fact, the Word says that the whole world cannot take it away from you.

Overcoming Discouragement and Despair

The next time you find yourself discouraged or filled with despair, remind yourself that these feelings will usually pass—especially when you expedite their passing. Cooperate with God by binding your will, mind, and emotions to the will of God, the mind of Christ, and the healing balance of the Holy Spirit. Loose wrong patterns of thinking, wrong mindsets, and the effects and influences of wrong agreements you have been affected by. This is how you begin to move discouragement and despair out of your soul.

Then occupy any space that has been created within your soul through these loosing prayers by beginning to read the encouraging verses of the Bible. Seek out a brother or sister in the Lord who is strong in faith. Paul told the Roman Christians:

"I long to see you so that I may impart to you some spiritual gift to make you strong—that is, that you and I may be mutually encouraged by each other's faith" (Romans 1:11-12, *NIV*).

Jesus Christ, who is the same yesterday, today, and tomorrow, said:

"What I'm trying to do here is get you to relax, not be so preoccupied with getting so you can respond to God's giving. People who don't know God and the way he works fuss over these things, but you know both God and how he works. Steep yourself in God-reality, God-initiative, God-provisions. You'll find all of your everyday human concerns will be met. Don't be afraid of missing out. You're my dearest friends! The Father wants to give you the very kingdom itself (Luke 12:29-32, *The Message*).

Realize that these negative emotions come out of your soul; they are not evil spirits. They are not part of your born-again spirit. They come from the darker side of your emotions, which are resident within your unsurrendered soul. God does not guide you by these darker emotions, nor does He ever direct you by fear—another powerful negative emotion. He will, however, allow your soul's collection of darker emotions to pressure you when you are resisting surrendering to Him. Struggle and conflicted emotions always mean that a Christian's soul is resisting God. Peace and hopefulness in spite of your circumstances mean that you are resting in God.

When you are feeling stressed or down, you will need to keep reminding yourself that you know you are in a soulish mode of thinking that is not your reality as a child of God! Your reality is that God loves you and has renewed your spiritual man who happens to be shoved into the background at the moment. Think of your soul as the Los Angeles Lakers defending their basket, and your regenerated spirit as the Sacramento Kings trying to sink a basket (Go Kings!).

If you are not an NBA fan, think of your soul as trying to enforce all of the hopelessness it is convinced is true and wants validated, while your spirit is trying to push forward all of the good things it knows that God wants you to experience. The reality of your situation and your life is that God knows right where you are and He is working on your behalf. You just need to clear out the old stuff and make room in your soul for God's peace and love to change the way you are thinking and the way you are feeling at the moment.

This is the diagnosis of your state of mind and emotions when your soul is in distress. This is not the natural state of a child of God. We all need to remember to position ourselves so as to be ready to receive peace from our Father in heaven. We do this every time we bind ourselves to the Father's will and loose all self-agendas and wrong beliefs of our own wills. We need to shed whatever things that are causing us to live below our inheritance rights—which we are doing every time we loose our souls' hold upon their wrong patterns of thinking and wrong ideas. This means we have to let go of our pasts, walk in the Spirit in our present moments, and anticipate unspeakable joy and blessing in the future.

A Lifestyle of Prayer

Praying the Keys of the Kingdom prayers once or twice will not undo a lifetime of your soul's pack-rat activities. Since you were old enough to form a negative thought, your soul has been filing away everything that has ever been said to you, done to you, and taken from you. You will need to pray with these keys every day, and you will need to support, cooperate with, and reinforce the good work they begin in you.

You need to regularly read the Word, memorizing your favorite verses so that you can quote them to yourself wherever you are. You should be aware that you need to break up the recycling patterns of your soul's negative thoughts the instant it begins to run them. One good way to do this is first pray:

"I bind my mind to your mind, Jesus, and I loose and shatter all of the recycling patterns of thinking that my soul is exercising. I loose all negative thoughts; I loose all critical and judgmental thought patterns. I need to hear your thoughts, Lord. Thank you for ~~helping~~ me. Amen."

[handwritten: living your life through]

Then begin to praise the Lord and sing your favorite Christian choruses. Praying, praising, and singing is a wonderful way to disrupt your soul's attempts to get its "stuff" together to launch a new onslaught of negativity at you.

[handwritten margin note: Key]

The unsurrendered human soul is thoroughly convinced that the entire human being belongs to it and it can run the whole show just fine, thank you! Strangely enough, this proves that the soul is doing what it was created to do—that is to manifest to the outer realm of life what it has accumulated in its inner realm. It gives out what it has stored up inside of its chambers.

"A good man out of the good treasure of his heart (the soul) *brings forth good; and an evil man out of the evil treasure of his heart* (the soul) *brings forth evil. For out of the abundance of the heart* (soul) *his mouth speaks"* (Luke 6:45, *NKJV*).

Unfortunately, most unsurrendered souls have an abundance of anger, fear, bad memories, traumatic happenings, unforgiveness, doubt, anxiety, and more stored up in themselves. Out of that negative abundance, they manifest what they are filled with. If you are going to live out a life of God-ordained impact upon this world, you need to let Him clean out all of the old and wrong "stuff" in your soul and replace it with His gifts and resources. Then your soul will manifest His gifts and resources to the outer realm of life around you. Proverbs

4:23 tells you to *"Keep your heart (soul) with all diligence, for out of it spring the issues of life" (NKJV)*.

God is very picky about where He is going to deliver those resources or spiritual gifts that you need. He will insist that you get rid of all of your soulish praying, soul power tactics, soulish coping mechanisms, soulish agendas and schemes, and sometimes even your soulish acquisitions of money, power, and influence before He begins to really bring in the best stuff. On paper right here, that sounds like a pretty good idea, doesn't it? That is not really too much to exchange for the abundant life that Jesus came to give us, now is it?

Ha! Just wait until your unsurrendered soul gets a good look at that list of what it has to give up—it will set off sirens, whistles, and fire bells in its rush to distract you from considering such foolishness (it thinks).

Are You Ready? *Yes now!*

If you are a relatively new Christian, these pages will help you get off on the right foot, helping you to understand why you need to overthrow the power of your unsurrendered soul early in your Christian walk. If you are a dissatisfied, wounded, fearful Christian, these pages will help you understand what is keeping you dissatisfied, wounded, and fearful so that you can break through to freedom in Him. If you are a Christian of many years who is seeking understanding of the deeper purposes of your living for God at this time, these pages will help you get a lifetime of clutter and residue out of your unsurrendered soul to get to those answers with God. In any case, I'm quite sure you are a believer with some degree of hunger to know more about God and His ways, or you would not even be reading these pages.

Get Ready For a Life Check Up

It is interesting that we will admit that we believe God had enough power to create the universe—including the sun which is more powerful than thousands of atom bombs, I'm sure. Yet we struggle to believe that He can work out the sticky situations that we, as frail little human beings, get ourselves into. I recently read a newspaper cartoon strip called "Hagar," which made me think of how often we miss the big picture, because we're self-focused on our own things. Hagar (a Viking warrior) and one of his friends were in a fishing boat on the ocean, nose to nose with a monstrous fish looking at them like they were lunch. Hagar says, "Drat! Just when we run out of worms!" Now that is losing sight of the big picture.

The big picture for us is God's will contains His wonderful good plans for our lives. The part of that picture that I'm focusing on in this book is to reveal what drives you and me to stumble all over ourselves trying to get to where we are walking in His will.

I have already written extensively on the Keys of the Kingdom and how to use them in your daily prayers, but this particular book is particularly exciting to me. It contains an in-depth explanation of the X-Ray of the Unsurrendered Soul Chart that I have been teaching from since 1995. This colorful chart lays out (in graphic form) the understanding I received from the Lord about the interactive workings of the entire human soul. It also reveals much of the reason for the baggage in our souls.

It doesn't matter how stylish our souls' luggage may be—Versace, Vuitton, or Gucci—there is nothing of our souls' baggage worth holding onto. We hear every day that people are breaking up marriages, relationships, and business agreements. These people say they have found out that they are not compatible with their partners in the marriage, the relationship, or the business agreement. This is really saying, "Your soul's baggage conflicts with my soul's baggage, and I don't like it!" If your baggage is like my baggage, that's okay. Then I can predict how you will react and what sets you off. I won't push your hot buttons and I can be pretty sure you will not push mine, either. You know the unspoken agreement: "I won't mess with your baggage if you don't mess with mine." What we should be saying is, "I need to get rid of this baggage of mine. It is really causing me and you a lot of problems."

When you see a doctor for things that are not working right in your body, what does he or she do? The doctor begins to diagnose your problem with examinations, blood tests, and x-rays. The Bible is full of good words about examining our motives, our beliefs, and our attitudes. Life is full of tests, continually prompting us to consider whether or not we will walk in our own wills or in God's will. It is a good idea as well that you get some kind of spiritual check on whose blood is coursing through your soul as well—your own or His. This book is about all of these things, but especially about reading an X-Ray of Your Unsurrendered Soul and choosing to submit to spiritual diagnostic tests for sickness in it. You may find things on the x-ray of your own soul that you didn't want to know, but the treatment program always effects a complete cure when you cooperate with it. Let me now share a story of how using these prayers to "treat" some deception in our souls' understanding produces a great outcome.

Things Are Not Always What They Seem

God wants us to learn to understand that things are not always what they seem. He wants us to see that what appears to be visible in the natural is not always what is really happening. When you bind yourself and others to God's will, you are always near His will. When you wholly believe the previous sentence is true, you are nearer yet.

I've reached a point in my walk with Him that I know that no matter what things look like, He is still at work in my life when I have chosen to align myself with His will. I don't always know what He is doing, but I know He is doing something and it is good. Binding my will to His will, I find it easier to stand and wait until it becomes clear what my role is in the solution of any situation I get into.

In the year 2000, two of my ministry staff, Evelyn and Marian, accompanied me overseas for a month of meetings in the United Kingdom. After we arrived in London, Evelyn realized that one of her expensive hearing aids was missing. She believed she had been wearing it on the plane, and it seemed that this was where it had been lost. She was very concerned, so we prayed in agreement for God's intervention in some way. We also prayed for Evelyn's hearing and for her peace of mind as we fulfilled our ministry obligations.

Preparing to speak one night, I was in my room in a beautiful home where we had been having meetings. Before going downstairs to the meeting, I wanted to reassure myself that a large amount of cash from our book table sales at several meetings in Scotland was still safely tucked away where I had hidden it a few nights earlier. I usually never carry much cash with me, but we had not been able to get to a bank to convert the English money to a U.S. funds cashier's check.

I was very shocked when I could not find the money. I began to tear my room apart looking for it, but the cash was nowhere to be found. The meeting was about to start in fifteen minutes and I was extremely upset. These meetings had been maxed out with over sixty people in our hosts' basement recreation room—including several strangers who had heard about the meetings. I worried that any of the strangers could have slipped upstairs and gone through my room while we were all praying together on previous evenings.

I knew I could not minister freely if I was so upset, so I forced myself to sit down and pray. I had previously prayed for God to use what I was going to say to cause life change in the people who were waiting. I had to get a grip on my soul, which was racing in circles, so I began binding my will to the will of God. I bound my mind to the mind of Christ so that I could hear His thoughts and not be engulfed with my own. I bound myself to the truth of the matter, and then I loosed all doubt, worry, and fear about the missing money. Most of the fear came from the fact that I had to pay a large portion of that money to my English book distributor in a few days as he had been sending my books out ahead of us to all of our meetings in Scotland and England.

I knew that God would be in control of everything if I could get my soulish reactions out of the way. Having prayed, I sat down and forced myself to wait until I began to feel His peace trying to filter through my mind and to my emotions.

Then I went to Marian's and Evelyn's room and told them we needed to come and pray in my torn apart room. They followed me and we began to bind our minds to the mind of Christ as we also loosed wrong ideas, wrong beliefs, and wrong patterns of thinking about the situation. Having been very aware of a lot of dark spiritual activity in the area we were in, we also prayed and loosed all interference and hindrances from demonic forces and particularly territorial spirits. As we bound everyone who had anything to do with the missing money to the truth, Marian suddenly said, "Liberty, you have to look through your suitcases again."

Frustrated, I told her that I had already looked through them many times and found nothing. She said, "It doesn't matter, you need to look again. I know you need to do that." Grumbling about people who don't listen, I began to search the many pockets of my suitcases again and reaching deep into one large pocket, I found the money. As we began to jump and leap around rejoicing, I heard the Lord say, "*Things are not always what they seem.* *Learn that!*"

The following day, I received e-mail from Linda back at LSM headquarters in California, saying that she had found Evelyn's hearing aid on the floor behind a chair in her office. We all said at once, "Things are not always what they seem, are they?" We had all been convinced that she had lost it on the plane flying over to England, yet it was back in our offices all the time.

Lost Keys

My designer from my publishing company in Florida, Andy Toman, happened to be in England at that same time visiting his family. He volunteered to drive us down to London where we would sightsee for a day and a half and then drive on south to Croydon for more meetings. It was great fun having a "native" Brit show us around London. We did the double-decker, open-air bus, touristy thing to make sure we saw as many landmarks as possible in one day. Andy introduced us to "pub grub" in a wonderful old English pub, we shopped at the famous Harrods Department Store (unbelievable!), and we saw castles and bridges and many other marvelous things. Andy was a great tour guide.

The last night we stayed in London, I was startled awake at about 2:00 a.m by someone knocking on my hotel room door. I opened it slowly and peeked out to see an extremely distraught Andy. "I've lost the keys to the van, Liberty, they're gone. I've looked everywhere! Without them we can't get the van out of the parking lot (which was costing $75 U.S. dollars for the one day we had wanted to use it), and I've called the car rental people about a new key and it will take days to get it here. That's $75 a day, Liberty. The car rental people will charge us $200 to drive a replacement van to us, and the replacement key will cost … we'll never get you to Croydon in time and …" Worries and dollar amounts and missed engagements were pouring out of poor Andy's mouth like an open floodgate!

I said, "We'll find the keys, Andy, don't worry. Did you look …?" Andy interrupted me and immediately began to relate how he had been tearing his room apart for hours looking for the keys until he finally felt he had to come and tell me about our predicament. I told him that I would get my robe on, we would wake up Marian and Evelyn, and all pray together. Everything would be all right, I kept reassuring him. Andy stood out in the hall to wait for me, looking so pitifully worried. He knew that prayer was the only answer, but he still wasn't convinced that God could get us out of this one without some serious consequences.

Back in my room, I suddenly realized that this was very much like the missing money incident a week earlier. I remember clearly what God had said to me: *"Things are not always what they seem. Learn that!"* I felt an assurance that everything would be fine, and that poor Andy was about to get the lesson we had already learned. Soon we were all in Marian's and Evelyn's room praying with great fervor. We bound Andy's mind to the mind of Christ, we bound his will to the will of God, and we loosed anxiety, tension, and worry from him. We loosed the enemy's influence from the situation and we asked God to tell us what to do.

We kept assuring Andy that things were not always what they seemed, and we were quite sure that this was the case with the missing keys. Andy was not sure at all, but he tried to look like he was for our sakes. We decided that we might as well all get dressed and make some plans. We weren't sure what plans to make at 4:00 a.m. in the morning, but I felt God was going to move and direct us.

Andy went back to his room to look for the keys one more time, bless his heart. I had just finished dressing when I heard loud banging on my door and muffled laughter. I opened the door and there stood Andy, Marian, and Evelyn, with huge smiles on their faces. Andy had banged on their door as he ran past it to mine. He was triumphantly holding up wet car keys while jumping up and down. "I found them, I found them," he shouted.

Shushing him, I pulled them all into my tiny room and turned on the electric hot water pot that you will find in every room in the United Kingdom. Over hot tea and some shortbread biscuits we had bought earlier, Andy related his victory story with great delight.

When he had returned to his room right after we had dinner that night, about 9:00 p.m., the phone was ringing. All of our rooms were extremely tiny, and the only place to hang up his jacket was on a hook on the bathroom door. Andy threw his jacket at the hook before answering the phone where he found that no one was on the line. A couple of hours later, while preparing for bed, he began to look for his keys. Searching everywhere, he began to panic—thinking that he had lost them in the restaurant or at Harrods Department Store. Andy nearly destroyed his tiny little room searching for those keys. But they were nowhere to be found. Finally, at 2:00 a.m., he had come to my room to tell me the bad news.

After we had all prayed and assured Andy that everything would be all right, that things were not always what they seemed, that was when he returned to his room one last time. Stepping into the tiny bathroom, he happened to glance into the toilet where he saw the van keys nestled in the bottom of the toilet bowl! Grabbing them and rushing to our rooms while they were still dripping wet, Andy was triumphant with his found keys. Evidently when Andy had thrown his jacket up on the door hook, the keys flew out of his pocket and landed in the toilet.

The funniest thing to me is that all of the toilets in the UK have an extremely powerful flushing action. I was sure, the whole time I was there, that any one of those toilets could have dragged a medium-sized dog down the pipes. Andy had actually flushed his toilet twice after the van keys had landed in the bowl.

I immediately had this mental picture of a small angel in that toilet bowl hanging on to those keys with all its might every time Andy had flushed the toilet, grumbling, "I wish they would hurry up and pray, so they can find these keys. This is almost too much for even an angel to bear!" We all rejoiced and had a victory party at 4:15 a.m. in my tiny room with hot tea and Scottish shortbread biscuits. It seemed like a banquet. Andy had the keys that once were lost—but now they were found!

One of God's consistent lessons here was first of all that things aren't always what they seem, and secondly, missing something does not always mean you have lost it. God is always in control and knows exactly where things are and what He wants to do about them. Binding your will to His will and your mind to the mind of Christ are the first steps to getting you into agreement with that truth.

Since this whole book is about demonstrating how we must come out of our "old creature" existence and transition ourselves—through effective steps of life-change—into "new creature" living, I want to share these following quotes. Please also allow me the audacity to include my own words in such impressive company.

Albert Einstein once said, "What you call a fact depends on the theory you bring to it."

Winston Churchill once said, "If we open a quarrel between the past and the present, we shall find that we have lost the future."

Liberty Savard says, "What you have chosen to believe about yourself—based upon your past—can be more powerful to your soul than the truth of who you are in Christ today."

As you read on through the pages that follow, you will read of the diagnosis of the problem our unsurrendered souls present to us. You will learn the solution or "soul treatment program" that our Father offers and how you can cooperate with it. You will find that after doing so, your prognosis will be a complete healing. Enjoy the journey to wholeness!

2

Diagnosis: Born–Again, Unsurrendered, and Earthen

Come with me now to the virtual-reality office of Dr. Soul Care. He is about to read an x-ray of your unsurrendered soul and discuss it with you. Dr. Soul Care begins to speak, "We need to go over your x-ray today," as he holds a film of it up. You can follow along with your own personal X-Ray of the Unsurrendered Soul on the inside cover of this book.

"It appears that there are several areas in this x-ray that we need to discuss immediately. I see some fairly significant areas of 'soul-disease' and many old wounds here. You've been through some things that happened long before you had any idea of how to deal with them, haven't you? It is always so sad when these things work out this way. So much brokenness occurs in the soul when you don't get all of the 'soul nutrients' that are necessary to make you strong and whole so that you can resist such wounding.

Illustration 1 - TRAUMATIC FACTS

Original Causes: Cannot be Changed	Traumatic Facts: Lack of Love or No Nurturing, Abuse, Word Curses, Generational Bondage, Neglect, Betrayal, Rejection	Original Causes: Cannot be Changed

"Because of so many Traumatic Facts happening to you, you probably didn't get all the love nutrients and nurturing nutrients that your soul needed. I also suspect that you didn't get any affirmation nutrients or security nutrients from the looks of all the other weaknesses I see here. No one ever told you how valuable you were as a person, did they? That would certainly account for such a breaking down of your soul's stability. This kind of early wounding in a soul causes three kinds of Sources to form nasty holes in the soul. See, here they are right here," and Dr. Soul Care invites you to take a closer look.

Illustration 2 - THE SOURCES

Unhealed Hurts	Unresolved Issues	Unmet Needs
Source # 1	Source #2	Source #3

"Yes, I see some serious unhealed hurts. I also see some throbbing unresolved issues. Then over here on the right are some significant unmet needs still festering, although it does look as though there may have been some healing here — but it was very temporary."

Dr. Soul Care looks at you to see if you are agreeing with what he is saying, "Until recently, we didn't have this technology to 'see' into the unsurrendered soul. But there is a Doctor Liberty out on the West Coast who has discovered a revelation breakthrough in this area, and we are able to do a much better job at diagnosing the soul's problems now. Tell me, have you been experiencing any symptoms of restlessness, dissatisfaction, discontent, some fear and anxiety, perhaps even insomnia? Hmmmmmm?"

Dr. Soul Care peers at your face again, then says, "I understand that you gave my Soul Care Nurse a copy of a spiritual insurance policy that says you cannot be sick, you cannot be hurt, you cannot be upset, and you cannot be frightened." Dr. Soul Care studies a piece of paper in his hand, "She gave me your insurance paperwork. I see that your policy says that you will not experience any personal problems as long as you keep your 'good works' clauses active. Let's see here, your good works clauses that are in force are: You're born again. You're filled with the Holy Spirit. You pray every day. You regularly attend church. You participate in praise and worship. You tithe regularly. You study your Bible. You help out at the homeless food bank.

"Your spiritual insurance policy says that if you keep these 'good works' clauses in force, nothing bad can happen to you. Interesting, but you can't get such guarantees in writing, you know. I hate to have to tell you this, but this so-called spiritual 'insurance policy' is just a deception of your own soul. 'Good works' clauses or not, it is quite obvious that some pretty bad things have happened to you even since you got your so-called policy in place. So, why don't we get on with the truth of your actual x-ray now?

"You have some unhealed hurts, unresolved issues, and unmet needs here from the Traumatic Facts that have happened to you — and it is very clear that they are still festering. They lie deep down underneath these layers of what is almost like scar tissue. The actual diagnostic terms for these scar-like layers are self-control (manipulation), self-reliance, self-protection, self-centeredness, self-defense, self-image, and self-understanding.

Illustration 3 - THE LAYERS

CORE OF POWER STRUCTURE
LAYERS:
self-conrol, self-reliance, self-protection, self-centeredness, self-defense
SOUL'S bottom line defense system

Dr. Soul Care continues, "This layering section of your x-ray is quite astounding. We still are at a loss as to how the soul actually creates these layers." Dr. Soul Care stops speaking while he appears to be studying the layers on the x-ray for a few minutes. He seems very perplexed. "It also looks like your unsurrendered soul has fabricated a fake scar tissue to try to hide your unmet needs and unhealed hurts in some way. Yes, this is certainly interesting—not good—but certainly interesting.

"When these layers give out, as they already have in some places here, several rather nasty symptoms just pop right up through them. At the stage your soul is in, it looks like some rather forceful drives have already shot all the way up to your mind. I'll bet that produces some painful reactions and responses."

Illustration 4 - THE SYMPTOMS

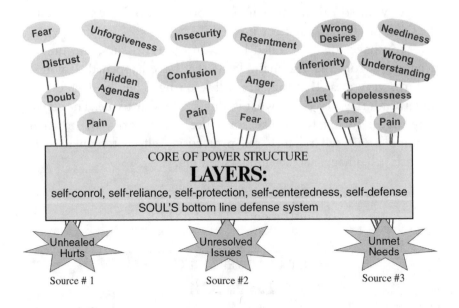

Dr. Soul Care seems to realize that he may be causing you some anxiety, and he clears his throat and tries to offer you encouragement: "But I know we have some solutions for you. Please don't get upset; we will work closely with you here."

Dr. Soul Care then says with amazement, "Do you know that we have even found scar tissue from this kind of 'self-protection' that appears to be a self-inflicted form of attempts to 'just suck it up,' 'just buck up,' and 'just grow up'? Amazing suggestions, but completely ineffective for dealing with the infection and acidity in the sources' holes. Still, I've heard that this is what many people advise each other to do and then just get on with their lives. Such nonsense, such painful nonsense indeed!

"It is quite evident that your 'scar tissue' type of layers as well as the fake layers were not strong enough to protect your soul from further damage coming up out of your unmet needs and unhealed hurts. See how the symptoms managed to crack through the soul's bottom line of defense? That's one of the reasons you are here today—your soul's Bottom Line Defense System failed. Just look how those symptoms bubbled up through it.

"Unmet needs occur when you don't get all of the 'soul nutrients' that you should. It's obvious that your soul's immune system has been extremely malnourished for a long time. The symptoms coming up out of these unmet needs are serious—wrong desires, neediness, inferiority, hopelessness—very serious. Your soul has a rough way of trying to compensate for such symptoms, but we'll get to that in a minute. The Good News here is that it doesn't matter what caused these unmet needs, because the treatment will be the same whatever caused them.

"Now over here, just look at these unhealed hurts! My, my, they look awfully raw and even bruised, don't they? You must have had some really traumatic things happen to you quite unexpectedly, things so hard and cruel that some of the soul nutrients you did get got zapped right out of your soul. That can be very painful, not like a nice clean incision with some anesthesia, that's for sure. Look at those symptoms bubbling up out of your unhealed hurts—suspicion, doubt, and fear. You have some distrust and hidden agendas growing in here, too, I'm sorry to say.

"It can be especially traumatic when you have no idea of what caused the bad happenings that destroyed some of your soul nutrients, because then you have no idea of how to prevent them from happening again. We have found that this can make any soul extremely anxious, never knowing how it should try to protect itself from something it doesn't understand or that could strike again without any warning."

Dr. Soul Care responds to a question you have just asked, "You say you want to know what those unhealed hurts are and what caused each one? Again, the Good News is that you don't have to know; in fact, it probably isn't even possible to track them back at this point. Whatever the causes were, all unhealed hurts will respond to the treatment we have to offer to you.

"Now, we get to an unusual area of trauma in the bottom of your soul, the hole that was created by your unresolved issues and unanswered questions. Can you see right here how brittle and sharp the edges of that hole are? These ugly holes are caused by unanswered questions that your soul just keeps trying to process, over and over. Questions like: 'Why did that happen to me? Why do I feel this way? Why didn't you stop that abuse, God?' As near as our other soul medicine teams can determine, based upon Dr. Liberty's original findings, this hole gets filled with rigid boundaries and self-protection rules that are trying to compensate for the confusion and the insecurity that grew out of it.

"These artificial boundaries and self-protection rules seem to give the soul some feeling of countering the fact that you felt like you grew up in the 'dark.' That means you probably never knew what your family's rules were, you didn't know where your family's land mines were hidden, and you had no idea of how to stay out of the line of fire when your family got combative. Some of the symptoms of such unresolved issues are very harsh, like the anger and the resentment.

"Your soul has quite a cover job going on here to try to hide that anger, which leads me to believe that you work very hard to seem to be in control of your emotions. These symptoms are closely connected to your emotions, you know, and it must be exhausting to constantly try to control them. In fact it's a wonder you are still trying.

"It wouldn't be unusual at this stage of the unsurrendered soul's deterioration if you were experiencing some guilt over the self-remedies your soul has turned to in trying to get rid of your pain. You can get into all kinds of wrong behaviors when you let your soul get into that sort of damage control.

Illustration 5 - WRONG BEHAVIORS

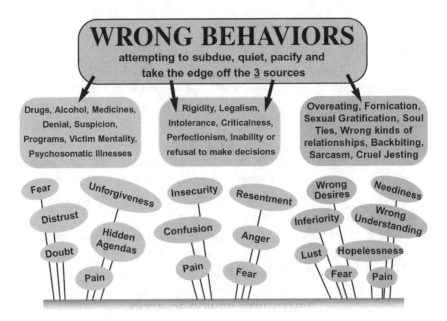

"See here on the x-ray how your soul has tried to revert back to the old wrong behaviors you've used in the past to try to subdue, quiet, pacify and take the edge off the symptoms of your pain? These are some pretty alarming actions your soul has taken to try to fix itself—drugs, denial, legalism, intolerance, fornication, soul ties, wrong relationships. That is sort of like setting the cat on fire to get rid of its fleas, isn't it? Oh, I'm sorry, I didn't mean to offend you. Just trying to lighten things up a little.

"There just aren't any soulish self-remedies that can heal the wounds you have or protect you from further wounding. You see, once you have unmet needs, unhealed hurts, and unresolved issues, you will always have them. Well, that's true except for one rather radical procedure that we'll talk about later.

"You've tried to get by with some drug and alcohol use, haven't you, perhaps tranquilizers and muscle relaxants, too? I'm not a bit surprised that your soul's pain has telegraphed itself to your body—you've had some pretty severe headaches, sore back and shoulders, and things like that, right? I'll bet you've also tried some recovery groups and programs, too, but ... (Dr. Soul Care peers at your x-ray) it doesn't look like they helped very much, either.

"There are also some signs of more self-remedies and wrong behaviors right here (Dr. Soul Care points to the Wrong Behaviors box over your unresolved issues) because of those really uncomfortable unresolved issues. Yes, I can definitely see the scarring from your soul's use of judgmental thinking and criticism. I can also see that your soul tried to resolve some of those issues by driving you to try to be perfect, but it's pretty clear that this hasn't worked either. Oh, dear, you have some really sharp shards of rigidity cutting up your soul in there, don't you?

"Well, the last source of all your distress is all these unmet needs over here. You've tried to feed them to death, haven't you? That would explain why your weight has continued to climb over the years. Do you know that I had one patient who tried to starve her unmet needs to death? We caught her just in time and pulled her out of it with our radical procedure. It looks like you've also indulged in some wrong sexual activity at some point in your life, or at least you've gotten awfully close to it with unsavory relationships—yes, there are clearly some scars from that."

Peering closely at your x-ray, Dr. Soul Care tsks tsks as he says, "I also see some connective tissue here that's all threaded through your unmet needs. You haven't been exposing yourself to soul ties, have you?" Peering intently at your x-ray, Dr. Soul Care shakes his head and says, "Yes, you have, there they are right there. I can see them twisted all through your unmet needs. Now that's no way to help the problem, you know. Soul ties just let other people control and manipulate you. We're going to have to cut those out." Dr. Soul Care stops, scribbles on a sheet of paper on his clipboard, and then hands it to his Soul Care Nurse.

"These wrong behaviors—your soul's self-remedies for its distress—are the product of your self-will trying to handle things. The self-will is the enforcer of the soul, you know, and if it is not surrendered, it causes all kinds of wrong choices to be made. What you are generally seeing here are the consequences of its multiple wrong choices.

"There is one last thing that the soul does to try to defend what it has done: it begins to build strongholds to justify and rationalize all of its actions. Dr. Liberty has found proof that stronghold building, or the attempt to defend everything the soul has been doing all through here," Dr. Soul Care sweeps his hand over the entire x-ray, "actually opens you up to an outside source of extreme distress and even terror. There is something about these strongholds that allows demonic forces to apply external pressure and increase the pain in all of your wounds. Nasty stuff, I tell you.

"I do see some signs of your born-again spirit trying to break through and help here. Yes, it has tried very hard, but the soul panics and shuts down your prayer lines every time your spirit prays that your soul would surrender. I can see that your soul has actually been so desperate, it has even considered praying, but only briefly. Still, that is good.

"It looks like your spirit has been praying for God's will to be done, but your soul has just prayed for Him to fix its symptoms and its pain. God won't deal with your symptoms and pain first, you know, because they would just come back if those three sources are not healed. He's waiting for you to agree with Him that He knows best how to fix you and where to start—and that's right down here in your unhealed hurts, your unresolved issues, and your unmet needs. He won't force His way in there, but He does need to get to that starting place.

"Ok, now let's just look up here at the top of your x-ray. We have looked at the unsurrendered soul's bottom line of defense down here (points to the layering area of the soul), now we're going to look at the soul's first line of defense up here—its strongholds."

Illustration 6 – STRONGHOLDS

STRONGHOLDS
Soul's first line of defense

Logic	Reasoning	Arguments
Wrong Ideas		Wrong Attitudes
Wrong Beliefs		Wrong Motives
	Wrong Patterns of Thinking	
Justification	**Denial**	**Defensiveness**

"Your emotions get all tangled up with the symptoms and drives coming up out of the sources in your soul, and your will has flooded your soul with consequences of wrong choices it has made. Here's where the mind kicks in with its input.

"Whatever you 'choose' to believe in your mind, that belief system will always control how you live out your life. God has designed our whole being in such a way that we cannot 'live' or behave in a way that is inconsistent with what we believe in our soul—well, not for long, anyway. The unsurrendered soul tries to fabricate different attitudes and characteristics to reflect different beliefs about itself, but such false traits have to be constantly reinforced and the soul wears itself out doing that. As a man thinks within himself, so he is, you know (Proverbs 23:7). Our souls have been trying to change their 'so he is' traits to what they 'wish we were' for years.

"The soul's first line of defense is its strongholds—its logic, reasoning, arguments, justification, defensiveness, and especially its constant denial that it needs to change anything. Yes, your unsurrendered soul tries to justify every dangerous thing it does. See these things entrenched within your stronghold walls—the wrong ideas, wrong beliefs, wrong attitudes, and wrong patterns of thinking? Look at the thickness of those protective walls your unsurrendered soul has built around them.

"Your soul is terrified that any change you might try to make would cause everything to fall apart and thereby reveal its culpability in the whole mess. So, to keep you from doing that, it is destroying itself by defending and denying the deception it has been accumulating for years. Ridiculous, isn't it?

"Yes," Dr. Soul Care nods his head wisely, "this is verrrrry serious. I'm afraid that you are looking at a life and death situation here. Oh, don't worry; this is not your eternal life that is at stake. It is the abundant life that you could have had right here, right now, but you don't. Any tiny slice of hope that you ever had of a glorious life here on earth, or of being overwhelmingly loved by Him right now, is ebbing away even as you sit here. We have to do something to stop that drainage at once!

"We have a Great Physician on call here who has given us some spiritual keys, spiritual medicine and treatments actually, to use. He works closely with a Spiritual Surgeon who is willing to perform spiritual surgery on an unsurrendered soul if He finds the right verbal authorization and agreement to do so. This is a very unique surgery. When this Spiritual Surgeon finds you have agreement with the power of the Word of God in you, He will do the surgery on you. He uses an excellent anesthesia called Grace and Mercy.

"This incredible surgery, which can only be performed by this Great Physician and the Spiritual Surgeon, removes all of the soul's toxic waste and scar tissue and thoroughly cleanses and heals all of your needs and wounds. Then He actually transplants a new system of belief, new attitudes, and a new patterning of thinking into your soul. I understand that these transplants are priceless, but He is willing to give it to us for free. The only thing He requires first is your actual agreement with His Word.

"*His Word is very, very powerful—it is actually alive and full of power—sharper than any two-edged sword, penetrating to the dividing line of the soul and the spirit, and of joints and marrow—exposing and sifting and analyzing and judging the very thoughts and purposes of your heart and soul*" (Hebrews 4:12, *Amplified Bible*).

ord has the ability and power to open up your deepest wounds and scars, divide them asunder, and do the spiritual surgery you need to be healed and whole.

"I'll bet you would like to know how to agree with the Word of God to get yourself ready for this surgery, wouldn't you? I thought so. Let's start your pre-op preparations right now. The Great Physician has given us some keys to give you to use every time you get nervous or concerned about your surgery. He said, *"Tell the patient that I said—I will give you the keys of the kingdom of heaven; whatever you bind on earth will be bound in heaven, and whatever you loose on earth will be loosed in heaven"* (Matthew 16:19, *NIV*). Now let me help you form your verbal authorization and agreement with these keys. Just pray these words after me." Dr. Soul Care smiles at you to encourage you to pray these words after him:

"Lord, I've hurt for so long. I've been afraid and angry for so long. I just can't manage this pain and anxiety any more. I come to you now, believing you want to heal me, and agreeing with your mighty power to do so. I bind my will to your will, Father God, which I know means I am putting myself under obligation to your will. Your Word tells me that your will for me is good. I bind my mind to your mind, Jesus, which I know means I am choosing to embrace your thoughts; I am choosing to reach out for your comforting words. I bind my emotions to the healing balance of the Holy Spirit, which I know means I am trusting Him to heal my tattered and torn emotions and restore them to newness and wholeness.

"I bind myself to the truth in your Word, and I confess that your Word is true, it is good, it is powerful, and I cannot live without it. I loose all lies, deception, half-truths, wrong teachings, and the effects and influences of wrong agreements that have wounded and lacerated my foolish soul. I know I cannot loose the actual unmet needs, unhealed hurts, and unresolved issues within me—but I can loose all of my soul's fabricated 'scar tissue' over them so that you can get to them and make me whole.

"I do not know why my soul has made so many wrong choices to embrace so many lies and deceptions, but I am loosing all of them right now. I loose all stronghold thinking, and all other wrong thinking that would try to protect any ungodly thing within my soul. I loose all of my soul's layers and facades of self-importance, self-will, self-understanding, self-reliance, self-protection, and self-defense.

"I tear it all down so that you might know I am making a choice to agree with you. I am choosing your help and healing, and I want you to give me a transplant of truth and joy and love and peace right into the center of my soul. I am choosing to surrender my soul to you for whatever purposes you have for it. Thank you, Lord, for this truth and for your love and care. I'm yours, please help me and hold me close until I'm all healed and fixed. Amen."

Dr. Soul Care then asks, "How do you feel?" while looking intently at your face. Smiling, he continues, "He's already started the transplant process, you know. You're already under the sharp scalpel of His Word and He's meeting your needs, healing your hurts, and resolving your issues. Yes, you're going to heal up just fine. You say you want to know what my fee is? Just the opportunity to see you running out of here to embrace your destiny."

Then acting more business-like, Doctor Soul Care says to you, "Now, I'd like you to look back at your whole x-ray just one more time, please." (You will find your personal copy of the x-ray inside the cover of this book.)

"Take a good look here. Do you realize how far you have managed to make it in life with all of this infection, gunk, and toxic waste inside of you? Well, that means you are a lot stronger than you thought you were! Now—think of how strong you will be and how far you can go when the Great Physician and the Spiritual Surgeon cut it all out and replace it with love, joy, peace, and obedience! Think of how it will be when you are working with Him instead of always being worked on by Him? There's no limit to how far you can go now, you know. Isn't that Good News?

"You ask if there are there any hidden costs involved in *Shattering Your Strongholds, Breaking the Power* of your unmet needs, unhealed hurts, and unresolved issues—and *Producing the Promise* that you have always carried inside of you? No, none at all for you. Jesus paid the price a long time ago and the written Word of God is your Paid-In-Full Receipt for that transaction. That's your guarantee in case you want one. No one has ever come back and complained yet when they have diligently followed their post-operative instructions to keep binding themselves to the will of God and the mind of Christ. It's been a joy to serve you, now go with God and be whole."

"Unless the LORD had been my help, my soul would soon have settled in silence. If I say, 'My foot slips,' your mercy, O LORD, will hold me up. In the multitude of my anxieties within me, your comforts delight my soul" (Psalm 94:17-19, NKJV).

Let's Just Do It

Whatever we apply these Kingdom keys to in prayer, if our prayer request is in alignment with God's will, then the answer is a done deal. Praying right prayers always means that you are agreeing with God's already established will in heaven. This takes a lot of pressure off you when you're praying because you do not have to know the details to pray rightly. You can pray with trust and confidence in the outcome of His divine plans for yourself, others, and situations. You can come out of a "problem mode" and move into a "problem solving/ problem solved" mode! You will be using the keys for life change and that is sweet!

Here is a basic Keys of the Kingdom prayer for you to begin praying as you are reading this book. This will definitely help you get a jump on the reactions of your own unsurrendered soul by doing so right now. Remember, reading this prayer is not the same as praying it:

"Lord, I thank you for the Keys of the Kingdom, binding and loosing. I bind my will to your will, and I am so grateful to be able to put my will under obligation to you. I bind my mind to your mind, Jesus, which helps me slow down my soul's self-centered thoughts, stop the recycling of old patterns of thinking, and helps me rest in your thoughts. I

bind my emotions to your healing, balancing control, Holy Spirit. I bind myself to the whole truth of your Word, Father God. I want to know it in purity, without any twisting or perverting of its meaning by my soul.

"I loose all wrong beliefs, ideas, and patterns of thinking that my soul has cherished and flown like banners. I loose all wrong attitudes I have had, and I loose all of my wrong motives and agendas. I loose all word curses from myself, dissolving the residue of any and all harsh, cruel words spoken to me, about me, and even by me. I loose the effects and influences of all wrong agreements made about me or by me. I loose all soul ties I have allowed myself to develop. I loose all of the layers and facades that my soul has established to try to bury my hidden unmet needs, unhealed hurts, and unresolved issues. I want to throw open every square inch of my soul to your healing power and love.

"Father, I cannot fix myself. My soul has tried to do this for so long, it has become scarred and bitter. I am ready to take down and dismantle all barriers, self-defense systems, and self-protection devices that my soul has learned to use to keep my pain in and you out. I choose to do that right now! I surrender to you, Lord, and I thank you for loving me even when I haven't been lovable. I want everything you want to give me, and I will loose everything you want me to give up. Thank you for these keys which empower me to do this. Amen"

The Contender

There is a powerful contender within each one of us fighting for control of our lives. It is the human soul. The devil only takes advantage of its rebellion to God's will. Each one of our human spirits were birthed into this world as spiritual orphans, with deep, unsatisfied yearnings to be linked to their Creator. Our poor unregenerated human spirits had to put up with being subjected to the unrenewed minds (ability to think), the unsurrendered wills (ability to choose), and the unhealed emotions (ability to feel) of our souls—often for decades until our spiritual salvation occurred.

I believe our regenerated spirits are now pushing back when the soul starts throwing its weight around. Our regenerated spirits love God, but Paul told the Roman Christians that the unsurrendered human soul wants nothing to do with God, *"Because the carnal mind is enmity against God; for it is not subject to the law of God, nor indeed can be"* (Romans 8:7, *NKJV*).

One translation of that verse says that the carnal mind (no God in it) is hostile to the things of God.

After the fall in the Garden of Eden (which severed the spiri-to-Spirit communion that Adam and Eve had with God), the "liberated" soul of mankind both then and in all of mankind to come began to flex its mental muscles and ratchet up the power of its will. The unsurrendered soul's desire to try to control others, run things, and deal with what it fears is still very strong in every human being alive today, and it is willing to fight any outside intervention. When you accepted Christ's sacrifice for your sins and became a believer, only your spirit became perfectly aligned to the Spirit of your Creator. Your soul stepped back, determined to start a war within you, and then began to fight.

It will fight very dirty if it has to, even to impersonating the Holy Spirit or to the impersonation of a demon. David's soul resorted to that sort of impersonation when he was fearful of being recognized in the city of Gath. Human souls can resort to that same type of impersonation today when they are feeling threatened and frightened by the spiritual demands of some personal deliverance ministry formats. Because the unsurrendered soul will go to extreme lengths to deceive if it is fearful enough, Christians need to be free of preconceived ideas and wrong teachings that would hinder the operation of the spiritual gift of the discerning of spirits.

This is a gift that is misunderstood by many. This is not the gift of discernment as many have written to me and told me that they have. This is a spiritual gift for a specific use: that a believer would know if any manifestation, behavior, or words has a demonic spirit, the Holy Spirit, or a human soul influencing them. Few Christians today seem to realize how crafty their unsurrendered souls really are and to what lengths they will go to try to gain or maintain control in their lives. How important is it to know whether or not you are acting out of your soul or your spirit? Watchman Nee said, "The greatest advantage in knowing the difference between our spirits and our souls is in perceiving the latent power of the soul and in understanding its falsification of the power of the Holy Spirit."

Do Our Souls Really Have a Part in Our Destinies?

It is such a paradox that the unsurrendered souls of born-again Christians work so hard to avoid God's attempts to heal them, give them eternal purpose, and cause them to walk into wonderful destinies. He created our souls with definite eternal purpose. Yet even as a redeemed child of God, the Christian's unsurrendered soul—the center of everything self-oriented—can be:

key

- Still full of the neediness, pain, and questions of a lifetime.
- Still full of the memories of every bad thing said about, done to, or taken from it.
- Still full of suspicion, distrust, and doubt.
- Still full of all of the ungodly input of the world's ways and rules.

This unsurrendered soul still sees the intervention of a forgiving, healing, loving God as terrifying. That is a paradox if ever there was one! Paul spoke of this in his letter to the Roman Christians.

"Those who think they can do it on their own end up obsessed with measuring their own moral muscle but never get around to exercising it in real life. Those who trust God's action in them find that God's Spirit is in them—living and breathing God! Obsession with self in these matters is a dead end; attention to God leads us out into the open, into a spacious, free life. Focusing on the self is the opposite of focusing on God. Anyone completely absorbed in self ignores God, ends up thinking more about self than God. That person ignores who God is and what he is doing. And God isn't pleased at being ignored" (Romans 8:5-8, *The Message*).

Considering that all of your problems today stem from the toxic waste that has been accumulating for years in your soul, it is good news to learn how to do get rid of that gunk. Acknowledge this accumulation of "stuff" within your soul, and then confirm to yourself that you believe the Word of God which tells us that Jesus said:

"I will give you the keys of the kingdom of heaven; whatever you bind on earth will be bound in heaven, and whatever you loose on earth will be loosed in heaven" (Matthew 16:19, *NIV*).

This verse means that you have some spiritual weapons to undo the damage that has been done to your soul. With these keys, healing, freedom, and liberty cannot be withheld from you. You are not a permanent "victim" because of the works of the enemy, abuse from your past, or control from authority figures—you've only been a "victim" of your soul's record keeping and the pressure cooker that your soul has used to cook those records! You now have keys to deal with all of that effectively and permanently!

In Ephesians 2:10, *Amplified Bible*, Paul tells the Ephesian believers:

"For we are God's [own] handiwork (His workmanship), recreated in Christ Jesus, [born anew] that we may do those good works which God predestined (planned before hand) for us, (taking paths which He prepared ahead of time) that we should walk in them—living the good life which He prearranged and made ready for us to live."

Our souls have tried to follow their own paths, kind of like little steam engines puffing around without any tracks to follow. Sometimes these soul trains end up in the ditch, sometimes in the desert, and sometimes in the swamp. It can be rough going when your inner dictator has no clear set of tracks to parade around on.

God has laid down preordained spiritual "tracks" for us to follow. That is so exciting! Good works, godly paths, and a good life all prearranged ahead of time and sitting somewhere for us to find and leap into. Where are they? I believe these "tracks" exist in heaven, and that is where they will stay until we reject our souls' aimless wanderings in the desert and in the swamp, and cry out for His paths, His will, and His ways. That brings us into alignment with the divinely laid tracks of our destiny. You begin to align with God's destiny tracks every time you bind your will to His will, crying out, "Not my will, but thy will be done in my life, Lord!"

God's Tune Up

Our souls are not going to give up easily. Years ago, I remember hearing one Christian young man exulting exuberantly over a "foolproof" plan he had hatched. He began to enter all of the sweepstakes he could find (this was in pre-lottery days), praying fervently as he filled them out, "God, if you will just let me win this sweepstake, I promise I will give half of the money to you!" He absolutely crowed about how God would not be able to resist such an offer to finance His Kingdom work.

All of us have prayed at one time or another, "Dear God, if you make me rich, I will donate lots of money to your Kingdom work!" We don't understand that our financial circumstances are often used by God to refine our self-interests and reveal hidden things in our hearts. If God gave us what our wills wanted instead of what He knows we need, we would never grow. You don't grow and you don't get up and head out to meet your destiny when you are comfortable and have everything you want right where you are. Sometimes we are in lack because that is the only way God can get us to get up off our backsides and get serious about finding out what He is doing.

You need to be confronted and challenged to grow. Some of those people you thought the devil sent your way are really people God sent to cause you to grow. When you find yourself involved in difficult situations with difficult people, that is when your soul is most likely to want to run its facades and fronts. Your soul will want you to either be strong and assertive or maybe meek and vulnerable, whichever role best suits its purposes. The best thing you can actually do is pray like this:

"Lord, I bind everyone, including me, who is involved in this circumstance and its resolution to your will. I bind my mind and the minds of everyone involved in this circumstance to the mind of Christ and to your timing. I loose all personal agendas, all self-motives, and all wrong patterns of thinking and attitudes from each one of us. I loose the effects and influences of all wrong agreements made

by any of us, and I affirm that your will shall be done on earth in each of our lives. Thank you, Lord, for the Keys of the Kingdom that allow me to do this."

Pray this, and then continue to agree with, and affirm that God's will is going to be done. Don't worry about telling Satan what he can and can't do in the circumstance, like so many want to do. I don't ever acknowledge his presence when I pray like this. I let him try to figure out what he can and can't do in the face of these kinds of prayers by watching my attitude of agreement with God.

A New Image

In Colossians 3:9-10, Paul was speaking to Christians when he wrote, "*You're done with that old life. It's like a filthy set of ill-fitting clothes you've stripped off and put in the fire. Now you're dressed in a new wardrobe. Every item of your new way of life is custom-made by the Creator, with his label on it. All the old fashions are now obsolete. Words like Jewish and non-Jewish, religious and irreligious, insider and outsider, uncivilized and uncouth, slave and free, mean nothing. From now on everyone is defined by Christ, everyone is included in Christ*" (*The Message*).

The old life consists of everything ungodly from your past—all the wrong ideas, the wrong desires, the wrong agendas, and the wrong agreements that lead to wrong behaviors and actions. Can we actually loose these old things permanently—putting them off as it says above? Can we really be done with them? According to the Word of God, we can!

We can stop walking around wearing an iron collar around our necks, an oxen's yoke on our shoulders, and dragging long chains behind us. Believe it or not, those things can become so familiar to us that it makes us nervous to think of giving them up.

You do not have to carry guilt and shame for your past anymore. You do not have to fight habits and behaviors from your past anymore. Heartbreaking behaviors ranging all the way from drug abuse to pornography to adultery to homosexual activity can be put away. All of these wrong behaviors come from the unsurrendered soul's belief that it must find some kind of behavior to compensate for and pacify its neediness and pain. The unsurrendered soul has a kind of mantra that sounds like this: "No more pain, no more pain, no more pain!" However and whatever it takes to achieve that goal is fine with it, regardless of who might get hurt in the long run.

Jesus knew what His destiny was and He knew what He had to do according to the plans of the Father. Did He want to go all the way through His destiny clear to the final end? Matthew 26:39-42 tells us that He asked the Father two times if it was possible for the cup of bitter drink (His death on the cross) to be taken away from Him. He did not want to die as a human sacrifice. But He also said, each time, if it was not possible to do what needed to be done any other way, then the Father's will was the only one to be considered. He was prepared to obey His Father, regardless of the personal cost. His obedience paid for all of our pasts that we could be free from their shame, free from repeating sinful patterns, free from guilt, and free from sin's death penalty as demanded by a righteous and Holy God.

What a Savior!

three

X-Ray of the Soul's Distress

The history of the Unsurrendered Soul Chart (found inside the cover of this book) began in 1995. During that year, I had begun holding 24-Hour Women's Invasions in my house, bringing up to 15 women into my home for an overnight lockdown. This invasion concept was basically geared to exposing and tearing down the hidden strongholds and control tactics of the unsurrendered soul.

I will never forget the night that the Stockton AGLOW women came to one of these Invasions! These 24-Hour Invasions always began at 6:00 p.m. on a Friday night and ended at 6:00 p.m. on Saturday night. Most of the souls of the women who attended these intense times of lockdown with the "Soul Busters" (myself and my staff) were glad to bail out of there by 6:00 p.m. on Saturday night. Some unsurrendered souls even tried to make a break for it sooner! Very few seemed to want to hang with the teachings about the sources of all of their struggles, wrong behaviors, and strongholds any longer than they had to.

The interactive dynamics of this process in the unsurrendered soul were very familiar to me, as I had been teaching them in meetings for a few years. I hadn't really considered that others might struggle to mentally grasp the whole interactive concept just from my words. But the Stockton AGLOW women were determined to understand all of the dynamics of this whole process in one setting! They kept asking, "But how does the soul's bottom line of defense affect the wrong behaviors?" "Why does the soul want to protect its wrong beliefs?" "Why do you call self-centeredness and self-reliance layers?"

I kept patiently answering their questions even after the Invasion was officially over at 6:00 p.m. on Saturday night. I was still answering their questions far into the night. Finally, at 1:00 a.m. the following morning, I said, "Look, you guys—either you get your sleeping bags back out and sack out on the floor right now or you have to go home! I love you, but I can't take any more." They actually weighed those two options while I held my breath. The blessed Holy Spirit intervened and they decided to go home. This truly was a group of women who wanted it all!

I didn't go to church the following morning; in fact, I could hardly move. I was drained, yet exhilarated in a feeble sort of way. These women wanted everything they could get regarding these concepts. I just sat in my living room with a cup of coffee and contemplated their hunger, a genuine treat for any teacher. Finally I asked the Lord, "What can I do to help them understand how these things all work together? Please give me a graphic picture of what happens in our unsurrendered souls. Lord, I need some kind of a teaching tool to help them understand."

I felt that He told me to get my big tablet of graph paper and all of my colored markers. I quickly retrieved them and sat down, ready for whatever He was going to say. I remember envisioning all the areas in the unsurrendered soul and how they related to each other. I began to diagram what I was seeing in my mind as He spoke to me. The chart poured out of me and onto that paper like I was a color printer.

The Chart

I still have that original colored-marker drawing, which is approximately 13"x17." We've had it laminated and it now hangs in our LSM Bookstore. To this day, the unsurrendered soul chart is one of my favorite teaching messages. I lovingly call those Stockton CA AGLOW women my favorite "lab rats" because they forced the creation of this new teaching tool during the longest 36 hours of my life! Today, as I teach from the Unsurrendered Soul Chart, I can almost see myself in a lab coat with a stethoscope, going over the x-ray of a Christian's wounded, malfunctioning soul.

As you look at the chart, realize that 99 percent of us have had some version of that entire chart churning around inside of us—and still do to differing degrees. We were born just prior to the bottom of the chart, before we were ever impacted by the authority figures in our lives. However, we were born into this world intimately known and loved by our heavenly Father.

"For you created my inmost being; you knit me together in my mother's womb. I praise you because I am fearfully and wonderfully made; your works are wonderful, I know that full well. My frame was not hidden from you when I was made in the secret place. When I was woven together in the depths of the earth, your eyes saw my unformed body. All the days ordained for me were written in your book before one of them came to be" (Psalm 139:11-16, *NIV*).

Incredible, wonderfully made little human creatures are born into this world to be raised under the guidance of authority figures with unsurrendered, hurting, needy souls. Each little child surely has a future planned for the purposes of God, a future that has been written in the heart of God before the child was born. Yet, because of the ways of mankind ever since the days of the Garden of Eden, little children are being raised by hurting, angry, fearful souls who know nothing of the preordained potential they are quenching.

In Ephesians 4:18, people who are separated from the life of God are said to be darkened in their understanding. The most loving of parents who have darkened understanding share their darkness, their deceptions, their confusion, and their pain with their children. Is it any wonder that so many of us, for generations too numerous to recount, have grown up with misconceptions and preconceived ideas about God, about ourselves, and about others? Is it any wonder that we struggle with so many wrong ideas and deceptions about where we fit into God's plans?

But, hallelujah, we do not have to remain deceived. We can make room within our unsurrendered souls to receive an inpouring of the truth and the light, and God will be only too happy to fill up the space you create for Him.

The Chart – Traumatic Facts

Across the bottom of the Unsurrendered Soul Chart (which you will find inside the front and back covers of this book), you will see a box labeled Traumatic Facts. Most of us have had some traumatic events in our lives. Some have had more, some less. Whatever you have experienced throughout your life, each thing that actually happened to you is a fact. You may not have all the truth about that fact, but it happened and you cannot change the fact of that. You cannot loose a fact.

Illustration 1 - TRAUMATIC FACTS

Original Causes: Cannot be Changed	Traumatic Facts: Lack of Love or No Nurturing, Abuse, Word Curses, Generational Bondage, Neglect, Betrayal, Rejection	Original Causes: Cannot be Changed

Perhaps you were raised by parents who did not know how to express love or nurture you. Perhaps you were in line for yet another generation cycle of bondage thinking. Generational bondage thinking sounds like this: "None of the girls in this family have been pretty. So, be sure you get a good education." Or, "Your grandfather was an alcoholic, your father is an alcoholic, and you're going to be one, too." Or, "You're just like all the other women on your mother's side—give you a 50/50 chance to do something right, you'll get it wrong every time." Or, "All the Johnson men have died of cancer. It's a Johnson curse. Mark my words, Peter Johnson, you'll get it, too."

You might have been betrayed or abandoned when you were young. It is a hard thing for a child to understand why Jerry, Judy, and Johnny all have parents who seem to care so much about them, but Mother gave you away. It is a hard thing for a child to understand why Father walked out one day and never returned. These children invariably ask themselves what was so wrong with them that Mommy or Daddy wanted to get away from them.

Perhaps you were neglected as a child or even despised. If that is a fact of your life, the first step you take towards truth is to admit that it did happen to you—but it wasn't because of something wrong with you. Don't accept the lie that you deserved it or earned it. Just accept the fact that one or both of your parents had unsurrendered souls that no one ever taught them to surrender to God. Too often we learn as children to alter our perspective of the reality of things too hard and too painful for us understand. We begin to deny the truth of the actual fact and believe that it must have been our fault. Then we built strongholds to protect our recreated false realities.

When a parent physically or emotionally abuses a child, often that child cannot correctly process this kind of behavior from the one who is supposed to be the source of all that is good and safe. The only source of care and security a child has ever known needs to be believed to be loving and kind. If the parent or authority figure is not loving and kind, for the child to actually admit this to himself would mean that every scrap of security the child knows might be false as well. That is very frightening, even terrifying, for a small child to contemplate. So a small child will embrace a comforting lie rather than face a frightening truth.

A little child who is not capable of caring for or protecting himself needs to believe that his parents really do want to take care of him. Small children are not capable of processing a lack of nurturing as being the result of an adult's soul being out of alignment. The child in this type of situation may begin to rationalize and justify the situation in a manner that he can process to give himself a sense of security, even if it is false.

A small abused boy, Robby, begins to rationalize that Daddy would never have broken his fingers if Robby hadn't bugged him. The boy deliberately caused this distraction out of fear for his mother's life, because Daddy is a wife beater. Robby's Daddy really seemed so sorry for breaking Robby's fingers, and he told him that he really did love him. Then Daddy told Robby that if only he had not bothered him, Daddy would not have had to hurt him. Robby, desperate to believe his father is telling the truth about how he is sorry and how he really loves Robby, also accepts the lie that the broken fingers really were his fault.

Robby determines that he just has to try harder to be good; then maybe Daddy won't get mad at him or at Mommy anymore. Robby becomes an anxious, nervous child who is brutally hard on himself when he isn't perfect or when things blow up around him. He believes the lie that he can regulate the behavior of the people around him by perfectionism; this child can actually feel that his mother's safety is his responsibility. If she is harmed in any way, he can feel great guilt.

The little abused girl, Lucy, begins to rationalize that Mommy wouldn't have screamed that she was so stupid and then beat her if Lucy hadn't been stupid enough to break Mommy's favorite dish. Lucy also believes that Mommy wouldn't have kept drinking if Mommy felt she was smarter. Children can understand the consequences of their misbehavior and perceived inadequacies, even believing that bad things keep happening to them because they are so stupid. Lucy may grow up believing that if she can just get smart enough, then she won't upset anyone anymore. Lucy is on her way to becoming an overachiever and an intellectual junky.

It may never occur to Robby that he didn't do anything wrong in wanting to distract his father from beating his mother. It may never occur to Lucy that she wasn't stupid and the broken dish had nothing to do with the fact that her Mommy was an alcoholic. These children often fall into the wrong patterns of thinking that if they just try to behave or perform better, Daddy and Mommy will be happy. Robby may grow into an adult who constantly helps and does things for other people with the hidden agenda of trying to control the emotional climate around himself. Lucy may become an intellectual snob with no ability to emotionally connect with other people

When small children are sexually abused by a parent, the child often places the guilt over the act upon themselves. After all, how could Daddy or Grandpa do something so bad to them if they were not such terrible, unworthy beings in the first place? If these children never learn that this is a lie, they can carry that guilt the rest of their lives. Sometimes a child abuser will speak word curses or threats to the child to devalue the object of his or her abuse. The abuser continues to tear down that child's self-esteem so that the abuser's acts no longer seem so bad because the child wasn't worth anything anyway.

Perhaps a mother does not like one of her children for whatever reason, and she withholds love, affection, and treats from that child. She rejects that child's attempts to connect with her, never being able to explain to the child that the problem is hers, not the child's. Perhaps a father is so angry with his wife for getting pregnant again that the child who is born becomes the scapegoat for the father's anger and the abuse of the older siblings.

There are many different forms of trauma that can occur in a young life, a teenager's life, or even an adult's life, but the chart lists the most obvious ones. Lack of love, no nurturing, abuse (in all forms—physical, mental, emotional, sexual), word curses, generational bondage thinking, betrayal, rejection, and abandonment.

Chart – The First of the "Un's"

As I was graphically capturing what I believed I was hearing from the Lord regarding these teaching points, I heard Him say Unmet Needs, Unhealed Hurts, and Unresolved Issues. Out of the hard things of our lives come the three sources of all of our messed-up thinking and acting. These three sources are like holes in our souls where every good thing we try to hold onto and believe about ourselves can drain right out of us.

Illustration 2 - THE SOURCES

Source # 1   Source #2   Source #3

Some people have asked if I have a background in psychology. The answer is no, I've never taken any college classes on the secular realm of dealing with the psyche—the human soul. The principles I have incorporated into this chart have come from being an avid reader and a copious note taker. All over my house, in pockets of my jackets, in my brief case, my computer case, my desk at work, my car, and my purse, are 3x5 cards with the latest information I have learned or gleaned regarding issues of the human soul in Christian terms.

As I thought and prayed about the unmet needs, I asked the Lord for a one-sentence explanation. I believe He told me that unmet needs are birthed when we do not receive the good things we need. In other words, we do not get all the "building blocks" (my term) that make up a complete and perfect soul.

Chart – "Perfect Soul" Model

Consider for a moment that there might be sixteen "building blocks" you need to have a complete and whole soul. Let me diagram a Model of these sixteen hypothetical "building blocks." Let's say that these building blocks consist of love, nurturing, security, trust, acceptance, encouragement, godly understanding, gender identity, spiritual identity, affirmation, hope, worth, creativity, purpose, goals, and a sense of destiny. These building blocks are not hereditary or genetic traits; rather, they are the character or personality traits that your parents (or the authority figures of your life) teach to you, express to you, or model for you. All sixteen of these blocks would go together like this to create our Model of a complete and perfect soul.

Illustration 1: Perfect Soul MODEL

LOVE	NURTURING	SECURITY	TRUST
ACCEPTANCE	ENCOURAGEMENT	GODLY UNDERSTANDING	GENDER IDENTITY
SPIRITUAL IDENTITY	AFFIRMATION	HOPE	WORTH
CREATIVITY	PURPOSE	GOALS	SENSE OF DESTINY

You probably did not receive all of these blocks when you were born, just as none of us did. If there is someone who was raised by perfect parents who were raised by their own perfect parents and received all sixteen of these modeled traits, I would like to meet that person and praise the Lord with him or her for a miracle! But, for now, let's consider how you and I probably grew up. There were a few things your parents, who gave you everything they could, were not able to impart to or model for you. They were actually missing the ability to encourage and inspire hope, having been raised themselves in the tough, no-nonsense time of the Great Depression. So, you were missing a few blocks right from the beginning, and your soul looked like this. You had no encouragement and hope blocks.

Illustration 2: Unmet Needs Weaken

The black holes above represent two things that should have been imparted to you by your parents, but were not — encouragement and hope. When we consider encouragement and hope as real needs of our perfect soul model, you now have an unmet need for encouragement which causes you to constantly check with others to find out if you are doing all right. You also have an unmet need for hope, something your parents were unable to model for you. You were never taught how to hope, and you never saw a fulfilled hope. You never saw hope. This unmet need causes you to cling to others who seem to know how to hope. Unmet needs are always birthed when something good that should have happened in your life did not. So you start out with a couple of holes right from the beginning, but you were able to compensate for those holes and get on with your life.

At some point, perhaps in your teen years, let's say that something very harsh and violent occurred in your life. You had always felt very secure and safe, almost feeling as if you were untouchable by the tragedies and traumatic things that happened in the lives of others. Now you were violently demeaned and your sense of security was so shattered that you lost all sense of having any worth as a person. You had always felt that if you lived a good life and were fair to others, life would be good and fair to you. Yet great harm struck you without warning.

You slowly lost your sense of purpose and one by one you gave up on the goals you had thought you could meet. Not understanding where such trauma had came from, you felt helpless as to how you could prevent such a terrible thing from happening again. Suddenly four of your soul's existing "building blocks" were torn away from you—security, worth, purpose, and goals.

Unhealed hurts are birthed when something bad happens to us that should not have happened. Now your soul is a little shakier.

Illustration 3: Unhealed Hurts Further Weaken

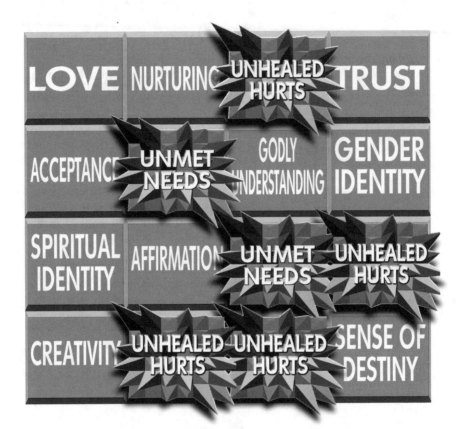

All was not lost, though, because you still knew that you were loved, and you still cherished the nurturing you had experienced as a child. Unmet needs and unhealed hurts were increasing in your soul, but you could deal with them.

Then, at the age of 30, you found out that your father has another family—a mistress and three other children. Shortly thereafter, your mother died; some said it was from a broken heart. The love you had cherished, the nurturing that you had felt was for you alone, the sense of destiny that your father had said was yours—all were shattered. The intensity of your "why" questions increased, but there were no answers—just unresolved issues. Unresolved issues are birthed when we do not know how to process unmet needs and unhealed hurts in a productive manner. You lost your "blocks" of love, nurturing, trust, and destiny to the explosive power of your unresolved issues.

Illustration 4: Unresolved Issues Further Weaken

Now your Soul Model is beginning to look kind of bad. Feeling the pressure and the stress that was running pretty high in your soul, you decided that maybe you should get your life right with God and try to get back on course. So you returned to the house of worship where you remembered attending Vacation Bible School. You were seeking the God of your mother, and you were seeking comfort and help. You accepted the Lord Jesus Christ as your Savior and some of the darkness seemed to recede from your soul, but you could still feel the holes in your soul throbbing with pain and need.

Time after time, you walked the aisles of that church to fall at the altar where you sobbed before the Lord. Then one day a well-meaning and truly kind Christian saint stepped up beside you and said, "I hear you asking God why all of those things had to happen to you. Why wasn't He there when they were happening? My friend, don't you know that God was always right there with you? He didn't leave you alone; He was there all the time. He saw everything."

Let's move out of the realm of hypothetical and into an actual experience I had at the altar in my earliest days of Christianity (I was saved in 1972). I, too, knelt again and again at the altars of my church after I was saved, trying to find out why God had allowed the things that happened in my own life that still seemed so alive and full of pain. One night a kind and well-meaning saint came and whispered the exact same words to me that I have written in the paragraph above. Kind words, well-intentioned words, even true words? Yes.

But at the sound of those words, my unsurrendered soul exploded in pain and rage, screaming inside of me: "You want to surrender your life to a God who would stand by and watch while such things happened in your life? You want to take me off the driver's seat and get down in front of God so that He can stomp all over you some more? You can't trust Him; you never have been able to. Get out of here now, you fool!"

I remember getting up from that altar with my face aflame with embarrassment. I felt like I had just been exposed as a fool and that even God thought I was a joke. Part of me knew that wasn't true, but there was just no way I could resolve the picture now seared into my thoughts of God standing by, thoughtfully watching all the pains and blows the world dealt to me.

I knew I would never make it with God if I was angry with Him or Jesus, so I gradually dropped the issue. I didn't resolve it, I didn't understand it, I just dropped it deeper into my soul's toxic waste pit. It became just one more unresolved issue to me. This unresolved issue began to erode away more of the remaining "building blocks" of my soul. Still I determined that I would go on with my relationship with

Him like before. I would just block this terrible question out of my thoughts and forget it.

I had just taken a couple more hits in my soul. Even though I determined I would not hold this against God, I felt I had lost something I thought I had received from Him. Because of the terrible questions I could not completely block out, I surrendered my godly understanding and even my spiritual identity as a beloved child of God.

If we now add this actual encounter that my unsurrendered soul had to the already damaged Soul Model we've been building, we end up with a poor soul which now looks like this. The godly understanding we had, along with the spiritual identity that had a tiny toehold in our soul—gone.

Illustration 5: More Unresolved Issues Further Weakening

The few remaining "blocks" or character traits of this person would be viciously guarded, maximized, and capitalized upon by this badly wounded soul. These traits would become very exaggerated because they were the only strength this soul had. The above soul now looks like a perfect candidate to become a workaholic who is very sure of himself, very good at what he does, very macho, and capable of rationalizing and bending the rules to accomplish his goals. Or this soul could belong to a highly motivated women's' rights advocate who had a genuine heart for women but no use for men, God, or family roles. Both of these hypothetical people might act very nice, be kind to others, and be highly successful, but they would be under great stress from their souls to continue to maintain their roles. They would actually be strong candidates for "Burnouts of the Year."

Chart – Layers

On the chart just above the three original sources—the unmet needs, the unhealed hurts, and the unresolved issues—we see what looks like a red war-zone bunker. This is what I call the layers. This is also the soul's bottom line, last-ditch defense headquarters.

Illustration 6 – LAYERS

> CORE OF POWER STRUCTURE
> # LAYERS:
> self-conrol, self-reliance, self-protection, self-centeredness, self-defense
> SOUL'S bottom line defense system

Here is where the soul carefully lays down its most serious defense layers like a hardwood floor over a rotten, scummy, mildewed sub-flooring. These layers of self-control (manipulation), self-reliance, self-protection, self-centeredness, self-defense, as well as self-understanding, self-promotion, self-image, and more, are the fake personas and false fronts we all put on from time to time. They are our "pretty" parquet hardwood floor that covers over the ugly dry rot and mold hidden underneath. We carefully cultivate a false front of self-reliance so that no one thinks we are needy and full of holes. We want to give the appearance that while we don't need anyone to do anything for us, we are ready to help them with their pitiful problems. We cover our own weaknesses carefully with self-defense systems so that no one can see our vulnerability and exploit it. Often we maintain this position with great self-control (manipulation), controlling our own feelings and responses as well as controlling and manipulating others who walk too close to our personal space. This requires a considerable amount of inward focus and self-centeredness to constantly maintain all the potential emotional fronts that we fear other people might try to breach.

This is the control room of our battlefront; this is where we practice and train ourselves with self-understanding, artificially pumping up our self-esteem, and remaking our self-image to line up with whoever we happen to admire or envy. This is where we try to convince ourselves that we have everything under control.

This is really like having the basement of your house filled with toxic waste and your idea of damage control is to lay down a new hardwood floor and top it with an expensive Persian carpet. You might even haul in a velvet sofa and hang a crystal chandelier just to set it off nicely. You would present a good front to any who might take a look into your windows, but you're really trying to cover up great gaping holes within your soul.

As you are showing off your new "living room," toxic waste fumes are coming up through the floorboards, up through the expensive Persian carpet, and poisoning your life every day. There is no damage control here. There is only a dangerous façade of safety and security. Your soul is in denial of the escaping toxic fumes, yet they keep coming up with increasing regularity.

These "fumes" or symptoms of the soul's distress are represented on the chart by the symptom bubbles. The red war zone bunker was initially established by the soul to prevent the escape of any symptoms from the unmet needs, unhealed hurts, and unresolved issues. It doesn't work, though, because these symptoms surface right through the soul's layering just like the bad odor of stinking garbage would float up to gag you even if you had covered it with a lace table cloth and linen placemats. These symptoms are the proof of a soul with toxic waste in its basement.

Illustration 7 – THE SYMPTOMS

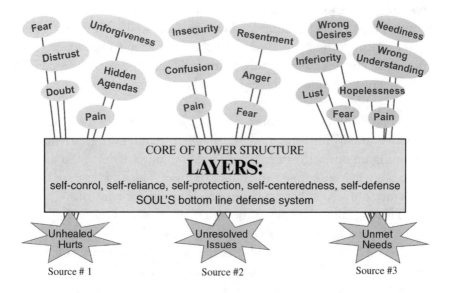

Look at the symptom bubbles coming up out of the unmet needs first. People with unmet needs in their souls will manifest symptoms of wrong understanding, neediness, wrong desires, a sense of inferiority, lust, fear, hopelessness, and pain just for starters. The wrong desires are for things that the soul mistakenly believes will meet the drive of its unmet needs. The sense of inferiority emanates out of never feeling whole, never feeling that enough is enough. The ongoing sense of neediness never abates, never lessens, and the hopelessness that any relief will ever arrive grows heavier and heavier.

The person with unmet needs will seek out material things, hoping that a new car, a new mate, a new job, a new boat, a new big screen television set will finally make up for that underlying sense of lack and emptiness that never goes away. This source hole of the extremely needy person makes me think of the black holes in the atmosphere that they worried about on Star Trek. Get your spaceship too close to one of those babies and you were sucked in and gone forever.

In my early days in the body of Christ, I wanted to fit in but just didn't feel that I really did. There was a great deal of initial acceptance and affection from the people at my church, but when it began to ebb, I became nervous. For the first time in my life, I had felt somewhat accepted and it seemed to be fading away. I began to rather frantically retell the stories again of how I'd been treated wrong, what I had never had, and how I just wanted to belong. I retold them with more and more frequency as I felt more distance growing between others and myself in my church.

It seemed that people started buying answer machines to keep from answering my persistent phone calls. The pew we all sat in together every Sunday was now empty except for me. When the pastor said Amen and I turned to see where my usual lunch companions were, they had already left. Finally I cornered one of them and asked what was going on. The person sighed and said, "Well, if you must know—you're just too needy. You've been draining the life out of all of us."

That was so painful to hear, and I went home and processed that hurt and humiliation for a long time. The problem had been identified, but no one had told me what to do about it and I didn't know what to do, either. So my soul decided it had to come up with a solution. I would no longer appear needy to anyone, I would become extremely self-reliant, self-focused, and self-sufficient! I would need no one.

I became Super Christian (translate: Super Pain) for the next few months—definitely an overreaction. For most of my life, whenever I would react to something painful, I would swing my mental and emotional pendulum as far in the opposite direction as I could from what I perceived to be producing the pain. Reacting wasn't good enough; I had to overreact. In my new Super Christian mode, when someone in church would ask me how I was, I would reply, "I'm just fine, thank you. Why, I'm highly blessed and favored of the Lord. Couldn't be better. Just great! How have you been since, well … you know. I mean, did you ever get over that bad time with your husband? Has he gotten another job yet? No? Um, well, how about your son?

Have they let him back in school yet? No? That's too bad; do you want to talk about it?"

I was dangerous to everyone, and I set myself up for more pain and rejection before I worked through that cycle. That is what the soul does—overreacts, setting itself up with a painful cycle of self-defense and facades. It was a long time before I could admit to anyone that I needed help after that. When our soul does this to us, it reminds me of the old pinball machines. The ball hits one bumper, which throws it into another bumper, which throws it into another bumper, and on and on. There is nothing you can do to stop that cycle until the ball loses momentum and falls through the slot in the front of the machine.

Getting God into these areas to meet your needs is not just important so you will be a nicer person to be around. Unmet needs make you vulnerable to those who know how to exploit them. Cult leaders prey upon people with unmet needs because they are so easy to manipulate. Any time you can convince needy people that you have the answer to their unmet needs, you can play those needy people like violins, or like a deck of cards as my friend, Jackson, would say. Unmet needs can cause you to place yourself in very dangerous situations.

One major benefit that I have realized in my life from understanding the workings of my soul and praying the binding and loosing prayers to open up to God's healing is that I have felt a tempering of my over-reactor. Hallelujah! My mental and emotional pendulum can still swing, but it no longer swings from one extreme to another when it gets thumped. This is a very good feeling.

Chart – Unhealed Hurts

Look now at the symptom bubbles that are coming up from the unhealed hurts on your chart. They, too, blow right up through the war zone bunker, hardwood floor and all. These symptoms include fear, unforgiveness, distrust, hidden agendas, doubt, and pain for starters. The symptom balloons emanating out of the three different sources are not exclusive of each other. In fact, they may cross over from source to source in some people. But this layout came from what I believed God was leading me to list.

For example, when someone has been wounded and ripped apart by a happening that results in a long-term unhealed hurt, the fear is understandable. All of us have experienced fear of being hurt again. Fear and pain are actually listed in the symptom balloons from each of the three sources. Unforgiveness is easy to understand when you have been hurt and you do not know how to get over the pain. Distrust and doubt ensure that we keep others at bay, refusing to allow them close enough to hurt us in any way. The tendency to have hidden agendas in the unhealed hurts' symptoms stems from the desire to always be prepared for any contingency so that you will never be caught off guard.

Chart – Unresolved Issues

As a result of our unmet needs (birthed when something good that should have happened to us did not) and our unhealed hurts (birthed when something bad that should not have happened to us did), unresolved issues come out of not understanding why these needs and hurts happened to us. Unresolved issues are birthed when we are unable to productively process the things that happen to us.

The symptom bubbles coming out of the unresolved issues probably began coming up following the other two areas of wounding to the soul. They come into being as the soul begins to realize that things are not working out the way it wants and it feels angry and cheated. The symptoms surfacing out of the unresolved issues come from the painful questions of your life that seem to have no answers. Sometimes we are heading towards our thirties to fifties before we even know what the questions are.

The person with major unresolved issues in his or her soul very often comes from a background where not only were there more surprises and shocks than normal; there may well have been another dynamic at work. This person frequently has grown up in a home where the boundaries were unclear, the rules were unspoken, and you never knew when you might step on a land mine. This is also the atmosphere of many alcoholic homes. I have firsthand experience with that dynamic as I grew up in one.

This person can go either of two ways as time passes. He or she may grow up with a lot of unresolved resentment and anger because nothing could ever be counted upon to be the same from situation to situation. The "rules" were always changing, and there was always a strong sense of everything being unfair. While this person may become very aggressive with their own "rules," others may retreat into the confusion of a life that seems to make no sense, yet still feeling the pain and fear acutely. This person will battle insecurity in many areas of his or her life.

The soul tries to establish false personality traits to compensate for these symptoms bouncing around inside of it. An insecure woman may force herself to become a risk-taker, always trying to be in "control" of her relationships and activities. The angry man may "act" very gentle, projecting a false front of peace and calm as he holds open doors, pulls out chairs, and hands you roses. A spiritual leader with deep unresolved issues may become legalistic and critical, establishing his or her own boundaries and lines drawn in the sand. The person filled with unhealed hurts may become cynical and suspicious, dropping out of life on drugs or alcohol while berating society in general for its insensitivity and lack of caring.

Wrong Behaviors

The unsurrendered soul begins to panic as it realizes that it cannot contain the toxic fumes or symptom bubbles any longer. It begins to search its memory banks for former behaviors that were once able to take the edge off its pain and panic. The soul decides that the only answer is to revert to former behaviors (pre-Christian), which it insists it can control. After all, the soul reasons, since this is a desperate situation, isn't it better to control a small wrong behavior rather than to have a complete massive meltdown?

Illustration 8 - WRONG BEHAVIORS

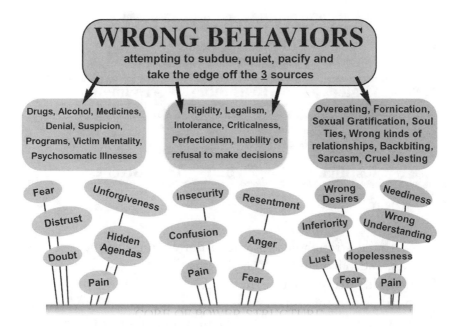

Eventually, the wrong behaviors become bigger and bigger, and what began as a simple coping mechanism takes on a life of its own. Soon the person is trapped on a soulish merry-go-round.

Eventually the person begins to realize that his or her behavior patterns are becoming too hard to hide anymore. Others who are concerned begin to speak to this person about getting a handle on some things they are seeing. This prompts defensiveness, rationalization, and justification of any suspect behaviors. The soul can become quite arrogant and prideful about its complex system of controlling everything.

Illustration 9 – STRONGHOLDS

STRONGHOLDS
Soul's first line of defense

Logic	Reasoning	Arguments

Wrong Ideas   Wrong Attitudes
Wrong Beliefs   Wrong Motives
Wrong Patterns of Thinking

Justification	Denial	Defensiveness

We build strongholds to defend our actions, our beliefs, our excuses, and our inability to make positive changes in our lives. Strongholds are probably the most powerful form of coping mechanisms that the soul engages. In fact, strongholds are built to defend the soul's entire crazy system of trying to run our lives.

Stronghold patterns of thinking and stronghold-protected mindsets need to be loosed—smashed, shattered, and torn down. If they are not, many half-truths (don't ever forget that a half-truth is also a half-lie!) and deceptions can remain hidden away in the soul. Just knowing about strongholds and knowing how the soul runs its craziness won't change anything. Knowledge is only knowing facts. Wisdom is knowing what to do with your knowledge. But nothing will happen if you don't have integrity to make you do something with your knowledge and wisdom. So, now just do it.

"Lord, I bind my mind, will, and emotions to your will and to your truth. I know I have been making excuses, denying wrong thought patterns, and trying to defend myself. I cannot defend myself to you. You know everything that is going on in my soul. I want you to be able to use all of me—even every corner that I have tried to hide from you. I loose, smash, and crush all stronghold thinking that I have used to defend myself when I have tried to hide ugly thoughts from you. I tear down every high thing in my soul that has tried to exalt itself between you and me.

"I choose to accept your thought patterns, Jesus. I bind my mind to you. I do not want any more crazy thought patterns; I want yours. I choose to surrender all of my defensive thinking, my denial, my excuses, my rationalizations, and my justifications. I cannot defend my soul; I must surrender it. I choose to do that, Lord. I am ready to get my soul train onto your tracks. Please help me do this, so that I can begin to fulfill my destiny purposes. I want to be whole, I want to help others become whole, and I want to tell the world about the God who could change even me! Amen"

These binding and loosing prayers will enhance what you are already doing right and show you what you are doing that is not as effective as it could be. How can anyone go wrong with a win-win deal like that? The hardest thing about the Keys of the Kingdom prayer principles is simply to make the choice to use them. Your soul will not go quietly into the night on that battle, trust me.

How do you know if the praying of these principles is working in your soul? How do you know if you are actually pulling down some of your strongholds? You will find that you can meet someone (or run into some thing) who sent you into meltdown the last time you ran into him or it, and you do not feel affected or reactionary anymore. You walk right through a difficult situation or meet up with a difficult person, and you come out the other side of such a meeting without so much as the smell of smoke on your clothes.

That is the best way you can know for sure that you are making progress with your unsurrendered soul's stuff. There is no way to take your soul's temperature, and there is no qualifiable test or examination you can undergo to gauge how you are doing. Spiritual growth and the diminishment of your soul's craziness are only visible when you realize that you are walking through canyons you've walked through before, but now you are just wanting to get on through them instead of going into meltdown in the middle of them.

Let's Stop Fussing About the Symptoms

Too much of the help people are being offered today is to simply treat their souls' symptoms. I have had many distressed mothers and fathers ask me if I will pray and "loose" the drug habits or promiscuous behaviors of their spouses or their children. I tell them that this kind of praying is really not effective. These wrong behaviors are only attempts to mask the symptoms of a deeper problem, a much more basic source of distress. That is what we need to be praying about.

I have even told people that they should try not to worry about the symptoms that are manifesting in their lives or in a loved one's life. They should focus all of their prayer energy on creating an opening in their own souls, and in their loved one's wounded soul, so that God can work on healing the sources of their distress. God will always begin meeting needs, healing hurts, and bringing resolution to issues and unanswered questions when He is given room to do so. That is the whole reason to be tearing down strongholds, loosing wrong beliefs and wrong ideas—so you can voluntarily open up and get God into the sources to fix them.

If you have ongoing headaches, it can seem to make sense to take aspirin to try to mask the pain. It seems to make sense, unless the pain is coming from blood vessels that are being restricted by the pressure of a brain tumor. By taking the aspirin, you are trying to treat the symptoms of the problem. If you do nothing to fix the source of the problem, the brain tumor would continue to grow and become even more dangerous. That is how we have often tried to deal with the pain of our souls. We have tried to treat their symptoms that are manifested in our thinking, our feelings, and our actions. And their craziness gets more and more dangerous to our lives.

Let's do a little review here before we go on to the next chapter. The unsurrendered, unrenewed, unregenerated soul has little understanding or concept of godly truth. Truth to your soul is whatever it has determined it should be. The unsurrendered soul perceives truth through the filters of the experiences it has recorded in its data banks. This kind of truth is never perceived the same as other peoples' ideas of truth because the filters of their life experiences are different.

We probably started life without a full array of psychological "building blocks" due to the unmet needs and unhealed hurts of our own parents. This caused some holes within our soul. Most of us were able to handle this as we grew into our roles in life. Our souls had enough blocks to give us the foundation we needed to go on. Life then began to tear at our souls' building blocks, snatching away some of the good and important things that were imparted to us by the authority figures who raised us. Now there were more holes in our souls.

Unmet needs probably existed first because we were deprived of some of the basic needs that are necessary to having a whole and complete soul. We have "holes" in our soul wherever one of these basic needs is missing.

Unhealed hurts began to occur in our lives when unexpected acts of loss, destruction, or cruelty came into our lives. We might have been physically hurt, perhaps we lost someone we love, we were betrayed, we were rejected, or we were abandoned by those in whom we had placed our trust. When the hurts are deep enough, they can rip out some of the soul's "building blocks" that we had been fortunate to acquire in our early life. Being deeply hurt can cause us to lose our grip on our sense of security. Being betrayed can cause us to lose our sense of being loved. Being abandoned can cause us to lose all sense of trust.

We are unaware of having done anything to deserve such a powerful loss, and we do not understand how to prevent it from happening again. We begin to question the fairness of our lives, even the fairness of God. We begin to lose even more of the "building blocks" that we had started out with. We all grow up with questions about our lives, and some of them become unimportant to us. But many do not and they only increase in intensity as we grow older. Unresolved issues often rise up in the souls of new Christians after the glow of the honeymoon with Jesus wears off and we began to seriously look at the promises in the Word of God that seem so out of our reach.

Perhaps we began to question God regarding our need for a godly mate. The Church often seems to preach that marriage is the ultimate goal for a Christian, and that some of our mental and emotional needs can only be fulfilled through marriage. Marriage is also often portrayed as a source of God's purposes being fulfilled in us as Christian men and women. If this were true, why wouldn't God make sure that each person not only got married, but that each person married someone perfectly suited for him or her in every way? Otherwise, wouldn't some of us be playing the same "game" everyone else was playing, but we were only allowed to play on one slanted corner of the field?

A true need in God's eyes is anything that is *essential* for the fulfilling of His purposes for us and for making us whole people (whole in soul and spiritually healthy). The greatest Apostle in the Bible, Paul, never married. God obviously did not seem to think that marriage was essential for fulfilling His plan and purposes in Paul's life. I'm not anti-marriage, I am just using this example to get you to consider that many things that we think are unmet needs in our lives really are not. That does not mean that we won't experience such an event at some point in our lives, it just means we need to quit obsessing about not having the experience now and get on with what is at hand before us.

One last bit of Good News to review here. All of your soul's "building blocks" that were never given to you (causing your unmet needs), or that were taken away from you (causing your unhealed hurts)—God can restore them to you. He will if you will just surrender and allow Him access into your soul to do so. Even your unresolved issues and questions that may have blown so many holes into your soul—He will resolve them if you will let Him in to do so. Okay, let's go on to the next chapter.

four

Façades and Wrong Behaviors

The soul creates many façades to cover up how we really are thinking and feeling inside. It often designs these façades based upon two false beliefs that many of us have grown up with. They are both lies. As long as these wrong beliefs remain unchallenged in our souls, they will continue to negatively impact our relationships to others and to God.

The first lie is that we must meet certain human standards to be approved and accepted. The second lie is that we must be humanly approved and accepted to feel good about ourselves. When you feel that you have been approved and accepted because you have performed up to a certain human standard, *you have not been approved and accepted*. Your performance has! As soon as you stop performing at that same level or better, human approval and acceptance will be withdrawn.

Each of us should always try to do our best in whatever we do. We must, however, stop expecting our validation as being a worthwhile being to be given or withheld because of our performance. You and I, as believers, are validated because of our relationship to the King of Kings. Period! From this point on in reading the book, agree to accept the truth that God never validates you because of your performance. He validates you simply because of your position in His Kingdom.

One wrong façade that our unsurrendered souls will establish is the façade of agreement with God when it is a deception. Our souls will put forth ideas and prompt actions that appear to be in the will of

God, but they are actually self-promoting. The human soul can be extremely convincing that there are certain self-willed decisions that God agrees to let us make, certain ungodly things that He agrees we can have, and that wrong agreements we have entered into can be adjusted and prayed into alignment with His will.

I talk to so many people who have entered into a relationship, started a business, or have some kind of a ministry which they acknowledge probably was not done in God's will. They are convinced, however, that they can pray and convince God to bless their endeavor if they do everything right from now on. That is an intriguing proposition, isn't it? Thinking that we can pray and make God bless something that never was His will for us.

That opens up a discussion of God's "perfect" will and God's "permissive" will, doesn't it? I think that this proposed understanding of the will of Almighty God is a very smart deception of the human soul. It helps it get what it wants if it can convince you that this is okay in God's permissive will. God does not have two levels of will for His children. It is human parents who have four or five levels of decision-making regarding their children. God's will was established for us so long ago that we cannot conceive the actual time involved. We are either in His will or we are not. Did not God say several thousand years ago, *"I know the thoughts that I think toward you, saith the LORD, thoughts of peace, and not of evil, to give you an expected end"* (Jeremiah 29:11, *KJV*)? God's will and plans for us are designed to move us towards the end result that He expects—not the end result He hopes for.

Hard Lessons for Hard Heads

God can certainly use the hard situations that arise out of us having pursued our own wills, but the lessons may be hard and the blessings may be few. Still, the lessons are all designed to turn your footsteps and thoughts towards His expected end—your destiny. When you find yourself slogging through the hard lessons of consequences, this is a good time to bind your will to God's will and your mind to the mind of Christ while loosing preconceived ideas you have about letting God be God.

The Bible tells us to: *"Cast your cares on the LORD and he will sustain you; he will never let the righteous fall"* (Psalm 55:22, *NIV*). We are also told in 1 Peter 5:7, *"Cast all your anxiety on him because he cares for you"* (*NIV*). This casting can be very difficult when you do not realize the strength and power being exerted by your soul to hang onto everything you are trying to cast off. It builds smoke screens, defense systems, and strongholds to protect its "stuff" from your casting off.

These soulish screens, systems, and strongholds must be brought down for God's healing to flow through our unsurrendered soul. It might seem more logical to you and me if God would just smash through them for us, but God's ways are not our ways. He is waiting for us to voluntarily surrender them to Him. Even if He were to take these obstacles down, if our souls were not surrendered they would immediately try to sabotage any acts of His grace and mercy.

"Because the old sinful nature within us is against God. It never did obey God's laws and it never will. That's why those who are still under the control of their old sinful selves, bent on following their old evil desires, can never please God" (Romans 8:7-8, *TLB*).

If God was to smash through our souls' strongholds and walls so as to flush His healing and gifts through us, our soul would begin to scream violation! Hear what God tells us we should do through Paul's word to the Corinthian church, *"We use our powerful God-tools for smashing warped philosophies, tearing down barriers erected against the truth of God, fitting every loose thought and emotion and impulse into the structure of life shaped by Christ. Our tools are ready at hand for clearing the ground of every obstruction and building lives of obedience into maturity"* (2 Corinthians 10:4-5, *The Message*). This says that He has given us *weapons and tools* for us to use to pull down the strongholds, barriers, and obstructions between Him and us.

I believe the situation is as simple as this: *"You built them, you tear them down."* He is waiting for us to voluntarily break open a way of access for His entrance into our innermost parts. If we will not, He will work on us in other ways. He will put obstacles into our paths and close doors in our faces to get us to realize that He is still God, He does know best, and we need to cooperate with Him. I am very grateful to God that He keeps on trying to push us to receive His best. The Lord spoke to me once saying, *"Tell them that if they will not come out from behind their strongholds and walls willingly, I will put frustration, stress, and anxiety in their way until they are forced to flee to me for deliverance."*

How many times have we pursued our own wills, heading down wrong paths with our faces set like flint towards our own goals, and suddenly we were blocked and frustrated in the way we were pursuing? How many times have we all chosen to believe it was the devil blocking our paths, and we began rebuking and carrying on and casting out—trying to remove what we thought the obstacle was. It was the Holy Spirit all the time, keeping us from charging around the next bend where the "bridge" was out over a deep rocky gorge of circumstances.

You can cooperate with this whole process of casting off wrong beliefs and wrong behaviors by loosing wrong patterns of thinking and wrong agreements that you may have made about having to take care of yourself. You can also loose wrong beliefs about what kinds of actions and behaviors will make you feel better. Then you can choose good actions and behaviors like praying, exercising, and laughing so that you can get a flood of God-ordained endorphins rushing through your body. In my office, where we often have up to five people working on separate yet interconnected deadlines, the stress and tension can really build. The enemy is always hanging around trying to maximize that kind of tension. We all try to remember when it must be time for an endorphin break and someone tells a joke or does something silly which causes everyone to start laughing. It really helps.

Body and Soul Getting Into Mischief

Paul also told the Roman believers that all things were not completed and made new at the point of their spiritual salvation—there was more to be done in their souls: *"Be not conformed to this world: but be ye transformed by the renewing of your mind, that ye may prove what is that good, and acceptable, and perfect, will of God"*

(Romans 12:2, *KJV*). Paul was saying to us that we need the renewing of our minds. This is also saying that the will of God is good, acceptable, and perfect.

This renewing of the mind does not come from simply binding your mind to the mind of Christ and loosing wrong ideas and wrong patterns of thinking. That gets you ready to begin occupying your soul's space with some serious reading of the Word. You feed your body three times a day. How many times a day do you nourish your poor, cranky, pinched-up, desolate, unsurrendered soul with God's life-giving love letters? Washing your mind and your heart/soul with the Word to calm it and transform it even affects your body's health.

"A calm and undisturbed mind and heart are the life and health of the body, but envy, jealousy, and wrath are as rottenness of the bones" (Proverbs 14:30, *Amplified Bible*).

Whenever your soul/mind feels neediness, the soul searches for a fix. Depending upon what your soul thinks will "fix" its distress, your body learns to respond to the distress signal. Once the body acts out a behavior or acquires a substance that alleviates the distress of the soul, a "track" is actually laid down in the brain. The brain remembers the behavior or the substance that brought relief to the body and the soul. Every time that same behavior or substance is accessed again, the track is etched deeper and deeper into the brain and requires more and more of the behavior or substance to bring relief. This is how addiction builds.

Doctors have now proven that some people are deficient in the natural "morphine" substance in our bodies that God created to give us a natural mental, emotional, and physical sense of well-being. This is an internal body chemical called endorphins. The word "endorphin" means "morphine within." Endorphin-deficient people are prone to depression and addictive substances such as drugs or alcohol.

Endorphins are naturally released, per God's plans for us, by creative activities such as exercise, laughter, prayer, and godly sexual relations within marriage. All of these activities elevate natural endorphin levels. Endorphins are incredible little guys, acting as painkillers by disrupting your body's pain pathway back to the brain, performing as antidepressants, and strengthening your immune system. Our ability to cope with stress relates directly to the endorphin levels in our bodies. When you are under prolonged stress, your immune system's efficiency is reduced dramatically. Some doctors have said that endorphins improve the circulation of blood as well.

The human body's ability to produce its own opiates may explain how someone severely wounded in battle can continue to fight or have the strength to save someone else. Some scientists feel that endorphin release may be another reason some people pursue dangerous activities such as bungee jumping. So-called thrill seekers and adrenaline junkies may not just be addicted to the rush of adrenaline; they may also be addicted to endorphins.

Exercise, meditation, relaxation and a good sense of humor may be more helpful than what those in the medical communities once believed. Norman Cousins reported that ten minutes of solid belly laughter gave him two hours of pain-free sleep when he was battling a painful degenerative disease.

If you have a very low tolerance for pain, you may have an endorphin deficiency. The incredibly good news is that you can pump up your own endorphin release level with exercise, laughter, and prayer. We have the Keys of the Kingdom to bind ourselves to the truth and to loose deception and wrong beliefs from ourselves, and we have endorphins to make us feel better about the whole process. What a great God!

Internet Ministry

Working at my internet question and answer ministry keeps me in close touch with Christians who are struggling with their unsurrendered souls today. When people can write anonymously about their struggles, there is a gut-level honesty that you rarely hear from someone in a church setting. Many people say that the internet is the work of the devil, and he certainly is willing to take advantage of anything that has such enormous power to reach into millions of homes around the world. So are many people who lack spiritual and moral understanding, but who are obsessed with a drive to cash in on a lucrative commercial market.

The internet has enormous power to connect the hurting and fearful people of the world with those who are putting out the Good

News. As I daily answer questions from people around the world, I am reminded that there are psychics and shamans and cultic web sites offering the same services for money. Even if there is no money asked for up front, the spiritual and financial costs of accessing those sites will come further down the line. People are in such distress and confusion today that they are actually paying people to help them destroy themselves.

I recently had a very angry woman e-mail me that she was so angry with Christian ministry sites that said they wanted to help people, but never answered e-mails or questions. She told me that if I didn't answer her, and quickly, she would go online and ask a psychic. She admitted she knew that was not right, but said she wanted somebody to tell her what to do. Such confusion should not exist even in an angry Christian. I exchanged several e-mails with her until she finally retreated from the truth I kept offering her. I believe she is still thinking about what she heard and it will bear fruit some day.

Extreme confusion also existed in a young woman from the East Coast who e-mailed me. I'll call her Monica.

QUESTION: "Dear Liberty, I had the privilege of talking with you when you were in my city. I told you that I was confused over your description of God wanting intimacy with us. Having worked years ago as a prostitute, I always thought that intimacy meant sex. You encouraged me to believe that I was confused about intimacy. You said that true intimacy was based upon mutual trust, voluntary submission to another person, and the giving nature of true love.

"Trust has always been difficult for me, and I tend to sabotage a lot of things in my life. I would really like to be totally surrendered to God, but it seems that life is so hard and the weeds in my soul have become like a jungle. I'm too tired to fight and I'm too tired to run. Monica"

ANSWER: "There is nothing in your past that can destroy your present and sabotage your future unless you let it. I want to encourage you with the knowledge of this truth, because it puts you in control of whether or not you want to trust in and surrender to God. You can bind your mind to the mind of Christ and then loose your way out of that jungle in your soul. You can trust God, Monica. No man, woman, child, or devil can keep you from doing that—only your own soul can.

"I was so encouraged when I finally realized, once I became a Christian, that I wasn't anybody's victim; it was only my soul preventing me from being completely free. I felt empowered to change, knowing that I held the keys within myself to break free. I felt empowered to break into a relationship with a God who loved me and wanted that relationship more than I did.

"You say you have read my books, Monica. Reading them is only the doorway into the knowledge of how to be free. You could read all about how to be a figure skater, studying the terminology, view videos of the technique, and be encouraged by Gold Medal Olympic winners to do it! BUT if you never put on a pair of skates and ventured out onto the ice (perhaps to fall, perhaps to appear foolish, perhaps to even hurt yourself a little), there is no way you could ever become an ice skater. You have to become personally, actively engaged with the prayer principles you read about and practice what the books are teaching.

"To learn how to be free from your past to embrace your future requires some practice. All things are possible with Jesus Christ, but many of those possibilities require involvement and practice on your part. You practice getting victory over your unsurrendered soul by using the Keys of the Kingdom in prayer, and by studying the principles of those prayers to know what is happening as you pray. These prayers can strip away the piled-up bushes and tall weeds and old junky 'vehicles' from your past that are clogging up your soul.

"Your very own unique, specific life plan has always existed in heaven. When you bind your will to the will of God (I sometimes do it ten times a day, particularly when I realize that my will is determined to make a manic jump off God's tracks), you are committing your will to being under obligation to God's will and plans and purposes. Liberty"

QUESTION: "Since I heard you, I now know that soulish attitudes and family dynamics have taken over a huge part of my soul. Can one ever escape that? My mother died a drug addict. Why did I become a prostitute and a drug addict, too? Monica"

ANSWER: "You need to loose wrong patterns of thinking about who you are and why you are the way you are. You need to loose the effects and influences of the wrong agreements and wrong actions of those who were in authority over you and contributed to the forming of your earliest understanding. Wrong ideas, patterns of thinking, feelings and emotional reactions were formed by your soul as a result of being exposed to the facts of your mother's confusion and behavior. You cannot loose those facts, but you can loose the effects and influences from them that are still impacting your concept of who you are today.

"I would say that you are still feeling the pain of those wrong thoughts and feelings because you were never made aware of them and told how to get rid of them. You can be made aware that you have termites in your house's foundation, but if you don't know how to get rid of them—all the awareness in the world isn't going to stop them from trying to destroy your home. You have to both have knowledge and act upon it."

QUESTION: "Something in me believes that my life should end as my mother's did. How can I know that I won't end up committing suicide like she did?"

ANSWER: "You need to loose that wrong belief and the resulting thought patterns and attitudes that come from thinking those thoughts. You need to bind your mind to the mind of Christ and let Him begin to filter His thoughts into your thinking. You need to be reading the Bible daily, looking up the Scriptures that tell you who you are in Him. If you don't know how to do that, read the Gospel of John and the book of Ephesians over and over and over until you see some things beginning to change in your thinking. Liberty"

QUESTION: "I have chosen to forgive my mother, and I can't help but wonder about the sins of the forefathers or foremothers in my case. The effects and influences of these sins are still evident in my life today. What can I do about that?"

ANSWER: "They are only in your life because you have not yet loosed, released, stripped their hold, and severed their ties to your soul. When you accepted Jesus Christ, He gave you the chance to have a fresh start, a new slate, and a 100 percent chance to begin anew. Second Corinthians 5:16-21, *The Message*, tells us this: '*So from now on we regard no one from a worldly point of view. Though we once regarded Christ in this way, we do so no longer. Therefore, if anyone is in Christ, he is a new creation; the old has gone, the new has come! All this is from God, who reconciled us to himself through Christ and gave us the ministry of reconciliation: that God was reconciling the world to himself in Christ, not counting men's sins against them. And he has committed to us the message of reconciliation. We are therefore Christ's ambassadors, as though God were making his appeal through us. We implore you on Christ's behalf: Be reconciled to God.*'"

"As one who has walked with God since 1972 (give or take a few squabbles and hissy fits and grumbling on my part), I am extending to you the true message of reconciliation. Bind your will to the will of God and bind your mind to the mind of Christ to help you shut out the old tapes of your soul and the death-filled words of the world as you learned to perceive it. Loose your old patterns of thinking, loose your old mindsets, loose the wrong teachings that you have heard, loose the deception and denial from your soul, and LOOSE WORD CURSES from yourself, Monica! Then pray the same thing for your children. Do some soulish housecleaning to make room for the new creature within you to stand up, stretch out, and get comfortable with its role.

"Focus on what I said above. You are being 'soul scattered' by all of your concerns. That is a favorite tactic of the unsurrendered soul, to get you to focus on worrying about so many things that you couldn't see one answer coming through if your life depended on it. Loose your distressing thoughts. Keep reading the Word, keep asking God to help you navigate this new course to victory, and keep praying like you have learned. Deal with your life in the natural as you have to, binding your mind to the mind of Christ and loosing wrong thought patterns when you feel overwhelmed."

This woman has written to me several times since these exchanges by e-mail. She is learning to lean on God and stop being pushed around by her unsurrendered soul. She is also learning to disengage from the wrong examples and wrong role modeling of her earlier years. It is a blessing to have actual keys in prayer to share with others who are being torn up by their own souls. I appreciate solid keys that I can give people to help them attain a walk by faith (which is a very abstract thing if you think about it).

The Unsurrendered Soul's Hidden Secrets

I get many questions from people regarding sexual promiscuity, adultery, pornography, homosexuality, and masturbation. I have covered all of these issues in former books, except one that I am being queried about more and more lately: masturbation. It appears that this behavior is common even in Christian circles. It is never talked about openly, of course, and perhaps that is why so many people do not understand how to overcome this behavior. I received the following question on my internet ministry page. It was from a truly anguished woman, and her painful guilt prompted me to introduce this subject here.

QUESTION: "Why do pastors, teachers, and counselors refuse to speak or teach about self-control and the guilt that is consuming so many church people because of practicing masturbation? The guilt is horrible, but I don't know how to stop."

ANSWER: "Masturbation is an issue that both men and women struggle with. Perhaps one reason that it is not spoken about in sermons, classes, or therapy groups is because there are people who do not want to believe that masturbation is a sin. There is no direct Scripture verse in the Bible that condemns it by name. Yet, it would seem that any secret behavior practiced to achieve sexual satisfaction outside of the area of married sex would not be the will of God. There is no reference in the Bible recommending physical self-gratification of any kind. The act of fornication (sexual activity with someone other than a marriage partner) is certainly addressed in the Word. Perhaps masturbation is a form of fornication, too, as it is seeking sexual satisfaction outside of married sex. Not all people would want to believe that. Paul told the Roman Christians, *"In the same way, count yourselves dead to sin but alive to God in Christ Jesus. Therefore do not let sin reign in your mortal body so that you obey its evil desires. Do not offer the parts of your body to sin, as instruments of wickedness, but rather offer yourselves to God, as those who have been brought from death to life; and offer the parts of your body to him as instruments of righteousness. For sin shall not be your master, because you are not under law, but under grace"* (Romans 6:11-14, *NIV*).

"The Word also tells us that the believer's body is the temple of God. In 1 Corinthians 6:18-20, Paul told the Corinthian Christians, *'Flee from sexual immorality. All other sins a man commits are outside his body, but he who sins sexually sins against his own body. Do you not know that your body is a temple of the Holy Spirit, who is in you, whom you have received from God? You are not your own; you were bought at a price. Therefore honor God with your body'* (*NIV*). The temple of God seems to be an unlikely place to pursue self-gratification of the sexual kind. It also seems unlikely that masturbation could be a way of honoring God with our bodies, doesn't it?

"Paul told the Ephesian Christians, *'Don't waste your time on ... the barren pursuits of darkness. Expose these things for the sham they are. It's a scandal when people waste their lives on things they must do in the darkness where no one will see'* (Ephesians 5:11-12, *The Message*). An activity that consumes one with guilt, a secret thing that would devastate a person if it were revealed in public, and an act that must be hidden in darkness where no one will see it cannot possibly have the light of Christ within it.

"Now, having addressed the subject, what is the answer to stopping this behavior? Until people are taught or learn on their own to open up to letting Christ live in them and through them, many will continue to struggle with unmet needs and unhealed hurts. When those needs and hurts get too strong for them to control in acceptable ways, many give in to the temptation of resolving the drives of their needs and pain however they can. Pornography and masturbation are sensation-producing behaviors that can be practiced in complete privacy, which can make them more difficult to control. That Christians are attempting to deal with their unmet needs and unhealed hurts in this manner is not too hard to believe when full-blown pornography is available in our homes on the internet and near-pornography is available in our homes every night over network television, on videos, and in the magazines we read.

"The human body reacts to everything going on in the unsurrendered soul—good, bad, or otherwise. Much of the body's reactions to the pressures and drives of the unsurrendered soul are manifested in behaviors that seem to bring a temporary sense of well-being so that the unmet needs and unhealed hurts seem to calm down for awhile. Desires to repeat these behaviors are not just psychological, coming from the soul (*psyche*), as I once thought. Masturbation produces a release of endorphins, feel-good hormones that our own bodies (*soma*) manufacture and store. Pornography also produces a release of endorphins.

"God created our bodies to release these feel-good hormones through certain godly behaviors. The problem we can get into is that endorphins are released in the body whether a release-inducing activity is God-ordained or not. The opiate receptors of the brain that receive these feel-good 'hormones' have no idea of whether or not they are even natural opiates, such as endorphins from within your body. The brain's opiate receptors also happily accept chemical stimulants such as drugs and alcohol as well.

"The answer is not to stress and feel great guilt over the masturbation or pornography. *That might sound strange, but stress and guilt have never healed anyone of the sources of their wrong behaviors.* The answer to stopping these behaviors lies in deconstructing the soul's self-gratification patterns by using the binding and loosing prayers.

"You need to understand how to tear up the actual pathways that have been laid down and etched into the brain by each repeated act of self-stimulation. This is a wrong mind/body agreement and can be very hard to break if you do not have the understanding of the Keys of the Kingdom prayer principles to help you. Pray this prayer whenever you feel that you are beginning to be tempted to indulge in this form of behavior, or any other self-gratifying behavior that does not honor God:

"Father, I want to be free from trying to comfort myself with acts of physical self-gratification. The best way I know to get close to your strength to overcome this desire is to bind my will and my body to your will and to bind my mind to the mind of Christ. I choose to do this; I choose to place

myself in your will that I might be free. I bind my emotions to the healing, balancing control of the Holy Spirit.

"I loose all wrong mind/body agreements that I have made knowingly or accepted ignorantly. I loose, strip, and tear up the psychological and physiological tracks that my brain has laid down, even deeply etched into itself, turning back to them every time I long to physically console myself. I loose wrong patterns of thinking and wrong beliefs that I deserve to be consoled and stimulated in this manner to make up for other things that I have never had. I loose all layering and stronghold thought pattern building that my soul has put in place to protect its right to try to appease my unmet needs and unhealed hurts.

"I loose soul ties that I have ever had with any sexual partners from my past. Lord, thank you for these keys that give me something to hold onto in prayer when I am seeking to change. I want to change, Father, and I am asking for your divine help as I make the transition to being free from these thoughts and behaviors. I want to stop all wrong behaviors and I want to be healed. You are my Healer and you are my Lord. Bless you, Lord, and thank you. Amen."

"I do not think that the best form of praying is ever the guilt-filled, begging, or fearful prayer. God hears those prayers, too, but I am sure that faith-filled prayers brimming with confidence in His loving care are the prayers He loves the most—actually the prayers that agree with His will. Binding your will to the will of God, binding your mind to the mind of Christ, and binding your emotions to the Holy Spirit places you into a position to become aligned with His will. His will is that you would experience the blessing and satisfaction of the fruit of the Spirit as listed in Galatians 5:22-26, '*But the fruit of the Spirit is love, joy, peace, patience, kindness, goodness, faithfulness, gentleness and self-control. Against such things there is no law. Those who belong to Christ Jesus have crucified the sinful nature with its passions and desires. Since we live by the Spirit, let us keep in step with the Spirit*' (*NIV*)."

QUESTION: "I read your books in early 1998 and I am in agreement with your teachings. I am a single (never married) adult. In your books, you said that you encourage people to believe that God will bring the right person into their life as a mate in His timing (I agree with this). But are you saying that we are to remain passive regarding initiating a relationship with someone? As a young boy, I remember praying to God asking Him to have the right girl walk up to me and introduce herself or to please, please, please remove all desire for a girl.

"Of course that never happened. However, I want to know if you are recommending (as does most of the teaching directed at adult singles) that single people become completely 'passive' regarding forming any romantic relationships.

"If this is so, is there any place for personal initiative in seeking relationships?"

ANSWER: "Well, this is a slightly new take on the subject of romantic relationships! I believe that we do need to be very careful about trying to get our unmet needs met through initiating relationships with other people. When strong unmet needs get tangled up with personal initiative, it can be dangerous to get in the way of that soul-perceived goal! My next statement is not going to win me any popularity contests, but getting your needs met or having your pain pacified by someone else is never the basis for a healthy relationship.

"The place for personal initiative is this: Use every cell in your body, soul, and spirit to become the best person you can be for God — not for a future marriage partner, not for a relationship partner — but for God.

"As far as remaining "passive" (as you say) instead of initiating a relationship on your own, I think being successfully single is never a passive state — it is a very aggressive state of action. I've been single since 1972, so I am not just proposing theory here. We should determine to be the best we can, to be all we can, and to be devoted to wanting to see God's will done in every area of our lives. This requires a seriously aggressive stand against giving in to all the strong psychosomatic (mind/body) drives that come out of the unmet needs, unhealed hurts, and unresolved issues that clutter up most Christians' unsurrendered souls.

"An aggressive approach to determining to be the most surrendered-to-God person possible should be the focus of our lives, with no regard for single or married status. Too often, we view marriage as God's ultimate goal for our lives. It is not. God has never married; Jesus has never married; Paul was never married. You will not go to heaven as a good husband or a good wife. You will not be a success on earth because you were a good husband or a good wife. You will go to heaven because you have surrendered your life to Christ, and received His forgiveness and salvation. You will be successful here on earth when you are aggressively seeking the will of the Father for your life.

"There is nothing wrong with wanting to get married when God has ordained you should. Marriage is an honorable and good state. But marriage is not God's ultimate goal for humanity here on earth. Every single person, and every married person as well, should be focused first of all on becoming the best person possible for God. The focus to become the best person possible for marriage comes after that.

"Until you get the green light from God with regard to a relationship—and you will know when you get it—focus on becoming the best at what you are currently being directed towards or being shown to do. In the natural realm of the world, people often feel they have to act quickly to snatch up a 'good' person for a relationship before someone else does. You never have to worry about that in God's world. He always knows which person He wants to match up with which other person. When both parties to a God-appointed relationship are aligned with His will, a glorious relationship will happen!

"Waiting on God is good, as God is never in a hurry. He wants us as healed as possible to be a blessing to Him and others. He never wants us to sacrifice ourselves to a relationship just so we don't have to be alone. He is not interested in providing mates to keep us from being lonely, or to keep us from feeling needy. He wants to heal our unhealed hurts and meet our unmet needs, because no human 'mate' will ever be able to do so. And here is the clincher! Those who surrender their souls to Him and allow Him to heal them are high up on His list of candidates for: Marvelous, Awesome, Glorious, Holy Matrimony!

"Ask God to show you everything you could be doing now to enjoy present friendships and relationships with others, whether they are male or female, old or young. God never puts us in a holding pattern where nothing is going on with regard to our destinies; He is always trying to teach us and mold us through every human interaction we experience in this life. God can teach you relationship wisdom while you are helping out at a senior residence. He can teach you relationship humor while you are volunteering at the zoo. God can teach you relationship patience while you are working with your church's youth group.

"There is a lot we can learn from others in all stations in life. Be about the business of breaking the power of your unsurrendered soul—that inner 'rascal' that keeps sending up needy, painful drives to push you to move in with personal initiative and find a relationship. Your soul always wants to convince you that God isn't working on your behalf for the best possible relationship of your life!"

QUESTION: "I have a problem of wanting compensation from God for the unresolved injustices of my life. I am convinced that God cannot fully bless my life on the basis that I might accept it as 'payback' for past, unresolved injustices. I know that I am somehow tricked into believing that good things have to be on their way to compensate for time that I have lost. I have forgiven those involved, but is that enough? I feel that the Lord has caused my soul to not react to future injustices, so I think I'm all right there. I received Jesus Christ in my heart back in 1992, but somehow I keep looking at life with the emotions of an idealistic teenager as though I am to live the rest of my life with a 'consumer mentality' instead of a 'producer mentality.' Jack"

ANSWER: "Jack, as you believe you have already lost time, don't set yourself up to lose any more. You must not look at what has happened to you in the past as open accounts that will come due some day. When you try to 'keep books' on God, your soul will always cry 'foul' because it will never be healed by trying to collect on its outstanding 'accounts receivable.' It will only be healed when you loose (rip apart and tear down) your stronghold thinking that is protecting your self-perceived right to a payback.

"Strongholds are rationalizations and justifications for holding on to wrong ideas and beliefs. You need to also loose your misconceptions about God and about what is 'fair.' God doesn't deal in fair like humans do. God once told me (when I was crying 'unfair!') that He dealt in what was right and best for everyone involved.

"The basic binding and loosing prayers (which I call training wheel prayers because they steady and stabilize you while you are getting your forward motion and balance in this type of prayer) are very effective at stripping away wrong ideas and beliefs. Your soul will fight this, however, and it will even try to get you to turn the prayers into 'mechanical rote' reading of them. These prayers must be prayed with focus on every word, committing yourself to every word you pray, and believing that God will respond.

"Now you have to determine whether or not you really want to give up those flawed expectations that are so crippling your thinking. If you do, you have the prayers and I hope you have the understanding of what you are doing to help yourself get free. Begin praying the following prayer as soon as you read this.

"Jesus, I don't want to think about what is owed me or due me because of what I have been through. I know this kind of thinking is not godly. Your Word says that you have given me the Keys of the Kingdom so that whatever I bind to your will here on earth is bound in heaven. It says that whatever I loose on earth will be loosed in heaven. In your name, Jesus, I bind my will to the will of God, that I will be constantly aware of His good plans and purposes for my life. I bind myself to the truth of God that I will not be deceived by my soul or the deceptions of the world and the devil.

"I bind my mind and my thoughts to your mind, Jesus, so I will be aware of how you would have me think this day. I do not want to react out of my own human, carnal thoughts when situations arise suddenly; I want to think and act, as you would have me act. I loose every wrong thought, wrong attitude, and wrong pattern of thinking that would keep me from receiving your peace. I loose all thoughts

of doubt, anxiety, stress, and confusion. I loose all the effects and influences of the wrong agreements I have come into.

"I want your grace and mercy, Lord. I want your will, so that I will always know that I am in alignment with your promises. Please speak guidance and direction to me, so that I can go forth in faith that you are leading me to wholeness and healing. Amen"

"After you pray this, Jack, then stop and wait for God to speak to you. Wait in silence, alone. No TV, no one else talking to you, just you waiting on Him. If you do not hear Him speak, then pray this prayer again with as much faith and agreement as you can, and wait. Every time you do this, you are forcing your unsurrendered soul to focus on hearing from God. If you sense your soul resisting your waiting on God like that—thinking of other things you should be doing—then bind your mind to the mind of Christ again so that you can hear His thoughts. Loose your soul's nonsense, clouds of words, and attempts to bring confusion by trying to distract you from focusing on God."

QUESTION: "Where does depression come from?"

ANSWER: "A soul that is trying to keep unforgiveness, bitterness, and hopelessness buried and covered over will always telegraph its distress to the body. Medical experts have found that the body reacts to this kind of psychological pressure by pumping toxic chemicals into the bloodstream.

"This creates a chemical imbalance in our bodies that can cause depression, and so much more—even lethal diseases like cancer— regardless of how much a person loves the Lord. This is the product of the soul's dangerous coping mechanisms of stuffing, burying, and denying. We must make a way to get God into the areas of our souls that need to be healed or de-stressed. The binding and loosing prayers show us how to do this.

"The Apostle Paul said that 'Abraham believed God and it was accounted to him as righteousness.' The phrase 'Abraham believed God' (in the original Greek) means that Abraham was in agreement with God's will in his every thought (soul), purpose (spirit), and action (body). Abraham was considered righteous because he was in alignment with the will of God in every aspect of his being. Isaiah tells us the fruit of such righteousness is peace! *'The work of righteousness shall be peace; and the effect of righteousness quietness and assurance forever'* (Isaiah 32:17, *KJV*).

"When I have no peace, I know I am not in perfect alignment—somewhere—with God's will. This always causes hidden stressing in my soul. The resulting toxic chemicals being released pull my body chemistry out of balance, not only giving opportunity for depression, but compromising my entire immune system as well!

"I believe the answer is to constantly maintain our souls with focused binding and loosing prayers, but not in trying to bind yourself to peace. Peace is a gift from above, and you cannot bind the gifts of God to yourself and thereby pass up the Giver. These prayers have power to bring us to a place where we can receive the peace Jesus has for us, and they also have the power to stop further compromising of our immune systems."

QUESTION: "I have been reading through your *Shattering Your Strongholds* book and I have come to the chapter on forgiveness. In my past I had a relationship that was verbally and mentally abusive. Although this was some time ago the memories still crop up from time to time, even though I have chosen to forgive this person. In praying the binding and loosing prayers to loose the residue of these memories, I hope to truly feel my soul has received from God. I get a little scared thinking that if I still think of these uncomfortable memories from time to time, I haven't forgiven completely. Do I just continue with the training wheel prayers of binding my mind to Christ's mind and loosing the old memories? I just want to be right with God and know I can go to the Cross and truly be forgiven. Can you give me advice on how to go about this??"

ANSWER: "I believe that when you have finally truly forgiven, those memories may still come back but they will not make you uncomfortable. They will be neutralized of any power to distress you in any way. Keep loosing all the effects and influences of wrong agreements, keep loosing soul ties, and keep loosing wrong beliefs you have about anything to do with this person.

"When you have let go of any and all residue in your soul regarding this, His peace will come and all memories will be like dry historic facts that you just archive in your mind. But, the fact that you are so concerned about this tells me you are going to be completely free very soon, because you want what God wants! Good for you!

"I had an exciting example of that complete freedom a few months ago. I thought of some old deep hurt someone had inflicted upon me, as it seemed to 'fit' the conversation I was then having with another minister. I tried to tell this pastor what had been done to me and try as I might, I could not remember any of the details. I got so excited that I couldn't remember these details. They had been archived in my historical archive memory!

"I still knew something had happened, but my soul had not been allowed to keep the details on artificial life support and it was over. This is when you know you have truly wiped the other person's slate clean of any personal accountability towards you. This is when you know you have truly given the person the gift of full forgiveness for all they did, wrapped up in mercy and grace. Even more so, this is a gift to Him, and how He must appreciate it when we can give it!"

QUESTION: "Regarding the forgiveness issue in your first *Shattering Your Strongholds* book, I was wondering what your viewpoint is on the following. In the Matthew and Mark verses, Jesus told people that God would forgive them only if they forgave others. And if they did not forgive others, He would not forgive them. We all agree that it says that point-blank. Don't you think that the time frame is the key to these verses?

"Jesus was talking to them before He died on the cross. There was no grace yet in place from His sacrifice because He had not gone to the cross. The people He was talking to were still under the law and they were required to make sacrifices by animal as they always had. When they would make the animal sacrifice, it would be for forgiveness of sins. I believe Jesus was telling them, don't ask for this animal blood to cover your sins if you have not forgiven others' sins.

"As you probably know, as part of their culture, people from that time were not kind and loving to one another and did not treat each other as God would want them to. Many of Jesus' teachings to them were in an effort to instruct them in how God would have them to live, such as the Sermon on the Mount. Many of them had never heard love preached before. It was a new concept to them, as was forgiveness.

"The Ephesian verses were after the atonement of Jesus' blood sacrifice on the cross. I note that in these verses it does not say that God will not forgive us as the Matthew and Mark verses do. These verses say, 'as God has forgiven you.' These two sets of verses do not say the same thing and I am surprised that you lumped them together in your book as saying the same thing. One says 'God will not forgive you' and the others say 'as God has forgiven you.' What do you think? Marianne."

ANSWER: "You have presented an interesting thought, Marianne. Actually, I have never heard anyone suggest that before. However, I don't think Jesus was talking to them only as still being under the Law. I think we could try to put too many things He said into that category, not just forgiveness, if we would subscribe to your suggested theory.

"Would you say that He was only talking to those people as still being under the Law when He said in Matthew 5:27-29, '*You have heard that it was said, Do not commit adultery. But I tell you that anyone who looks at a woman lustfully has already committed adultery with her in his heart?*' After His death, did that mean they did not have to worry about this anymore?

"And in Matthew 5:43-45, '*You have heard that it was said, 'Love your neighbor and hate your enemy.' But I tell you: Love your enemies and pray for those who persecute you, that you may be sons of your Father in heaven.*'

"After Christ died, does that mean no one had to obey this Scripture anymore? I could, of course, go on and on listing things that Jesus said before He died. If they were not relevant after He died, then why would God record these commands if they had no meaning to our walk before God today? I personally accept every Word Jesus said as applying to my life today. Jesus said He was the same yesterday, today, and forever. Jesus' teachings are that as well.

"For me, the clincher is that He was willing to die as a sacrifice that I might be forgiven and freed from my sins. How can I ever accept that kind of sacrifice as only for me, and say it stops with me? You admit that God says we are to forgive as He forgave us. How can I ever say that I don't have to make the sacrifice of dying to my own soulish self-interest that you or someone else might be free of my unforgiveness? I cannot. We are to be like Christ in every way, even to the sharing of His sufferings."

QUESTION: "My husband has left me and set up another home. It really hurts when he comes back to our house and takes things for his new house. I feel enraged when he walks in and ignores my feelings about boundaries right now. I feel powerless. I have asked God to forgive me for these feelings. My husband even asked if I would pack the rest of his things for him! Help me understand. Maxine."

ANSWER: "You should pray first to break all soul ties with your husband. This will help to reduce the pain in your soul in situations like this. Soul ties are not a healthy means of keeping emotional contact with any other person. The Breaking Soul Ties prayer is in *Breaking the Power* that you say that you have. Praying this will help strip away the clouds and confusion in your soul so that you can hear God.

"Listen very carefully to what I am about to say here, then pray, and unless God says NO, get ready to set up some boundaries. You say your husband has moved out and set up his new home. If he were still in your home trying to work things out, that would be different. But he has chosen to establish a new home for the time being. So pack up whatever is his along with whatever you feel he might need. Have it all delivered to some place where he can pick it up, and then change your locks. Tell him that you need some space to begin working with God to become whole. Let your answering machine screen your calls. Begin to spend time alone with God, behind these boundaries that you have set up for the time being at your home.

"Such boundaries do not mean you are unwilling to work things out according to God's direction. They only mean that you need to clear some space to allow God to help you think clearly. Many rejected wives are afraid to give themselves this space with God. They think ANY tie with the husband, no matter how emotionally difficult it may be for them, means that there is hope he will come back. I disagree.

"You have all the hope in the world for God's will to be done here, but God often works better when there are no confrontations going on between souls. Hold tightly to God, set genuine boundaries in the natural realm of your life, and let God be God. Bind your husband to God's will, bind his mind to the mind of Christ, and bind him to the truth. Loose wrong beliefs from him, loose stronghold thinking from him and loose the layers he has built over his unmet needs and unhealed hurts. That gives God a great platform to work from, and He can work quite well with your husband without you being present. How does He do that? His Spirit will be with the one you pray these prayers for."

five

Fine-tuned Prayer Principles
that Mend and Heal

R ight after being saved early in 1972, I began hearing a teaching that did very little to make me feel secure about my relationship with God. A pastor in my church repeatedly said that the Christian walk was like a tightrope and one misstep could plunge you off the rope into the abyss of sin. The good news was that you could be forgiven. The bad news was that as a Christian you would never walk as high as you had before. This same pastor also repeatedly said that to fall into sin was like falling onto one of those old-fashioned furnace floor grates that brought heat up into your house. If you fell onto one of those when the furnace had been on high for some time, you would be scarred from the grid marks on that grate. So, if you fell into sin, you would be forever scarred with the grid marks of your sin.

I was nervous every day about making a wrong step and losing my standing with God. I am so grateful to now know that God will always accept our words of repentance and our pleas for forgiveness. He will then chuck our sin into the Sea of Forgetfulness! He gives each one of us a one hundred percent chance to start over—over and over when we have the right attitude about not wanting to repeat our failures. Most people that we know, even the ones who love us the most, will eventually get fed up if we keep repeating our offenses. You might hear them say, "I've really tried with you. I have forgiven you over and over, and you just keep doing the same wrong things again. I give up. I just can't do this any more."

That's not how our God responds to our repeated failures, though! Hallelujah! He so wants us to succeed, to grow, and to know Him in an ever-greater manner. He wants to see us shine by reflecting His glory.

That's a high calling, you know—being a glory reflector! Our heavenly Father is always focused on who we are becoming, not what we've been or where we are now. We fall seven times—seven times He helps us get back up. There is a song that says, "We may fall seven times, but seven times we get back up. And we're back in the race, back in our place!" Those are great words. When our attitude and minds are set towards obeying and loving Him, our Father in heaven will take our hands, stand us up on our feet, brush the mud off us, and put us back in the race—back in the place where He has always desired for us to be.

While I do not fully agree with the doctrinal belief of "once saved, always saved," I do think it is much harder for a born-again believer to jump out of the hand of God than any of us have thought. I hear from so many struggling Christians who contact me through my website's question and answer pages to ask if they have lost their salvation. Sadly, it is clear that there is limited confidence in the incredible power of God's ability to hold onto one little wounded, confused, rascally human soul trying to outrun its own born-again human spirit. Remember, this is the same God who has the ability to create suns, stars, planets, volcanoes, and hurricanes.

So much of this confusion about God's power to hold onto those who have confessed their faith and belief in His Son, Jesus Christ, comes about because of believers' lack of understanding about God. He is not on stakeout in heaven, training binoculars on us to see who is going to fail next. So many of us have learned too well how to beat up on ourselves with self-condemnation over our mistakes. We have to stop that.

I heard one pastor say, "If my eighteen-month-old son comes running up to me with a full diaper, I don't get upset and legalistic about it. I scoop him up in my arms, lay him on the bed, clean him up and powder him sweet, give him a kiss, and then set him down to run off to play. I don't get all uptight because he hasn't learned how to use a potty chair yet. He's my kid and I love him."

Then he said, "Why can't we realize that we are God's kids and He doesn't turn away from us when we make a mess. He just picks us up, cleans us up and powders us sweet, gives us a kiss, and sets us back down to get on with life."

Our souls are not only responsible for self-condemnation; they get a lot of help from Satan as well. Any time you want to feel bad about yourself, to feel guilty or to be ashamed, Satan is right there to act as your ready buddy, your constant companion. He'll even help you come up with things to be ashamed of that you hadn't thought of yet.

I don't need a buddy like that. I need a friend, a savior, a master who says, *"I have given you the Keys of the Kingdom. Use them in your prayers to shut out Satan's words and to strip out your soul's negative thought patterns and wrong mindsets. That's why I gave them to you, so that you could be free of who you were in the world to become who you are to be in me."*

Time and Experience

There are at least twenty Christians I am aware of who have been using these Keys of the Kingdom prayer principles since before my first book, *Shattering Your Strongholds*, was originally published in 1992. Some of these believers talked me out of computer printouts of my early manuscript for their own study, and some asked me to hold teaching classes with chapter handouts. Several of these people are still using the prayer principles and have moved on into their destiny purposes. All of them have been fertile ground for understanding of how the unsurrendered soul tries to even override the binding and loosing surrender process.

Your soul cannot stop the power of these Kingdom keys, but it can mess with your head in other ways that cause you to be distracted from the purity of their use. One person I'll call Carolyn, very confident in the power of this message of these prayer principles, was always asking what she should be binding and loosing in different situations. Carolyn packed a laminated prayer chart out of *Shattering Your Strongholds* with her for years, so she wouldn't pray anything wrong. I kept reminding her why I called the binding and loosing prayers in my first book "training wheel prayers." That is because you use training wheels to help you learn to ride a bike only until you get your own sense of forward motion and balance. Then you put the training wheels aside and just do it!

Carolyn was so concerned about what she should loose in every new situation that arose. I would patiently remind her that the basic loosing prayers would work just fine. Troubled, she would say, "But I want to be very specific. This situation involves _____ (fill in the blank) and it's about _____ (fill in the blank), and I want to make sure I loose exactly the right things."

I would answer again, "Just loose stronghold thinking, wrong ideas, wrong beliefs, and wrong patterns of thinking. That will get it." After questioning me if I was really, really sure, she would always walk off looking slightly disappointed. One day, after she told me that she just didn't know what to do because she had loosed every stronghold and every thing she could think of, over and over, she still wasn't sure it was enough for this particular situation in her life.

I closed my eyes and sighed quietly, and then the Lord spoke these words to me. Tell her: *"You've loosed the walls of your stronghold, and you've loosed the remnants of all the wrong beliefs and thought patterns that were involved in its construction. God says that it is down, so walk out of it and get on with your life."* I did, and Carolyn looked rather amazed. Then we agreed together that this stronghold and all of its residue of rationalization, justification, denial, and human logic over wrong thought patterns was broken and collapsed flat. She walked free from that old recycling of her fears of not loosing things right.

There were three other people who had used these prayer principles for over ten years, but they were not getting breakthroughs in certain areas of their lives. This puzzled me, because I knew that they prayed the binding and loosing prayers on a regular basis, and I knew that the binding and loosing prayer principles worked. I have files full of testimonies from people all over the world that attested to this.

One man I'll call Clyde told me that he had been praying the binding and loosing prayers every day for eighteen months and nothing had happened. That challenged my thinking, but he insisted it was so. He just kept saying, "Nothing has happened! Nada. Zip." I told him that I didn't understand how that could be, because I knew the binding and loosing principles worked so well when they were prayed regularly and with faith. Clyde insisted nothing had happened.

I was first of all amazed that Clyde would continue to pray these prayers for eighteen months when he believed he was not getting any answers. Christians do that, though. They hear something that they think should work, and they will do it over and over, year after year, whether it does or not. Perhaps they are thinking, "Maybe if I hold my mouth differently this time, or if I face the north, or if I shut my eyes, it will work this time." That doesn't make sense and it isn't like God.

God is always ready to give encouragement and some form of an answer; we just don't always know how to hear Him. This block in our hearing ability is usually connected to our having very definite, preconceived ideas about how He is going to answer or should answer. That is something I think everyone should loose on a regular basis — preconceived ideas about how God is going to answer us.

As Clyde continued his litany of negativity, I held my tongue and just looked at him. Each one of us needs to learn these two things: You don't have to say something every time someone makes a statement. You don't have to answer every question someone asks you. Sometimes you need to just hold your tongue. The Word says, *"Even a fool is thought wise if he keeps silent, and discerning if he holds his tongue"* (Proverbs 17:28, *NIV*).

Liberty says, "Silence makes most people uncomfortable and often they begin to talk to fill the space. They frequently will give you more information when they do."

Clyde said, "Oh, well, I suppose you'd say that because I finally got a promotion at work after twenty years, that it was because of those prayers I prayed." I just looked at him. He continued, "And you would probably say that it was because I prayed the prayers that my wife and I are getting along better than we ever have before." I said nothing. He continued, "You probably think it was the prayers that had something to do with the unexpected inheritance I got so that we were able to buy a new house and send our daughter away to college, wouldn't you?" I just looked at him.

"And you would probably think the binding and loosing prayers I kept praying caused the people at work to start being more friendly with me, wouldn't you?" Then Clyde looked puzzled and stopped speaking. I said nothing. Finally he said, "Wow, maybe the prayers did have something to do with all that after all."

Clyde was so used to seeing himself as a recipient of hard things and "bad luck" that he couldn't even recognize good things and blessings from God when they came his way. Clyde finally broke into a new pattern of thinking about himself and his family that day. I think he also broke through to a new pattern of thinking about God. He began to look for good things, expecting them to come his way.

Another one of these three people I will call Brenda wanted to speak to me one night. Brenda was a woman who had a hard time praising, complimenting, or even thanking others. Feeling bad one day after a family gathering, she said, "I've been praying these prayers for years, and I just don't understand why my family is still so critical of me. My parents were critical of me and my children are critical of me. It hurts."

I said as gently as I could while still speaking the truth, "Do you really think that this critical thinking of your parents jumped right over you and landed on your kids? This is a generational pattern of thinking that has been passed from generation to generation in your family. No generation got skipped, however, because you really are kind of critical yourself. You need to start loosing critical thinking and other wrong patterns of thinking."

Brenda said, "I have been, for years, and nothing ever seems to change."

I paused for a moment, hoping that God would say something, and feeling that He had, I asked her, "What did you replace the critical thinking with after you loosed it?" She had no idea what I meant, and I only hoped I did. God still hadn't given me the final answer. Again, I practiced my "saying nothing and hoping to look wise" method of operation. I was hoping that either He would say something or that she would speak up and give me more information.

After a long pause, I heard the following words in my head and I said, "You know that you can't directly change someone else, but you can influence them to change when they witness a change in you.

So you need to start with yourself. After you loose critical thinking from yourself, then you need to replace it with something that is the exact opposite of being critical. That is how you occupy the space in your soul where your criticism and judgmental thinking had their roots. You can't just leave that space empty, or what was last there will grow back.

"The opposite of being critical is being an encourager, cheering someone on, being hopeful for their dreams, complimenting their efforts, exhorting them to keep trying, and urging them to believe for God's best. Since faith without works (actions and deeds) is dead, you have to take some good actions after you have loosed criticism and judgmental thinking from yourself.

"Call up your daughter and encourage her in those classes you didn't want her to take. Tell her that you know she will use them for something good one day. Call up your son-in-law and tell him how grateful you are that he has provided such a good home for your other daughter and their children. Call your mother and tell her how you appreciate everything she taught you. This is how you lay down tracks of good thought patterns in your mind, and you will be occupying the territory that you have just cleared out."

I was quite impressed with what God had told me to say, but her soul obviously wasn't. She said, "I'll tell that to my daughter the next time she calls me."

"No, Brenda, you call her—and do it today. Don't let your breakthrough depend upon her telephone patterns. Do it. And then call your son-in-law, and call your mother," I encouraged her.

"Well, I don't want to spend that much on long distance phone calls. I'll write them a note when I get some stamps," her soul weaseled.

"I'll give you some stamps right now," I said as I dug into my purse. "Here, take these and JUST DO IT." Brenda had some strongholds, indeed! The unsurrendered soul protects all of its "stuff" with personal strongholds.

Stronghold Protection

The original Greek word for strongholds, as found in 2 Corinthians 10:3-5, is *ochuroma* which means the logic and reasoning you will use to defend your arguments and the wrong beliefs that you want to protect. An excellent example of the consequences of building a stronghold of excuses for why you cannot deal with your anger before nightfall can be found in Ephesians 4:26-27, *Amplified Bible*. *"When angry, do not sin; do not ever let your wrath—your exasperation, your fury or indignation—last until the sun goes down.* **Leave no (such) room or foothold for the devil—give him no opportunity.***"*

If you choose to disobey this direct commandment of God, *"Do not let the sun go down on your anger,"* then you are rebelling. This verse gives a clear-cut command with no hidden meanings. In your rebellion, your soul will try to convince God that while you do care about His will you have really good reasons why you can't obey this command. Most Christians know better than to rebel and tell God you don't care, but rationalizing, justifying, and defending your excuses for not obeying Him can be dangerous whether you tell Him that you care or not.

The best thing to do when you are in this state is to pray and loose your angry thoughts, loose your wrong mindsets about the other person, and loose any word curses you may have spoken about them, and then forgive that person. But, if you are not going to do the best thing, rebelling with your mouth shut is better than trying to run your excuses on a God who knows you inside out. Rationalizing and justifying our refusal to obey is what actually builds our strongholds, which clearly give the enemy room, opportunity, and a foothold in our lives.

As believers we will get angry from time to time because we do not know how to handle this powerful emotion when we are filled with wrong mindsets and bad attitudes. The stronghold is not the anger—the stronghold is the rationalizations and justifications we fabricate to defend our right to be angry. As Christians, we have no right to be angry with anyone except the enemy.

These Prayers Make Me So Angry!

We hear from many Christians who have always felt they were living as close to God as they knew how until they found the Keys of the Kingdom principles of prayer in *Shattering Your Strongholds, Breaking the Power,* and *Producing the Promise.* After some serious praying to tear down stronghold thinking and the control structure of their unsurrendered souls, they call or write us saying they are having an acute identity crisis. One man, Benjamin, said that he found rage welling up in him and spilling over into things that were not even any of his business.

After living for years behind a façade of hiding his true feelings so he could be liked and approved, Benjamin found that he had no idea how to relate to people in a godly, healthy way. I assured him that the anger and rage had always been deep inside his soul, poisoning his thinking, his decision-making ability, and his feelings that God was working with him to clean out. He needed to let it come out and not try to stuff it back down.

I encouraged Benjamin to keep pressing his soul with these prayers and not to back off. He should try to watch his words and to ask for forgiveness quickly if he spoke too harshly, saying that God was doing a new thing in him and he was trying very hard to cooperate with Him. I reassured him that it is always amazing how God will allow grace and mercy to flood over those around us when we blow up if we humble ourselves and ask for forgiveness as we keep trying to surrender to Him.

Anger is one of the emotional façades your soul will use to throw up smoke screens. Anger is a very powerful God-given emotion, but anger is only good when:

- It gives you the boldness and courage to fulfill a direct command of God.
- It gives you the drive to face and dismantle a work of darkness.
- It causes you to be so disgusted with your own soul that you are ready for change.

Anger is:
- A natural element of passion, which becomes sin when there is no godly cause or use for it.
- Never to be rationalized to support unforgiveness.
- Never to be rationalized to support revenge or "getting even."
- Never to be rationalized and justified to show authority or power.

Anger can be like a jumper cable to jumpstart your action on an issue, but it must never be used as an ongoing source of motivation. When you use battery cables to draw power from another source to recharge your own car's battery, you can damage your battery if you do not remove the jumper cables after you get your engine started.

I'm Not Angry; People Just Keep Bugging Me

Many Christians are so full of stronghold thinking and mindsets that they cannot hear from God, and they are just barely able to get along with other Christians. These strongholds have to be pulled down. Paul tells us in 2 Corinthians 10:3-5, "*The weapons of our warfare are not physical (weapons of flesh and blood), but they are mighty before God for the overthrow and destruction of strongholds, (inasmuch as we) refute arguments and theories and reasonings and every proud and lofty thing that sets itself up against the (true) knowledge of God; and we lead every thought and purpose away captive into the obedience of Christ, the Messiah, the Anointed One*" (Amplified Bible).

This is a perfect scriptural example of how we can use our binding and loosing keys in prayer—our weapons of warfare that Jesus Christ has left for us to use. We loose stronghold thinking, argumentative thinking, wrong beliefs, and soulish reasoning. We loose every proud and lofty thing, such as arrogant attitudes and wrong ideas in our souls that would try to come between the true knowledge of God and us. We bind our minds to the mind of Christ as we loose all of these things out of our souls' grasp. This is how we tear down strongholds in our minds.

When we are feeling hot emotions running through our soul, we don't want to recognize that many of our most irritating circumstances with other people are really divinely strategized training sessions. God builds character and strength through hard times and difficult circumstances. After binding your mind to the mind of Christ, loose wrong ideas you have about whether your life is fair or not. Then bind yourself to God's will as you push yourself into a learning mode to understand what you can learn from the trial. When you do this, there is a good chance that you won't have to go through that same circumstance again. And who wants to go through hard circumstances over and over?

Praying with these keys will link you with God's divine empowerment to help you move from the abstract "wanting to change" to causing personal change to come about in your life in a concrete manner.

"Jesus, I thank you for leaving me the Keys of the Kingdom of heaven so that I can work with the Father instead of always having to be worked on by Him. Working with Him is exciting! Being worked on by Him can be painful because of my soul's resistance. I am grateful to be able to bind my will to the will of the Father, because this allows me to place my will under obligation to His will. I want His will to be done, not mine, because my self-will gets me into trouble.

"I bind my mind to your mind, Jesus, because the Word tells me to want the same mind that is in you. I am choosing your thought patterns over mine, because my unrenewed thought patterns always get tangled up with the unresolved issues of my life. I bind my emotions to the Holy Spirit's healing work. My emotions can still be raggedy now and then, but they are getting better all the time.

"Thank you, Holy Spirit, for your healing and balance. I loose (smash, crush, and destroy) all wrong patterns of thinking, wrong beliefs, wrong ideas, and wrong attitudes that are rooted down so deep in my soul. My choosing to do this uproots them permanently! I choose to believe that when I surrender all of my personal agendas and desires to you, you will give me new plans and exciting opportunities.

"Lord, I know it doesn't matter what things look like in the natural; I choose to believe that you are in perfect control in the spiritual realm. I do not want to mess up what you are doing, so I will hold steady and wait upon you. I can do this now because I have bound my mind, will, and emotions to you. I loose the effects and influences of wrong agreements that I have been a part of, and I loose all desires to be in control. I loose all of my stronghold thinking. So, now, Lord, I'm ready to be your vessel. Tell me that you love me again, and then tell me what to do. I'm yours. Amen"

Change Can Be Good

The Lord first revealed the principles of the binding and loosing prayers to me in 1985, principles I began to use right away to start working on surrendering my own self-willed soul. Since writing my first book which was released in January of 1992, He has continued to bring me to a time of refining the fundamentals of the binding and loosing principles. One thing about writing a book, as years go by you might change and refine your thinking, but the words you wrote in the thousands of copies of the books already sold remain carved in granite, or so it seems. They'll come back to flatten you from time to time. It is always interesting to explain why years later I have modified some stands I firmly took in 1988 when I wrote my first manuscript.

As an example of this, in my first book, *Shattering Your Strongholds*, I stated that I believed the "strong man" mentioned by three of the Gospel writers was Satan. Matthew 12:29 says, *"Or again, how can anyone enter a strong man's house and carry off his possessions unless he first ties up the strong man? Then he can rob his house"* (*NIV*). Mark 3:27 says, *"In fact, no one can enter a strong man's house and carry off his possessions unless he first ties up the strong man. Then he can rob his house"* (*NIV*). Luke 11:21 says, *"When a strong man, fully armed, guards his own house, his possessions are safe"* (*NIV*).

My conclusion that this "strong man" was Satan came from the many teachings I had heard to that effect. Many deliverance ministries use this same passage as scriptural "proof" that we can bind Satan. A couple of years after my first book came out, I began to question my own beliefs as to who the strong man was. I was more and more assured that we cannot effectively bind Satan, so then how could we bind the strong man if this was Satan? Also, if we could bind Satan, the thousands and thousands who have been trying to do this for centuries should have been able to stop him somewhere, shouldn't they?

When I became certain that the strong man of Matthew 12:29 was not Satan, this provoked the question: Who was the strong man, then? In early 2001, one of my staff members and Level II Certified LSM Teachers, Linda Cady, became intrigued with my statements that I wasn't really sure who the strong man was any more, but I was convinced that it was not Satan. I wondered if it could be the unsurrendered human soul. She began to research this sticky issue.

With Linda's permission, I share her research here coupled with views of my own. In Matthew 12:9, we read that Jesus went into a Jewish synagogue and began to teach the people, healing a man with a withered hand. Seeing this, the Pharisees left the synagogue and met together to figure out how to get rid of Him. In verse 15, we read that Jesus was aware of this and left the synagogue to go away from that place. Many people followed Him and He cured all of them.

In Matthew 12:22, we read that He was asked to help a blind and deaf man who was demon-possessed: *"Then they brought him a demon-possessed man who was blind and mute, and Jesus healed him, so that he could both talk and see. All the people were astonished and said, 'Could this be the Son of David?'"* (NIV).

The people were asking in this last verse, "Is this the Messiah?" The Pharisees, who had begun tracking Him when He went out from the synagogue, were probably quite upset at that question. If the Messiah really had shown up, then what would that do to the religious system that the Pharisees so loved? Their greatest concern now was that Jesus was a serious threat to their established religious lifestyle.

Matthew 12:24-28 tells us that after Jesus had healed this man and the people began to wonder if He was the Messiah, the Pharisees reacted. *"When the Pharisees heard this, they said, 'It is only by Beelzebub, the prince of demons, that this fellow drives out demons.' Jesus knew their thoughts and said to them, 'Every kingdom divided against itself will be ruined, and every city or household divided against itself will not stand. And if I drive out demons by Beelzebub, by whom do your people drive them out? So then, they will be your judges. But if I drive out demons by the Spirit of God, then the kingdom of God has come upon you'"* (NIV).

Jesus is describing what the Pharisees are trying to do to Him. They are trying to cancel out His divinity by saying that His power is not of the Holy Spirit, but is of the spirit of Beelzebub. This is done in an attempt to also negate His protection and authority over those who would choose to follow Him—those of His house or His household. Jesus tells the Pharisees that they are not doing the work of God the Father, but they are actually denying that the freeing of the man from a demon is the work of God.

Then Jesus turns to the people and begins to create a word picture for them:

> *"Again, how can anyone enter a strong man's house and carry off his possessions unless he first ties up the strong man? Then he can rob his house. He who is not with me is against me, and he who does not gather with me scatters"* (Matthew 12:29-30, *NIV*).

The word strong, as used here, is *ischuros, which* means strong, mighty, and valiant. In Revelation 18:8, this particular word is used to describe God. *"For this reason in one day her plagues will come, pestilence and mourning and famine, and she will be burned up with fire; for the Lord God who judges her is strong"* (*NASU*).

In Revelation 5:2 and 10:1, *ischuros* is used to describe God's angels: *"Then I saw a strong angel proclaiming with a loud voice, 'Who is worthy to open the scroll and to loose its seals?'"* (Revelation 5:2, *NKJV*). *"And I saw another strong angel coming down out of heaven, arrayed with a cloud; and the rainbow was upon his head, and his face was as the sun, and his feet as pillars of fire"* (Revelation 10:1, *ASV*).

In the following verses, the Greek word *ischuros* is used to describe men. First John 2:14 tells us, *"I write to you, fathers, because you have known him who is from the beginning. I write to you, young men, because you are strong, and the word of God lives in you, and you have overcome the evil one"* (*NIV*). The word "strong" as used in the verse above means "mighty, powerful, strong, and valiant— able to overcome evil." In Hebrews 11:34, *ischuros* is used in the Faith Hall of Fame chapter to describe Gideon, Barak, Samson, Jephthah, David, Samuel, and the prophets. When used of human beings, *ischuros* means "strong in body or in mind"; and it is also used of one who has the strength of soul to sustain the attacks of Satan.

There is no use of *ischuros* in any verses in the New Testament that alludes to Satan.

The people who had followed Jesus to this confrontation would have been familiar with the use of this Greek word *ischuros* as meaning mighty, valiant, and full of valor. It is also likely that these people knew that the word *ischuros* was used in reference to God, angels, and men. Because Jesus knew they understood this, He created a word picture using the word *ischuros* to describe Himself as protecting His own house. The word *house* as used here does not actually mean an abode, rather the Greek word *oikia* (oy-kee-ah) means "family" or the "persons dwelling in the house." This refers to the family that Jesus was gathering, people in whom the Holy Spirit might abide.

The people understood that the only way to plunder His house and steal from His family was if He were to lose His power. The Pharisees tried to convince those who were present that the works which were really of the Holy Spirit were actually the works of Satan. If they could discredit Jesus as the Messiah, their position as Israel's religious leaders would no longer be threatened.

"*Again, how can anyone enter a strong man's house and carry off his possessions unless he first ties up the strong man? Then he can rob his house. He who is not with me is against me, and he who does not gather with me scatters*" (Matthew 12:29-30, *NIV*).

For years, perhaps even centuries, we have taken this passage to mean that we can bind Satan and take back what he has taken from us, or we can bind him and stop his activities. It appears to me that the only one who can bind Satan will do so in Revelation 20:1-2.

With His word picture, Jesus was saying to the multitudes, "*How can anyone come into the house of a man who is powerful and strong, a man fully dressed in the armor of the Word of God, one who is counted with Gideon, Barak, Samson, Jephthah, David, and Samuel as well as the prophets—a man of valor?*"

There is only one way. First the *evil men* must try to bind the Spirit of the strong man. They must speak against the Spirit of God Who has made the man strong. If the evil men can convince the people to not believe in the true source of the power of the strong man, but rather to believe that the strong man has been using Satan's power, then the people who would become part of His household could be plundered. The Pharisee's intent was to take away the strong man's family, the household of Jesus—to keep the multitudes from believing in Him.

In Matthew 12:29, *ischuros* is used twice, *"Again, how can anyone enter a **strong** man's house and carry off his possessions unless he first ties up the **strong** man? Then he can rob his house"* (*NIV*). Does it not seem likely—from the consistent use of the word *ischuros* above— that Jesus is not talking about Satan here; rather, He is talking about Himself as one with God, an angel, or a good man?

Webster's Dictionary says this about our English use of the word "strong":

- Physically powerful.
- Healthy and sound condition, morally powerful.
- Strength of character or will, intellectually powerful.
- Able to think vigorously and clearly.
- Having special competence or ability.
- Governing or leading with firm authority.
- Powerfully made, built, or constituted.
- Holding firmly, tenacious, binding tightly.
- Not easily defeated or dislodged.
- Deep-rooted, having many resources.
- Powerful—in wealth, numbers, supplies.

Even in our own language, English, the word "strong" has far more positive implications of describing a good person than a bad person. In John 17:12, as Jesus spoke with His Father about those who were His, He said, *"While I was with them, I kept and preserved them in Your name (in the knowledge and worship of You). Those You have given Me I guarded and protected, and not one of them has perished or is lost except the son of perdition (Judas Iscariot)—the one who is now doomed to destruction, destined to be lost—that the Scripture might be fulfilled"* (*Amplified Bible*). Jesus tells us here that we were as possessions given to Him by God. The word "goods" as used in Matthew 12:29 means possessions.

If the above research is true, then the only Scripture in the Bible that would support the belief that you can bind Satan has just been rendered null and void. So have a lot of half-truths about spiritual warfare as it is generally being practiced. The key of loosing—the smashing, crushing, destroying, shattering, and bursting key—is the most effective means of stripping both the source of the demonic power and the power itself. A most basic prayer for effective spiritual warfare would be:

"Lord, I bind my will to your will. I bind my mind to your mind, Jesus. I bind my emotions to your balance and control, Holy Spirit. I bind myself to an awareness of the power of the blood and what it means to me. Thank you, Jesus. I loose all stronghold thinking and the effects and influences of all wrong agreements I have entered into and any soul ties that have come out of them. I loose, smash, crush, and destroy the effects and influences of wrong agreements made by others near me or far away, wrong agreements that territorial spirits have been feeding from. I declare that right agreement and your will shall be manifested in my home and my city.

"I loose and smash all hindrances and devices the enemy would try to deceive me with. I loose and crush all word curses, wrong prayers, witchcraft, and any incantations that have been spoken about me or against me, and I ask that you, Father, would turn them back upon the ones who spoke them with wrong intention.

"Thank you, Father God, for protecting me and keeping me aware of the need to pray these prayers. I ask that you teach me how to operate in the gift of the discerning of spirits, that I might be always be aware of the sources of any wrong activity around me. Bless you, dear Jesus, and in your Name, Amen." (See Chapter 3 of Breaking the Power and Chapter 9 of Producing the Promise for further understanding of prayers of spiritual warfare.)

Fine-tuned Keys

Human beings, bless our little hearts, always like to personalize and tweak things that work quite well as they are. That has been especially true of the binding and loosing prayers principles. People frequently send me "their version" of some of the prayers in my books, wanting to know what I think. Some have even collected all of the prayers, tweaked and reprinted them, duplicated my publishers' cover designs, and presented their book of prayers to me. Oh, dear. I believe the old adage that says: "If it isn't broke, don't fix it!"

Many people have wanted to bind themselves to inappropriate things, such as money, success, marriage, patience, love, and so on. I don't think you will necessarily hurt anything by such ineffective prayers, but you certainly won't help anything, either. I'm tired of ineffective, soulish praying—I want to pray prayers that place me in a position to be empowered by God to fulfill my destiny.

One good rule to remember is that you basically bind yourself to the good attributes and characteristics of God such as His will, His truth, the mind of Christ, and even the paths He has always wanted you to walk. Loose wrong things from yourself, such as wrong ideas, beliefs, attitudes, and patterns of thinking. Loose stronghold thinking, word curses, and the effects and influences of wrong agreements you have entered into and any resulting soul ties.

Some people have asked me if they could bind themselves to the promises of God's Word or to God's love. That is like binding yourself to air so you can breathe it. His promises exist and are yours when you have done what you need to do to receive them. His love is all around you like water is around a fish in the sea. You don't have to bind yourself to these things; they exist, and they are yours. You just need to believe in them and make room to receive them.

Do not bind yourself or teach others to bind themselves to "things" that are:
- gifts from God,
- acquired only from making a right choice, or
- acquired through experience.

It is very typical of the human soul that after you have been using the Keys of the Kingdom prayer concepts for awhile, your soul will want to "improve" upon the simplicity of them. That is not to say the principles cannot be improved upon, but some are unaware that they are allowing their souls to complicate their simplicity. This can lead to what I believe are presumptuous prayers.

Many want to bind themselves to God's healing or to Jesus' peace. You cannot bind yourself to healing. Healing is a gift from God that can require life change in the soul or the physical habits of the one needing healing. It is useless to bind yourself to life change and then do nothing to change. The binding and loosing prayers will never take the place of personal accountability or responsibility to do what is needed. But they will help you open up to receiving empowerment from God to do what you need to do.

To bind yourself to a gift is to say that you want to bypass the will and the timing of the Giver. How would you feel if you had purchased a gift for your friend and you were waiting for the right time to give it to her, but that friend sent a delivery and pickup service to get it from you right now?

If you are in need of healing, loose wrong patterns of thinking about infirmity, loose wrong agreements that certain diseases are inevitable in your family lineage, and loose conventional wisdom that says you are at-risk for the disease of the month. When you are in need of healing in your body, worrying about it is like rocking in a rocking chair. Worrying gives you something to do with yourself, but it never gets you anywhere.

When you focus on something negative that a doctor or someone else has said, that is like focusing your camera. When you want to take a close-up shot of someone's face, you focus on that person's face. Everything else other than the face gets fuzzy and out of focus. When you truly focus on God's love and His promises to you, then the negative things in the background get fuzzy and out of focus. When you focus on a negative thing, God's promises can get fuzzy and out of focus.

Instead of trying to bind yourself to peace, bind yourself to the will of God and the mind of Christ. Loose worrisome thoughts, and then stop focusing on them. Loose the wrong desire to keep repeating how terrible things are, and then stop saying those things. Loose the wrong desire of your soul to fixate on reports in the natural, which have no confirmation from God in the spiritual realm, and refuse to let your mind bring them back. Keep binding your mind to the mind of Christ, and focus on Him.

The peace Jesus said He had for you and me (that incredible true peace that the world cannot take away) will not generally settle down into your soul (where unrest and lack of peace occurs) if your mind and emotions are filled with negative activity. Jesus can do whatever He wants to give peace to anyone, but peace is a gentle thing, a soft emotion that generally will not fight strong negative emotions for the right to enter your soul.

To receive this gift of peace, you may have to give up certain things (loosing prayers are a big help here) such as the habit of worrying, a tendency to feed your mind with negative things, and coming into wrong agreements. As you loose all three of these behaviors of the mind, you are making room for peace to be given to you. The Lord can give peace to someone who is filled with anxiety; after all, He is sovereign, and He can do anything He wants. When we cooperate with Him by making room to receive peace in our souls—by loosing peace-destroying activities our souls are accustomed to engaging in—is a good thing to do.

Begin your cooperation with God by binding your will to His will with complete trust in what He has planned for you. Bind your mind to the mind of Christ and read His words of peace and comfort. Bind yourself to the truth of God's constant love for you, and then choose to act like you really believe you are loved. Begin acting out your trust by speaking positive words, refusing to think negatively, and by rejecting any form of activity that would let the world intrude upon your focus on Him. This helps you position yourself to receive from Him—receive what He knows you need most.

And finally, do not bind yourself to fame, which comes from making right choices. Do not bind yourself to satisfaction, which comes from making right choices. Do not bind yourself to wealth, which comes from making right choices.

Do not bind yourself to wisdom, which is gained through experience. Do not bind yourself to patience, which is gained through experience. Do not bind yourself to being skinny, which is achieved through experience.

Occupying Your Soul With Him

Use the key of loosing as your means of creating room within your soul. When you do this, you are removing old recycling patterns from your soul and you are creating room to receive more of the Lord within your soul. The room you create then *needs to be occupied* with right patterns of thinking to help you follow through on your choice to turn away from what you have just loosed.

The binding and loosing training wheel prayers can help you stop begging for things from God that your own stubborn self-will is blocking you from automatically receiving. I know that God is quite aware of all prayer directed towards Him, but I really believe that the prayers that get answered the easiest and the soonest are the prayers that agree that God's will should be done in every area of our lives and the lives of our loved ones. God wants us to get our wills surrendered and out of the way so He can perform His will on earth through us.

Do not worry about praying these binding and loosing prayers over and over. In the original Greek language, the word "vain" as used in Matthew 6:7-10, has a special meaning. *"And when you pray, do not use vain repetitions as the heathen do. For they think that they will be heard for their many words. Therefore do not be like them. For your Father knows the things you have need of before you ask Him. In this manner, therefore, pray: Our Father in heaven, hallowed be Your name. Your kingdom come. Your will be done on earth as it is in heaven"* (NKJV). Vain, as used in this passage, means full of folly, manipulative, and trying to squeeze, according to *Thayer's Greek-English Lexicon.*

This descriptive word meaning "foolish" and "manipulative" describes the wrong, soulish prayers that so many pray in ignorance. The word repetitious is not the point here; the type of wrong prayer is the point. To bind your will to the will of God is certainly not praying with folly, being manipulative, or attempting to squeeze Him. It is a verbal prayer of surrendering your will to His will, prayed in accordance with Scripture (Matthew 16:19).

It is a perfect example of praying that God's will would be done in you and on earth as He has already established it in heaven. When we pray for His will to be done, especially when we are praying

113

according to Scripture, we can expect Him to do what needs to be done in every instance.

They Are Just Keys

Because of the repetitious nature of our unsurrendered souls, I frequently remind people that they need to remember these are just prayers using scriptural keys. Some people get way too excited about the key aspect of these prayers. Keys are just keys—they are meaningless unless they will open up or start something. If you never use your key to open your mansion or start your new Corvette's motor, you are not any better off with the keys than you were without them!

These prayers are not to just be read, they are to be PRAYED with focus and concentration on every word that you are committing yourself to by the words you verbalize. You should always understand why you are praying with the keys of binding and loosing, as well as what the consequences of such prayers may be like. Understanding is vital here, not just repetitious repeating of the prayers.

If you just turn on a high-powered blender full of juice without knowing that you need to put the lid on, things are going to get messy. If you give a teenager a power saw without explaining that they are not to cut up the porch, the deck, and the fence, things could get messy. That is why understanding is necessary when you use things with lots of power.

Do you get up every morning and brush your teeth? If you don't, you should—but that's another issue. What do you use to help you clean the nighttime fur off your teeth? A toothbrush and toothpaste, most likely. Could you clean your teeth without them? You probably could, but it would probably take longer, be less efficient, and it would certainly be less practical. The speed, efficiency, and practicality of these two tooth-cleaning facilitators do not make the toothbrush and the toothpaste more godly or anointed. They just work best, and they work well.

This analogy holds true for the principles of the Keys of the Kingdom. They work, and they work well. You can eventually get your soul's stuff surrendered to God on your own terms and in your own time, but it may take your entire lifetime. Or you can learn how to use the Keys of the Kingdom and begin to surrender your soul much faster, more efficiently, and in an extremely real and practical manner.

What man has taught you of soulish understanding about what will and what won't work for your life brings you no guarantee of success. What God instructs you to do always brings spiritual success. Unfortunately, the unsurrendered soul is at war with God, distrusting Him completely. Romans 8:7: *"Because the carnal mind is enmity against God: for it is not subject to the law of God, neither indeed can be" (KJV)*. Enmity is described in the Greek language as hostility and hatred. So don't look for much cooperation with praying these prayers. Your soul will try distractions, sleepiness, headaches, and hunger to distract you from praying these prayers. Don't listen to it.

The ultimate goal of these prayers is that your entire soul would be surrendered to God for healing, guidance, and alignment with His purposes. This is a goal of reaching a place where you are able to say, "Not my will, but thine be done" to God—with your body, soul, and spirit in alignment with that statement. You use these prayers to reach the place where you can truthfully say, "God, I want your will to be done and I leave all the details up to you."

See The Big Picture

We must all learn to look beyond our own needs and desires when we pray with the binding and loosing prayers. Believers today have become so concerned with their problems and the problems within their churches that it seems we have forgotten there are hurting and dying people out in the world. We must be very careful that we do not forget the purpose of getting healed in our souls.

The purpose is that we could be servants and help others to hear the truth of the Gospel of Jesus Christ that they might be set free to be all He created them to be.

Paul told the Colossian Christians that it was time to get on with walking the Christian walk. He wanted them to get on with their lives! He wanted them to stop standing and sitting on the sidelines, worrying about if they were going to walk right. He wanted them to get on with the walking out of life! If you always stand at the side of the ice and worry about whether you are going to skate right, you will never get on with the skating.

Paul gave us good advice in Colossians 2:6-7, *The Message*, "*My counsel for you is simple and straightforward: Just go ahead with what you've been given. You received Christ Jesus, the Master; now live him. You know your way around the faith. Now do what you've been taught. School's out; quit studying the subject and start living it! And let your living spill over into thanksgiving.*"

The prayers do the work of bringing the spirit, soul, and body into agreement with God's word and His will. The bonus, the privilege, the blessing for those willing to pray the prayers is that God's will also includes the blood of Christ, all the work of the cross, and the Holy Spirit as your teacher, counselor, and friend.

We can pray, we can act upon what we have prayed to cooperate with God's empowerment, and we can do what He tells us to do. God is in us, He is available to us, but it is up to us to choose to cooperate with Him. We cooperate by renewing our minds with the Word of God. We cooperate by choosing right things to speak. It is up to us to make Jesus Lord of our soul life. If Jesus is not the Lord of your thought life, then He is not your Lord at all.

Most people in the born-again bunch are used to hearing the voice of their unsurrendered souls. It has become normal and natural for us to " hear" the voice of the unsurrendered soul telling us how to run our spiritual life/growth experience. This is living a double life, being terminally double-minded. Commit to being single-minded towards your Lord and Master, your Savior. You will be amazed at the response you will get.

six

Mother in a Mine Field

Aggressively believing and anticipating that God has a revelation or a new directive for you every day poises your faith for growth. Such anticipation can hardly wait for the next morning. Our perception of the future always defines how we live in the present, impacting how we act and think each day. If we are discouraged, filled with pain, unhappy, having no hope of things getting better, the future can seem massively overwhelming.

The Bible tells us that without a vision, or a revelation understanding of something about what is to come, God's people will perish. We need to realize that there is a divine plan already set in place for our lives, having been set in place for longer than we can imagine— even before the foundations of the earth.

> *"For you created my inmost being; you knit me together in my mother's womb. I praise you because I am fearfully and wonderfully made; your works are wonderful, I know that full well. My frame was not hidden from you when I was made in the secret place. When I was woven together in the depths of the earth, your eyes saw my unformed body. All the days ordained for me were written in your book before one of them came to be."* (Psalm 139:12-16, *NIV*).

Because of our souls' incredible stubbornness, the actual outcome of each of our days to date may not line up with what God had originally planned for us. That does not mean those days were useless and lost, it just means some of us have a longer learning curve than others. God will use every failure and every discouragement we have known to help turn our stumbling walks back towards His plans. He chose us to receive the Gift of Life in Christ Jesus, and He preordained and planned for us to do great works, walk good paths, and live good lives (Ephesians 2:10, *Amplified Bible*). That can be frustrating or liberating, depending on how much we believe that we have to personally locate and implement those works, paths, and lives. Good News! We do not have to know how to find our way to these good plans of God, because Jesus Christ within us knows how. We are packing the Hope of Glory around inside us—talk about being close to The Real Source!

When born-again Christians do not believe that God truly holds them in the palm of His hand, but believe that they must succeed or fail on their own—they can crash and burn mentally, emotionally, and physically. When we believe that we'll make it only if we can hang on until Jesus returns, then when we doubt we can hold on any longer, our souls begin to anticipate disaster.

Most Christians believe that spending eternity with the Lord is the future that awaits us after death, but how sad if that is the only thought that keeps a believer trudging on through life from day to day. When children of God do not know how to spend every day anticipating what good thing may happen next, they are easy prey for the bitter lies and harassment of the enemy from without. As if that weren't devastating enough, these believers are also hopelessly dragging around hundreds of pounds of unmet needs, unhealed hurts, and unresolved issues within themselves.

Try to imagine running a marathon race with hundreds of pounds of baggage on your back. What about just one hundred pounds? You might start out the race with expectancy, but the farther you ran the lower your level of strength and desire would fall. You might press on because you know you should, but you can only continue running for just so long on sheer willpower alone. Your body will cease to cooperate and you can fall helplessly by the wayside. The Christian walk is called " running the race" in the Bible. You may be managing to jog forward in fits and starts, sometimes running valiantly for days. You might fall, but you can pick yourself up and start onwards again.

Some, however, so fear the length of such a "race" that they become mentally, emotionally, and physically paralyzed. Others cannot muster any desire to run at all. "Just give up and get it over with," the soul says.

Can the human soul say that with authority? Can an unsurrendered soul override the life instincts of a born-again believer's spirit? In some cases, it can. Christians have opted out of life because continuing the race became too overwhelming for them. This is a terrible tragedy, even more so because of the presence of the Gift of Life within their spirits. Christians who commit suicide are rarely talked about in the Church. When they are, leaders usually tell us that a spirit of suicide overtook the one who is dead. There is no such spirit listed in any of my twenty Bibles. The Church has just found it easier to blame a demonic spirit than it is to acknowledge the incredible power of an unsurrendered soul intent upon stopping its own pain permanently.

How do we—witnesses, disciples, and believers of the God of life—address such deadly despair and depression in a born-again believer? We must first admit that the unsurrendered souls of some believers have the power to so magnify their pain and despair that they begin to consider death over life. We must acknowledge the fact that ignored unmet needs, unhealed hurts, and unresolved issues in an unsurrendered soul can become so all-consuming that, under certain circumstances, they can drown out the human spirit's ability to cry, "Life, choose life! Choose life!"

There are answers, but they require us to face the fact that we have not been taught all of the truth. We have not been taught about the power of all believers' unsurrendered souls that continue to fight the relationship between their born-again spirits and God the Father. The salvation experience of accepting Jesus Christ as Savior does not mean that Christians then become perfect in every area of their being.

It is a blessing that the born-again human spirit of the believer is no longer a spiritual orphan and has now become connected to the Spirit of its Creator. But we must acknowledge that the self-focused, self-reliant, self-defensive human soul wants no part of God at the point of the new birth. The unsurrendered soul is actually very startled

119

to recognize that God has come to take over its control of the believer's life.

When you understand and believe this, you can begin to deal with the controlling power within your unsurrendered soul. You can begin to loose, smash, and destroy its old wrong beliefs, deceptions, and stronghold thinking with binding and loosing prayers, by reading the Word, and through new understanding of the workings of the soul and the spirit. If you do not know that such power to control exists within you even after your new birth experience, you can be methodically defeated over and over by your soul's deceptions.

In addition to trying to avoid dealing with God, the human soul tries looking for many ways to deal with its overload of unmet needs, unhealed hurts, and unresolved issues. It will try revenge, chemical substances, anger, denial, and many other things to stop its ongoing internal trauma. It will also attempt to bury massive pain and fearful memories of the traumatic things that may have happened, overlaying them with façades and deceptions that everything is under control. When it does this, the stress, anger, fear, and pain will begin tearing down the body's resources.

The stress of these powerful emotional reactions causes an equally powerful chemical reaction in your body's chemistry. Your body can begin to release toxic chemicals into your entire system in response to the great mental and emotional distress that your soul is trying to submerge in its subconscious. Your immune system becomes compromised and your entire body begins to slowly fall apart.

The following story, which continues on through the next chapter, is an attempt to help those in trouble to realize that there are keys, there are means, and there are steps that anyone can take towards cooperating with God to become whole. Rosanne begins here to talk about facing the problems and teaching answers to those hidden members in the Body of Christ who need to know they can choose life. The following words come from excerpts out of an extensive eighteen-month e-mail dialogue between myself and Rosanne, a Christian mother of a born-again, church-attending, ministry group-involved, college-aged daughter who killed herself. After editing Rosanne's powerful words, I have chosen to delete most of my responses.

Dear Pastor Savard, my name is Rosanne. I have been downloading past issues of your newsletter from your web site, and I just wanted to write you. Eighteen months ago my daughter Sharon—a senior at a well-known university who was very active in a large, nondenominational church—a believer who was receiving ongoing teaching, mentoring, and discipling—picked up a loaded gun and shot herself in the head. She's dead and now I just have a "girl in a box." Sorry if that is too blunt.

I know there are others who are going to church, joining discipleship classes, singing in the choir, who are in terrible trouble as well. Why won't the Church recognize the possibility that their troubles could lead them to disastrous choices to stop their pain? Why won't the Church admit that born-again believers can and sometimes do commit suicide? I have to admit that it does seem we should be exempt from suicide, doesn't it?

I went to the leaders of Sharon's church to try to find out why no one saw this terrible act coming. While meeting with her pastor and members of her discipleship/mentoring group, I was given your books, although none of these people seemed to have read them. Unfortunately for me, I saw your books as a cop out at that time, "Here, read these books and don't blame us."

I was only in the room with those people for five minutes before I knew they didn't know any more than I did. In the current atmosphere of society's belief that "someone must pay," they were probably afraid that I would bring a wrongful death suit. But that day I was only looking for answers. I believe it was God's answer that I was introduced to your teachings at that time.

I had always believed I needed God's spiritual armor to protect my born-again human spirit from me until I read your books. Now I believe that our born-again spirits, containing the fullness of all that Christ's Spirit wants to impart to us, are alive and quite well. However, as you say, our unsurrendered souls can cut off any good thing from God that is trying to flow out of our spirits to them. Our souls are capable of viciously fighting against any intervention of God's power into their craziness. Pastor Savard, I think it is possible that God has already given us all the protection, healing, and blessings we need, but our souls just don't know it.

I agree. Rosanne, if our souls can convince us that we have no chance of the abundant life, then we will live as if there is nothing left but to survive until we die. Our unsurrendered souls are capable of twisting everything God has done for us, making it look as if it is our own doing (if it was good), or that God was out to get us (if it seemed bad). Sometimes our souls will go with "the devil did it" angle.

Satan loves all of these deceptive scenarios, because this type of rationalizing keeps us from receiving God's loving truth.

> The Holy Spirit told me two years prior to Sharon's suicide (during one of her earlier attempts to end her life) that Satan could not touch her spiritually. I completely misunderstood this in the context of the dangerous power of her unsurrendered soul. The power of God's everlasting Gift of Life was being withstood and forced to remain in one place within Sharon—her born-again spirit. That precious Gift of Life was being blocked from her mind, will, emotions, and her body by her unsurrendered soul's distrust of anything from God.
>
> I knew Christ was her only answer, but I just didn't understand how to work with that answer. I still don't. Even now I am only good at handing out your books to try to help people, not much else. Thank you for lending me your hope. I continue to talk to God about my willingness to share Sharon's life. The suicide of a born-again believer is not the most popular subject in Christian circles. The air can get sucked out of the room real fast because of the collective gasps when that word is spoken in relationship to Christians. I know.

Good description of the Body of Christ's reaction to such a frightening subject. I'm willing to help you and be your voice, Rosanne. I'm willing to write and teach whatever I sense God wants to use to help others. I believe God may be developing that same commitment to teach truth within you as well. He did not let Sharon commit suicide to build this within you, but He is the Master at using the tragedies of life for good purposes—those tragedies of life *that He was not allowed to prevent*. Keep pressing in to Him, keep praying the binding and loosing prayers, and stay in touch. Liberty

Dear Pastor Savard, thank you for continuing to respond to my frantic e-mails. I continue to pray the training-wheel prayers in *Shattering Your Strongholds* and *Breaking the Power*, and I am aware of a new ability to believe God that was not in me before. I thank you for finally explaining to me, in language I could understand, about the unsurrendered soul's opposition to the divine destiny of the surrendered soul.

I'm beginning to understand that the problem wasn't that I was asking everybody the wrong questions—the problem was that the people I asked did not have the right answers. I wanted the experts, the leaders, to tell me how a child of God could have such a devastating ability within herself to end her own life. They couldn't.

I am now beginning to understand the opposition within some wounded souls that so works against the power of the Gift of Life. His everlasting life and all of God's covenant promises are meant to be transferred from a born-again spirit to a surrendered soul and then outward to flood a person's entire being. This is not happening in so many believers. For the first time in my born-again life I am beginning to understand why so many of God's words are past tense—that is because all that He has for us has already been done.

He has already saved, healed, protected, and provided for us. Our unsurrendered souls just won't receive it. The surrendered soul must be where God meant the image of Christ to be reflected. I know He won't impart the image of Christ over the top of my unsurrendered mind, will, and emotions. There is not enough room for the two of us in there. I could try to imitate Christ in my unsurrendered soul, but my born-again spirit would never buy it. I realize now what my spirit kept whispering to me years ago, *"You are not spiritually real."*

Pastor Savard, I laughed with you when I read what you said about your conversion. You put words to my thoughts that the soul is not in charge of salvation. I clearly remember saying to my feet, as they propelled me down the aisle to get saved, "Feet, where are you going?" My spirit was large and in charge, whether my soul or body wanted to cooperate or not.

I, too, was saved in a fundamental church. Like you, I went down that aisle again and again seeking legitimate truth, only to be given abstract concepts that were not user friendly! I was told so many times, "You are just not spiritually mature enough to understand, but you will." It was like these folks had a spiritual secret, but they wouldn't tell me because I wasn't mature enough. I wanted to say, "Hey, folks, I was just born again. I didn't have a lobotomy."

I thank you for obeying God and writing your books. I have found the spiritual principles of binding and loosing and your teaching style to be immensely "user friendly." I have always believed that truth has to be transferable somehow, and you have validated that for me.

Since I have been so open about Sharon's suicide, you can't imagine how many people have come up to me and whispered how a son, daughter, spouse, family member, and even themselves had thought about suicide. These people are just the born-again ones. I need to firm up what is going off in my spirit when they tell me this. For now, I am talking to them about your books.

Because of Sharon I am so sensitive to suicide that I can't just give vague words and promises about prayer and then walk away. Each time someone says something about suicidal thoughts to me, I take a physical, emotional, and spiritual blow that hits me like a Mack truck! I feel helpless as I look into their faces, knowing that the unsurrendered soul can and will provide its version of power to stop the pain if no one else will. But how do I communicate that clearly to them?

I agree with you, Pastor Savard, that there is no spirit of suicide that you can cast out of someone. Even if there was, it would only be a momentary relief while the unsurrendered soul cast around for another angle.

People like Sharon and others who have talked to me speak of previous attempted suicides during their history with the Church. We're praising and singing about the God of Life, and here are these people in His Church openly admitting that they struggle with suicidal thoughts. Some huge alarms are going off in me, red lights and sirens, but I don't know what to do! Suicide is an attempt of the unsurrendered soul to do only what God can do—control life. It does this by offering its own deadly version of life-control. Bang, you're dead. Problem solved.

Thank you for trying to sort through my thoughts. Do you still want to help me tell Sharon's story? Are my questions too tough? I appreciate you, Rosanne

Yes, I will still help you with this story which needs to be told. Tough questions are fine, especially if they are questions that others need answers for as well. Liberty

I finished reading *Shattering Your Strongholds* again. I think my searching for answers and asking God how Sharon could commit suicide—a beautiful, born-again child of God, forever 21 now—is both ending and beginning. I always knew at some level there was something missing, something I didn't know. I spent three-quarters of a million dollars with secular medicine and psychology—and they all ran for cover when Sharon finally decided to stop the pain herself.

God spoke to me after Sharon's death that He had (again past-tense) healed her from a rape that occurred ten years before, but that she had allowed that rape to define her life until her death. God said that He had healed her, but Sharon didn't know it. I couldn't understand His answer, but I believe I do now. I think you are saying, Pastor Savard, that an unsurrendered soul can block God's healing process even though His power is present, ready, and willing to do its divine work. Is it really possible that an unsurrendered soul can hold its position of control even to death?

God told me that He could not stop Sharon from her choices, but He could save her and He did. He said that He had given her a will, and that He knew what it would cost Him to do that. I'm beginning to understand some of what God has been telling me with the help of the understanding He has given you. Right now I think I am saying that what we don't know can kill us. Is that too harsh? I am not ashamed or embarrassed about Sharon, only so sad. Rosanne

Thank you for your response and clarification, word pictures help me. Please feel free to use anything I have shared with you in these e-mails. I see people cringe with my hard questions, but I continue to persist. I appreciate your honesty with me. You didn't know Sharon, but she was very much like your cousin, Sarah, in *Shattering Your Strongholds*. Extremely fragile—emotionally, physically, and spiritually fragile. Her physical body was shutting down, and I knew that barring a miracle, she was dying. I had accepted that in the natural.

I knew suicide was not God's will. I also knew that He didn't take her home to be with Him, like some in my church said to me. My question from the beginning was not "why did it happen." My question has always been "how did this happen?" This had to be such a destructive power operating in a fragile woman-child who had never fired a gun that it pushed her to choose to blow away her physical life. If an unsurrendered soul could move us in this self-destructive direction, then how much more there must be when we allow God to move our souls into perfect alignment with Him?

It is this "how much more" that I keep trying to communicate, but I keep getting disqualified. I try to speak, but people say, "It's just Rosanne. You know, her daughter committed suicide. Just humor her, and she'll go away. She's so upset, poor thing."

You did a beautiful job telling "Sarah's" story in *Shattering Your Strongholds*. Sharon's ten-year fight is so similar in many ways. I am wanting to do something for others in this state, but something has been holding me back. It is this scenario I keep playing out in my mind: "Okay, your daughter committed suicide, and you couldn't help her. How can you seriously think about offering answers, help, and hope to someone else, huh? Maybe you could write a book about what not to do when your child is getting ready to commit suicide. Yeah, that would be good, wouldn't it?" Where is this thing hiding in me?

God spoke to me, using my name, *"Rosanne, I guarantee Sharon's triumph in her final outcome."* Imagine having God's personal, spoken guarantee—then realizing that there was no place in the Body of Christ where you could give a praise report about it? Later, while reading the *Amplified Bible*, I found the same words, *"The God who always causes us to triumph in our final outcome."* It's great to know the Holy Spirit uses the *Amplified Bible*, too—the woman's Bible as my pastor calls it. You know, so many more words than we might think necessary?

Sometimes I feel slightly schizophrenic. We're always talking about God's presence—needing it, desiring it, being in it, walking in it. But then when one of us actually gets there even momentarily, we can't talk about it. I want to talk about it.

The Holy Spirit has told me I should begin to use the word celebrate whenever I think about Sharon. Celebrate. He said that He and Sharon were celebrating and I was missing the party. His word—party—not mine. I've been writing these things down in my journal, and I think God wants to talk to all of us like this.

I received your book on tape series of *Shattering Your Strongholds* and your Leadership Training. Every morning I walk two miles and I take you with me. Today I listened to tape seven of the Leadership tapes. You said this tape series was a gift to me, and I guess it is. It has caused me to yield on yet another unresolved issue concerning Sharon's suicide. I am learning to do what you have taught me—when something sends my soul into orbit (you call them the soul's hot buttons), I am trying to stop and begin praying the binding and loosing prayers. You said to use the reaction as a doorway to healing by the Holy Spirit.

Your guest teacher on those tapes used the same scriptural references that were used on me by pastors, mentoring groups, discipling groups, and intercessory prayer groups from Sharon's church. She and her fiancé were active members there. That is what set off another soulish hot button in me, a big one. During the year and a half that Sharon was engaged to her fiancé, these same people who used those Scriptures prophesied, mentored, agreed with, and blessed them, saying that their pending marriage was made in heaven.

All the while, Sharon's destructive physical and mental symptoms were accelerating on a downhill course.

Rosanne, I don't know what Scriptures you are referring to, but that is not important. You took your reaction to hearing these Scriptures again to the Holy Spirit. That is good. Keep doing that. He doesn't want you buried under hot buttons and painful reactions. He is working to set you at liberty.

Pastor Savard, I knew that Sharon should not marry her fiancé or anyone else until she was healed. On a purely natural level, I could see she was dying unless God intervened. She and I talked a great deal about this intellectually. Sharon was home for four days before the suicide. She kept crying until she finally told me she knew she could not marry her fiancé and she didn't know what to do.

I told her that I didn't know what to do either, but I agreed that she should not get married at that time.

Over that same four-day period, her fiancé and his mentor had come to basically the same conclusion, only with a spiritual twist. Someone prophesied to him that he should not marry Sharon, because he was a stumbling block to her. The "prophecy" given said that Sharon loved him more than she loved God, and he should break their engagement to "help" Sharon get rightly connected to God first.

Her fiancé then used these scripturally sounding words to break his engagement to this physically, emotionally, and spiritually fragile lamb, Sharon. Unfortunately, he put it in writing, so I now have this priceless written document in my possession (you can just see my pain, right?). There is power in written words, yes? Sharon was also a writer, and she journaled. She made notes on every phone call she made to every one of the people in her groups who had personal contact with her during this difficult time. Then she put a gun to her head and blew her life away.

Even before I found your Keys of the Kingdom books, I knew that Sharon killed Sharon, not anyone else. I just didn't understand how until now. Thank you for explaining "how" this can happen to a born-again child of God. We have no "unsurrendered soul insurance policy" do we?

On a personal note, the Holy Spirit revealed to me that I had done the superficial, "Sure, I forgive you" routine with those church folks. The unsurrendered soul's forgiveness, I guess I'll call it for now. People helping people need to understand what you are teaching. Some hurting people in our churches are just dying slower than Sharon. Rosanne

I attended one of your meetings last week. It was a meaningful experience for me. The forum of the meeting did not allow me to ask any of the questions that I still have. I don't mean that as criticism, this is just a personal problem I have with my narrow focus right now. When you talked about Christian counselors telling you that your message was too confrontive to the soul, that is where I got up and left during your teaching session. Couldn't handle my feelings. My daughter is one of those who left a "nice" Christian counselor's office and put a bullet in her brain. How confrontive is a bullet?

My immediate concern right now is that last night a former co-worker (I haven't actually worked since Sharon's suicide) called to talk to me about her teenage sister, Ginia. Ginia has recently confessed to cutting herself and to having bulimic symptoms. She is now hospitalized in the psych ward under suicide watch as she told her parents that she wanted to kill herself. Ginia is not allowed visitors this week (I know this is standard procedure from my experience with Sharon).

Two days after Ginia was hospitalized, right after your teaching meetings, I was radically believing that I am dangerous with the Keys of the Kingdom principles of prayer. Ha! When my former co-worker called me, I tried to encourage her—but I didn't do very well. Then my soul started dragging me through the swamp after I hung up. You gave an example about how your soul talks to you? Well, mine was ranting: "Your daughter put a great big gun to her little brain, and you think you are actually going to say or do something that is going to impact Ginia's life? Who do you think you are? Your kid is dead, and now you are going to get involved in someone else's life? Here, I got something you can bind, okay? Bind your pitiful mouth shut!"

I don't feel very dangerous for God right now, Liberty. Is it dangerous to think I can help anyone?

Excellent application of understanding how your soul can talk to you! That is when you have to apply these prayer principles to yourself first, getting your own soul as much under control as you can. Then begin praying the Keys of the Kingdom prayers for the ones who are in great distress, even threatening to end their lives. If your soul begins to act up, start praying the prayers for yourself again. You are dangerous with the keys, Rosanne, and you do have the means of entering into heavenly places to conduct spiritual business for those who cannot help themselves. Isaiah 57:14-15 tells us this:

"Build up, build up, prepare the road! Remove the OBSTACLES out of the way of my people. For this is what the high and lofty One says—he who lives forever, whose name is holy: 'I live in a high and holy place, but also with him who is contrite and lowly in spirit, to revive the spirit of the lowly and to revive the heart of the contrite'" (NIV).

Rosanne, you and I, and every other Christian are called to do this. God never calls us to do something that He is not prepared to equip us to do.

I know we have the answers, Rosanne, because this is a spiritual problem. It is not a mental or an emotional problem. These troubled people are not mentally ill—they are spiritually ill. We have answers for spiritual problems. You said that no one seems to have any reasonable short-term answers for mental problems except to drug the mind. That, of course, does not "fix" anything.

Hold onto the fact that you just spent four days in teaching meetings hearing about what does work. The stronghold thinking of the unsurrendered soul has to be broken so that God can enter into the damaged areas of the mind to heal and restore it. He won't go in to do so without an opening. Our binding and loosing prayers can create those openings to allow Him to filter His love and mercy into a soul's wounds and diseased parts.

They have drugged Ginia to stop the pain, but it also stops everything else. Not knowing anything else to do, I cooperated when they did this to Sharon, too. Please, Pastor Savard, am I too close to this to be of any help?

Only if you are feeling extreme panic about letting someone else down, Rosanne. Are you feeling that you let Sharon down? If so, then the ride could get rough for you as you try to help this young woman and her family. I firmly believe that you did all that you knew to do for Sharon. You cannot come into agreement with feeling guilty over not doing what you did not know to do.

Binding and loosing prayers actually give us "keys" to speak in prayer into someone's mental state. These prayers also give us keys to speak in prayer into an emotional state and into the determination of the self-will. The loosing key can break off the effects and influences of doctor's negative diagnoses (regardless of how "correct" they are in the natural realm of medicine). If such diagnoses do not line up with the destiny purposes of God for the individual, then they are not right.

I am willing to try to work with this former coworker and her sister, but I feel terribly inadequate as to how to start. I am praying the binding and loosing prayers for Ginia now, but do you just give people the *Shattering Your Strongholds* book and tell them you are praying? Do you just say God bless you and have a nice day? I am not being facetious; I need help to know how to begin.

You begin praying the binding and loosing prayers for Ginia wherever you are. First, however, I ask you again to search your own soul and see if you are believing that Ginia's life depends upon you ministering breakthrough truth to her in a perfect way. This is a deception if any part of your soul is saying this. All God may be asking is that you let Him use you to help her bring her strongholds down a little.

You must break through any other deception that it all depends upon you doing exactly the right spiritual thing. You must recognize that you can pray wherever you are, or you can go to Ginia and pray the prayers with her, asking her to pray them after you. God will use what you do in faith, either way.

But, Rosanne, hear me on this! You are not the one who will save her from her soul's desperation! You are just the one who appears to be in line with the opportunity to help her open up to an infusion of God's love. Don't expect yourself to be perfect. Just try to hear what God is asking you to do. It may be nothing more than to sit with the family and share this way of praying by just doing it. It may be to go and pray with Ginia and ask her to pray after you. We often think that we are capable of doing great harm by not being a perfect messenger. Sometimes we do much more harm by not being willing to be a messenger at all.

I know the power of the unsurrendered soul to counterfeit dying-to-self versus killing yourself. This knowledge has to work in the mainstream of life. I want to use it to be able to impart "life words," or I don't need to be talking to them. Please don't give up on me, Liberty, I actually believe what you said, that I have an end-time message and ministry. Rosanne

Liberty, thank you for responding to my questions and quickly getting to the source of my unresolved issues. I am choosing to see these areas of fear and panic for what they are, and I'm telling my soul I know they are there and I can open them up to God. You're right, I do know what to do, thank you.

I went to visit my former co-worker yesterday. I encouraged her and assured her that this was a spiritual problem, and thank God, we have answers for spiritual problems. She said that her parents were insisting that Ginia be released to them in a couple of days. I told her that I had a tool (your *Shattering Your Strongholds* book!), which I gave to her. I told her I absolutely believed that if I would have known about the spiritual principles in this book, I could have saved myself ten years of walking the halls of counseling offices, emergency rooms, hospitals, psych wards, and intensive care units—both Christian and secular.

I told her that I didn't know whether Sharon would have responded or not, and I didn't have to know. Then I told her that while I wasn't exactly out looking for people who were talking about attempting suicide, I had promised myself and God that if someone called me, I would tell them about the Keys of the Kingdom principles. I told her I would be willing to help her and her family work through the book and pray the prayers with them if they wanted me to.

I also told her that I was praying the prayers for Ginia right now about the power of right and wrong agreements. I feel confident giving them your book and not reinventing the revelation God has given you. I believe God will continue to heal me and refine my rather confrontive message.

I have had doctors with more degrees than a thermometer look me right in the eye and tell me they didn't know why such and such a drug was or wasn't currently working with Sharon. They just didn't know why it worked on some people and why other people killed themselves while they were on it. I had wonderful, caring psychiatrists walk the halls of intensive care units with me while Sharon's life hung in the balance, telling me, "I'm so sorry, I never saw this coming." Frankly, I wanted better odds. I believe these spiritual principles give people better odds. I believe they are the "missing living link."

Would Sharon have embraced this truth in time? I don't know. What I do know is that anyone who calls me and uses the word suicide is going to hear about it! I wasn't in charge of Sharon's life choice, and I won't be in charge of Ginia's life choice. But I will have told Ginia and her family the truth about the body, soul, and spirit connection with God.

You wrote to me: "I would ask you to search your own soul and see if you are feeling that Ginia's life would depend upon you going and ministering breakthrough truth to her in a perfect way. This is a deception." That deception is exactly what was going on in me. Immediately after I confronted my soul with the above information, I was not afraid anymore. Absence of fear—a profound benefit and result of the Keys of the Kingdom principles working in my life.

I appreciate your candor. I am praying the ministry prayer every day, because I don't want to leak out any ungodly stuff. My sense of humor is returning, and although I don't find it listed in the Bible, I call it a gift. I have ordered more of your books because I see people all the time who need to read them. I will talk about this as long as I have breath. Sincerely, Rosanne

Thank you so much for everything you have invested into my ongoing process of understanding the unsurrendered soul. I am continuing to heal as I use the Keys of the Kingdom principles in my own daily life. I have not told you this before, but your first email to me was like a life preserver thrown out into cyber-space. I had been hiding in my room for over a year after Sharon's death, coming out only to search the Internet for answers. You remain the only person in spiritual leadership in the Body of Christ who ever answered even one of my questions.

I still have some unresolved issues about church/spiritual stuff that I keep processing. My soul thinks it just needs the right set of facts to process intellectually and then I will be okay. I know my soul is doing this, but I find myself unable to stop from writing more letters to ministries with my questions. No one but you has answered yet. I'm not trying to criticize them, and I only tell you this as a way of encouragement for what you are trying to do. We just don't know when someone else perceives us as their last hope. I know the discipleship group at Sharon's church didn't know that she walked out after talking to them to go and put a bullet in her brain.

Sharon went to rape crisis centers, wrote articles, and published poems. She believed that one day she would help others, and I think she still will through her story! Thank you for helping her to do so. Thank you for being willing to take on these tough issues. Rosanne

Thank you, Liberty, for being the voice in the wilderness. We have just had three guest speakers in our church, and guess what their message was? The spirit, soul, and body connection. But they all stopped short of the "how to work with God and be healed" information, just insisting that we must "suck it up" spiritually because we are Christians.

Your message, your voice, it is vitally important. ***Don't you dare ever think about stopping what you are doing!*** I'm praying for you, your family, and your ministry. Five years before Sharon committed suicide, I started this spiritual journey that led me to your door. I looked at my life, my family, my Christian friends, my church, and my pastor and I said, "If this is what it means to be a Christian, I quit. God, you are going to have to kill me, I can't do this anymore unless I can be spiritually real." I think this prayer qualified as my surrendering my will to God's will and giving Him that tiny opening He needed to begin fixing me. He used that opening to begin showing me how to bring down the limitations and strongholds I had erected in my soul.

This morning as I walked I listened to one of your teaching tapes from your last women's retreat. My pastor recently said that Satan comes to steal, kill, and destroy the Word in us through adversity. All Satan can actually steal is the Word in us, and all the benefits, privileges, promises, and blessings it has. I am encouraging you, in the only way I know how, to stir up God's Word in you. It's in there just like the example of the incorruptible seed that you gave in your tape I was listening to today. Listen to God's Word in you!

I was awakened at 2:30 a.m. with the impression to bind your mind to the mind of Christ. These things are still new to me, but I did it. I don't really understand why God would need me to pray for you, but I like it and it encourages me! I love it that God would be so concerned about you that he would wake me up at 2:30 a.m. to talk to me about it, and I wouldn't mind being awakened. Cool! In Christ, Rosanne

Liberty, I want Sharon to have a voice, and she will have that voice in your book. I have written two more ministries in the last six months. They didn't answer. This validates to me how important this information could be for other Sharons sitting in our churches. You remain the only person in ministry and leadership who seems to think so. Thank you, Rosanne

Liberty, I've been putting together some "teaching" points from your message for when I talk to other people. Here is what I have so far: The unmet needs, unhealed hurts, and unresolved issues in the unsurrendered soul are like bottomless holes. Regardless of how much good preaching, praise and worship, prayer, love, or attention comes into your life and uplifts you, these good things immediately begin to leak out of those holes in your soul. No amount of money, alcohol, drugs, medication, sex, material things, relationships, or food can ever fill up these holes.

When the soul becomes overwhelmed by the sustained intensity of the drives pushing up out of its unmet needs, unhealed hurts, and unresolved issues, the mind, will, and emotions simply can't take the overload. The mind, will, and emotions have been driven to try to fix that which is unfixable except by God. Having no backup support system, the soul simply begins to come apart under the pressure, right?

The corrosive acidity of the unmet needs, unhealed hurts, and unresolved issues eats away the soul's infrastructure as the holes get bigger and bigger. I think of them becoming like a whirlpool, slowly sucking everything down into darkness. When the soul collapses in upon itself, minds snap, emotions freeze, and the will to live is gone. (I heard you say that!)

Suicide is the final act of an unsurrendered mind, will, and emotions, isn't it? This soul no longer believes that if given enough time, it will find the right set of facts to process to "fix" itself. So it provides what it perceives to be the answer.

Sharon's sister (the buck-up queen) and I kept trying to encourage Sharon to at least try for "get-by" living. "Get-by" living is better than giving up, but it is always just one step away from the next crisis. The slightest slip or change in circumstances can hurl the "get-by" person into disaster. This person rarely tries to determine why things keep going wrong, and therefore never learns how to change their behavior patterns to prevent future problems. They are just constantly in a state of applying band-aids as a form of damage control. Band-aids for this kind of destruction within? I don't think so! The reality is that the soul must be painstakingly stripped clean and then restored by God.

136

This kind of "on the edge" lifestyle mistreats your soul, which can be compared to running an engine without oil until the engine freezes up. We can't repair a locked-up, damaged engine by simply adding more oil. It must be taken apart and rebuilt by replacing the damaged parts. God provides a way for this to be done in our souls more quickly than we ever dreamed, but it can become an agonizingly slow process when the uncooperative soul is not stopped from throwing its reactions into the mix.

Sharon's discipleship core group, intercessory prayer group, and pre-marriage mentoring group did not know how to help someone in her kind of a spiritual crisis. Neither did I. I knew the problem and the answer was spiritual, but I simply was not equipped to deal with my own daughter being in a full-blown spiritual crisis. Recognizing that they had reached the limitations of their own abilities, the people in Sharon's groups basically handed her a Bible, told her that she needed to find her own truth, and that she should not be dependent on them any longer. They all loved her and believed that God was going to heal her.

However correct they may have been in their conclusions about Sharon's dependency on them, to her they were her last hope. How did Sharon reach the place where she was so out of contact with who her real hope was—God? How did she place all of her hope on these frail human beings instead? She was completely dependent on them, believing they were her support system. They represented God to her, and they were probably frightened by this. They did not know how to take her past that spiritual deception.

Even though I was insisting and assisting Sharon to live, I did not have the knowledge or ability to help her get past it, either. The only difference between them and me is that I was relentlessly pursuing elusive alternatives that were never quite the answer. After three-quarters of a million dollars, we pretty much ran out of money to pursue any further alternatives—or I might have chased even more.

It really is unacceptable that something inside of us should ever be allowed to keep us from embracing all that God has pre-planned, prepared ahead of time, and pre-ordained for each one of us. I am convinced that we can be equipped to help others in spiritual crisis (for lack of a better term). I will never know about Sharon till I get to heaven. But I tell everyone I give *Shattering Your Strongholds* to here that if I had known the spiritual principles in this book, I would have had a powerful spiritual weapon to help Sharon in her crisis.

Suicide is a powerful and dramatic display of the ultimate workings of the unsurrendered soul, but the spiritual principles in the Keys of the Kingdom are even more powerful and dramatic. You are taking the difficult issue of suicide by a born-again believer to a public arena, and you are willing to be Sharon's voice and mine. It is my hope that someone will read it and understand that they don't have to die to get spiritually connected with God. They can do it here, and meet up with Him there when He says so.

I would like to see you come to my church and then to Sharon's church, but I am beginning to learn to walk in such things as divine appointments yet to be. How does it feel to see your words come back to you? Gotcha! Rosanne

Dear Liberty, I've been evaluating what you said about moving away from blaming those in the Church and from self-blame. I believe I am doing that. I am the Church; and I do desire to learn from a suicide by a born-again believer. It is just that no one will listen to me, not even my own pastor. No one except you has ever been willing to address this, but I already told you that, didn't I?

I kept wanting to find out who might be responsible for not having the correct information to save Sharon. The bottom line for me now is that the only answer is in Christ. I did not fail Sharon spiritually. She knew who Christ was, and now she knows who she was in Christ. She did, she does.

My now position is that the Church (me) should have answers. We say that we do. We should be able to back up that claim by imparting life-giving truth into people in spiritual crisis. Would Sharon have believed and surrendered her soul if she had known about the Keys of the Kingdom principles? I don't know.

Sharon was already living on the edge. The slightest rejection was enough to send her spiraling down into darkness. I read a testimony on your web site from "T" about an impending suicide. This person seemed able to grasp the concept of the spiritual keys and the unsurrendered soul. That was encouraging to me, and it meant that Sharon might have been able to embrace them, too. Even more encouraging is that others may.

I believe God means for the surrender of the soul to be an ongoing process. Not just to get some relief, but an ongoing process toward complete surrender. Identify, acknowledge, resist, renounce, deal with, accept healing, and move on. I would not have been able to do any of these things for Sharon. Her freedom would have been a result of what she believed, renounced, and rejected. I accept that.

God has been whispering to me to stop rehearsing the suicide. This is not about Sharon anymore; it's about what God can do now. I would like to be a part of that. I will accept correction and refinement of the truth so other people are not scared of me. I need to be able to teach others about the power of the unsurrendered soul. God bless you, Rosanne

Rosanne: You are truly an end-time messenger in the making. Your writings are so powerful, they often stop me in my tracks. Your letter below is strong, but filled with great insight. You have said that Sharon believed she had an alternate personality, "Polly," or something like that? Are you willing to explore that as to the type of counseling she received?

I have always maintained that this is a very dangerous diagnosis, allowing the soul to set up its own rules and call the shots on which "part" it will or will not put forward. I say dangerous, because this diagnosis both encourages and gives permission to the soul to further fragment the wounded mind's concept of reality. This diagnosis gives permission to the soul to counterfeit "personalities" to act out alternate roles. We should be insisting upon the coalescing of the already fragmented pieces back into wholeness.

Yes, I would be willing to explore Sharon's diagnosis of multiple personality disorder. I was being told at the time of her death to try to go along with the "Polly" personality. Polly was beautiful, poised, articulate, and self-sufficient. Polly was not clinically, chronically depressed; Polly did not suffer from ADHD. Polly did not suffer from post-traumatic stress disorder from the rape. Polly did not experience brain seizures that put her into an unconscious state for hours. When I met with the people from Sharon's church, it only took me about fifteen minutes to realize that they had known "Polly," and I was trying to talk to them about Sharon.

I was told that Sharon received blunt trauma injury to her brain during the rape. This was also mental and emotional blunt trauma. She was not conscious during the multiple rapes of her fragile, undeveloped fourteen-year old body. Not yet being allowed to date, Sharon took the screen off her window one night and went out to meet some high school boys. I had not really talked to her about some boys being sexual predators. Since she could be disciplined with a raised eyebrow, I had never made any provision in my mind for her doing something like sneaking out.

It is the brain that triggers each next stage of our body's developmental growth. Sharon's brain, I was told, did not trigger her next stage of growth, and she became unable or unwilling to move beyond the rape experience. To validate your teaching on the power of the mind-body connection, Sharon's physical body tried to come into alignment with what she believed herself to be. She matured chronologically, but her physical body stayed like the child she was at fourteen. She was child-like when she died at age 21. My "girl in a box" was still my child.

Dear Liberty, here are my lists of reasons that I felt God had to keep Sharon alive:

She participated in intercessory prayer group, discipleship group, pre-marital counseling, and premarital mentoring.

She was engaged to marry a Christian young man.

They were prayed and prophesied over.

She was born-again, Spirit-filled, tongues-talking, tithing, and attending every church service.

She participated in praise and worship.

She had ongoing Christian fellowship.

She read the books and listened to tapes she was given.

She kept a prayer journal, took notes during services, wrote down key Scriptures on 3 x 5 cards and memorized them.

She hung Scriptures from her mirrors, cupboards, refrigerator, and bedside table.

During the worsening of her problems, I mentally ticked off Sharon's "Activity List," over and over, to convince myself that she would be all right. I did this even as her outward behavior was changing, and she had a desire to go places and do things that Christians shouldn't do. I also clung to "My List" for Sharon, even while her already fragile physical and mental condition declined at an alarming rate.

My "Personal List of Spiritual Qualifications" helped me believe that I had met all the pre-conceived conditions or requirements to become legally entitled to the privilege of God answering my prayer—my way. I believed that "Sharon's List" and "My Personal List of Spiritual Qualifications" qualified me to claim all the promises, blessing, and privileges in the Word. Now I know that we can stand praying and claiming all day and night, but if we are standing there with strongholds, limitations, and restrictions in our unsurrendered soul, God will not violate our souls' defenses to do the very thing He knows we need for Him to do.

I was not praying for God's will to be done in Sharon's life at the time, I did not know how. After all, she met all my pre-conceived conditions of why God had to answer my prayers my way. I believed that because of "My List" and "Sharon's List," she could not commit suicide. She might die of her progressively deteriorating physical problems, but somehow "My Personal List of Spiritual Qualifications" protected her from suicide. "My List" was my spiritual insurance policy. Was "My List" stronghold thinking?

Just yesterday, this scenario was played out in front of me again. A dear friend of mine who knew Sharon, and had walked through her suicide with me, began relating to me about another acquaintance of hers. She spoke of a husband and wife who are Christians with a strong Christian home and a grandfather who is a preacher in our city.

Their daughter, Sunnie, was a talented gymnast, anorexic, and in great distress mentally, emotionally, and physically. My friend started reciting Sunnie's "List" to me, Sunnie's parents' "List," and Sunnie's grandfather's "List." I said to her, "Stop it, these lists do not obligate God to do our will." She looked like I had slapped her, but she didn't say a word. Somehow we have been led to believe that our "Lists" prove that we are qualified to insist that our problems be answered when we pray.

Rosanne, therein lies the truth, which has been diluted with deception. We cannot establish our own safety or the safety of our loved ones through our own spiritual checklists. Yet, we believe we can and this is an encouraged belief. Why? Because that is what all of our leaders have been taught to believe (to some degree). You asked me for truth, and you speak hard truth, so I must believe you will accept hard truth. Surely you do not expect to be blamed or condemned because you did not know that a spiritual checklist would not give you a guaranteed spiritual insurance policy. If you do, then we need to explore that, because it is a lie.

You must extend grace to the spiritual leaders of Sharon's church who probably had their spiritual checklists, too. Many, if not most, Christians today have never been taught what you and I are discussing here. If this truth is not being taught to leaders, how can they teach it to the body of Christ? You cannot condemn a leader for not teaching what he or she has never learned. Nor can you condemn them for not recognizing or embracing a new understanding that appears to invalidate much of what they have been taught.

I think the passage out of *The Message* that I often use in teaching is quite appropriate here (John 9): *"Walking down the street, Jesus saw a man blind from birth. His disciples asked, 'Rabbi, who sinned: this man or his parents, causing him to be born blind?' Jesus said, 'You're asking the wrong question. You're looking for someone to blame. There is no such cause-effect here. Look instead for what God can do (now).'"* You are definitely searching for truth, Rosanne, and you are blazing quite a trail in doing so, a trail that we will work together to try to smooth out and present to others. But, you may be asking some wrong questions, too.

Jesus was saying above that finding someone to blame was not the answer. *Finding who could be blamed would not undo what was already done.* I know you are aware of this to some degree, and I know you are trying to move away from blaming those in the Church.

I believe you are also trying to move away from self-blame. Hard as that is, it must be done. Finding out who might be responsible for not having had the correct information to save Sharon will never bring her back, nor will it make your grief any less painful. I feel that you know that.

Did Sharon have a faulty set of spiritual facts to rely upon in coming to the decision she made? Was she confused and disappointed at the conclusions her mind arrived at based upon her inadequate grasp on truth? Probably. But that cannot forever pin you to the tragedy that ensued. Liberty

> Even if we manage to pray, prophesy, and speak God's will into someone's life, Liberty, there are times that the person just doesn't respond by getting well. They don't get well because nothing has addressed the strongholds in their souls that are blocking the healing. So we then send these people out into the world's medical and psychological system, often to almost certain death. The weapons of our warfare are not carnal, yet we send them out to fight a spiritual battle with carnal weapons. We must stop!

seven

Woman with a Mission

Rosanne's story continues:

During the time of Sharon's problems, I attended a forgiveness conference, which was a very powerful experience for me. I experienced a new level of understanding about forgiveness there, and I truly felt I was walking in that level. I was taking Sharon through these steps to freedom also, at my level of understanding. Sharon killed herself with this material in her personal possession.

Until I read your explanation of what forgiveness is and what it isn't, in *Shattering Your Strongholds*, I didn't understand the truth. I never saw that I was deceived and had a stronghold in that area. Liberty, you helped me look where my soul refused to look with an unforgiveness issue with Sharon.

I never spoke it out loud, but I was angry because Sharon "gave up" before I could find the answer. See the deception? I allowed my soul to deceive me into believing that I was obeying God's command to forgive. God's promises are almost always dependent upon our keeping His conditions that come with them. His Word says, *"For if you forgive men when they sin against you, your heavenly Father will also forgive you. But if you do not forgive men their sins, your Father will not forgive your sins"* (Matthew 6:14-15, *NIV*). There are conditions in His covenant promise to forgive us — we must forgive others.

Christians often think that God will keep His part of a bargain whether they do or not. In His wisdom and in His grace and mercy, God may continue to maintain His covenant promises with us long after we have abandoned our part of the covenant. There is a limit, however, to how long God will excuse and extend grace towards the one who deliberately ignores His commands that are clearly defined in the Scriptures.

The Holy Spirit recently told me that I didn't have to wait any longer for validation of the Keys of the Kingdom spiritual principles. I am the validation. This painful journey has been about me being healed and restored in my soul, not Sharon. Sharon is safe. I have been holding back, thinking that I needed some kind of proof before I was brave enough to offer the keys in a spiritual crisis situation. He said, *"You told Sharon that you didn't understand her pain, you knew that it was real to her, but that you never really understood it. Now you do. It's now about you accepting My provision of healing for the worst thing that has ever happened to you."*

I thought Sharon's suicide disqualified me, but it qualifies me in a way. God has provided a way of healing for the worst thing that could ever happen to us. God bless you, Rosanne

The Lord continues to reveal things to me as I strip away restrictions and boundaries that my soul has put a " normal" label upon—the unresolved issues filed under "normal, no reason to look there anymore." Thanks to your teaching and persistent mentoring, I'm beginning to understand that if I'm not hearing from the Holy Spirit on all of my life issues, THAT isn't normal.

Some place between the first time I heard you in person and the second time recently, I have figured out that God's way of healing and restoration is only limited by the faith response of the person who is asking for help. At some point they must assume their own responsibility to choose the truth or a lie. What would their souls' response be if they were told they had only 90 days to live—how about two months, or just one week? Would their souls seek the truth then, or would they still deny it?

After I arrived home from hearing you teach this last time, I experienced a healing of a huge unresolved spiritual issue. I was ready to pack up and run for home after the session you did the last afternoon. If I had gone through with my panic plan and left the meeting early, I wouldn't have experienced a healing at that time. My unsurrendered soul would have talked me out of that encounter, and I would have gone home unhealed and wondering why won't God heal me.

Because of these unsurrendered areas of our own souls, we are the ones who sabotage God's plans for us. It's not another person, not Satan—it's our own unsurrendered souls. Sharon's unsurrendered soul took control and ended her life. Somehow she had the capacity and ability to listen to the voice of despair in her soul, yet could not hear the life-giving voice of her born-again spirit. Suicide is an example of an unsurrendered soul at critical mass.

I've been studying I Thessalonians 5:16, *"Quench not the Spirit."* What if this was a translation error, and it should not be an upper case "S"? We are not powerful enough to quench the Holy Spirit of God in us. What if the writer is saying here that we are to not quench our regenerated human spirits which are trying to get the words of life, God's life instructions, into our souls? Maybe I'm wrong about the translation error, but I think we can quench our own human spirits with a powerful unsurrendered soul.

In any case, I won't be able to stop talking about God's plan for the complete restoration of the unsurrendered soul. Please don't stop telling me the truth. If you can refine and define my thoughts and examples, I would consider it the same as if I were to teach it. This is my "if someone else does it better, then I don't need to" theory. (I didn't say it was a good theory.) In Christ, Rosanne.

Hi, Liberty. Recently two young Christian businesswomen related to my friend and I how they had gone out witnessing all morning. My friend had been inquiring as to their whereabouts because she had noticed people trying to get into their shop that morning.

These young women told us that they believed they didn't have to worry about the future of their business—even though they had not had it open all morning. They said that because they were obedient to God to go out and witness, God was obligated to make up the time, take care of their business, and make sure everything was delivered on time. They were convinced that God had to supply the money for the business plan they presented to Him because they witnessed for Him.

The unsurrendered soul wants to reason that if "I" am obedient to God when I want, where I want, how I want, in other words "my way," God will have to honor that and do what I expect. Seeing myself and my own list-making in this experience, I asked the Holy Spirit how have we all made such errors in judgment? How did I sit under some of the most amazing, Spirit-filled teachers and pastors and miss the truth? I do not control God's blessings and plans by my own self-willed plans and purposes — regardless of how "good" they may seem to be.

My unsurrendered soul continually wants to reason from the point of "what I am doing" as to whether or not God accepts me. This unresolved issue causes me to want to bring out "My List" of what my soul believes I can do for God. It wants to run my latest list of constantly changing feelings, thoughts, and actions as to whether or not God accepts me now. God has already (past tense!) accepted me "in Christ." I can't do anything, even a "good thing," to acquire any better standing. I can only believe what He says about me.

My unsurrendered soul has been trying to conform to the image of Christ based on "My List." It can make practical work for God, such as witnessing, into an excuse for escaping the salvation of the soul process. My soul reasons, "Remember how useful you are here, think of how much value you could be there, and add these things to 'My List' that proves how valuable you are to your church." My soul equates working for God in my church as part of my value to God.

My faith definition and my unsurrendered soul's ability to rationalize are still often in conflict. The only time I have actually reasoned that being strong-willed is a blessing is because I can use my strong will to choose God's will. Christ is my "life source." I'm really, really, In Christ, Rosanne

I sat at the kitchen table in the early morning sun in what was to be the last day of my summer job caring for my two grandchildren. It wasn't supposed to be the last day but their parents and I had made a decision that it was. Four weeks remained before school started and I was sick in my heart. My grandchildren had made it clear to me that they didn't like to do the things I liked to do. They said the things I liked to do were boring. They would rather do something else. Now they would live out the consequences of their choices.

With the decision made, I waited for them to get up as I had all the previous mornings of the past eight weeks. What would we do today? Would we have pancakes or French toast for breakfast? Perhaps we would go to the French restaurant and sit in the sun and eat French pastries and act like fine ladies and gentlemen. We had so many choices. We could use our all-terrain vehicle or we could carry our bikes, roller blades, swimming gear, and explore parks and recreation areas around our city. How about the Imax theater, or a movie?

We had season passes to a large amusement park where we could set a new park record for number of times riding the roller coaster. Imagine, a grandma who rides the roller coaster and swims in the wave pool. I was there to protect, provide, defend, and supervise their lives, and I liked my job. Every day I would be waiting for them to get up so we could decide what we were going to do that day. The summer had been planned ahead of time, designed for their fun, enjoyment, and happiness. I was there specifically for that purpose, and I was there because I wanted to be.

Sitting there at my daughter-in-law's beautiful kitchen table in the early morning sunlight, I poured these facts and more out to God, saying, "God, I just don't get it, how can this be? All my plans just aren't going to work out with my grandchildren. It's not a lack of money, time, planning, or desire. How can these children turn to me and say, 'Grandma, what you want to do is boring, we don't want to do what you want to do. We want to do something else.'"

God began to speak to me. He said, "*Rosanne, this sounds a lot like your life, doesn't it? I had plans, purpose, and a destiny for you and you basically said, 'God, your way is boring,' and you turned and walked the other way.*" I felt worse as He continued, "*I am sad that so many of my children do the same thing and then blame me for their messed up lives. They say, 'Where were you God, how did you let this happen? I thought you cared about me.' All those paths I imagined, planned for, and set apart for you, we're not going to walk them now, Rosanne. Does it change my love for you? No, but I'll have to watch you from a distance. I'll wait for news about your life, your choices, and your decisions.*"

"Oh, God," I answered, "that is exactly what I have done so many times. My unsurrendered soul said your way was boring. My unsurrendered soul said it had other plans that would be much more exciting." I had indeed listened to the voice of my unsurrendered soul, turned, and walked into the waste-howling wilderness where I stayed for ten years. God didn't send me there; I went there by choice. God kept calling me to come back, and I didn't recognize His voice. "*What are you doing over there in the waste-howling wilderness?*" God would ask.

"Not now, God, your way looks boring," I always replied.

He said, "*How often my children do not recognize my will and my healing when it comes into their lives.*" So, here I was, two and a half years after Sharon's suicide, and God quietly answered another question. My question had been, "How could she be healed and not know it?"

He said, "*I answered her prayer for healing of her mind and body, and she didn't recognize it. She had predetermined that her healing was going to come through her pending marriage, her church, and her mentoring groups. She had predetermined what her healing would look and feel like. Because she did not understand that her healing was in the broken engagement and in the broken relationships, she took her own life. I healed her, Rosanne. I answered her prayer; I healed her and she didn't know it.*"

Thank you, Liberty, for your relentless pursuit of The Truth, The Life and The Way! I am the recipient, Rosanne

Dear Liberty, another entry from my confessions of a " former" spiritual birth defect. Joshua 5:9 tells us, "*And the Lord said to*

Joshua. This day have I rolled away the reproach of Egypt from you. So the name of the place is called Gilgal (rolling) to this day." Joshua had been told by God to circumcise all the males in the camp before they could go into the Promised Land. The circumcision was a type of cutting away of the reproach (the shame) of the world from them. It was a cutting away of the old way of thinking and believing.

Today, September 30, 2001, God rolled away my reproach. I needed to be responsible and accountable personally as Sharon's mother, and I needed the Church to be responsible corporately. We failed her because we "knew" that His will, His plan, and His purpose for His children would never end in suicide. I failed, and I could not and would not accept absolution of my guilt and my shame. I wasn't letting "the Church" get away with it either. Me being "the Church" made this position even more difficult to defend.

In the previous verse 8 of Joshua 5, we read, *"They remained in their places in the camp until they were healed."* While my pastor was teaching on this particular passage of Scripture, you could literally see and feel his pain. It was no different for me that Sunday, Liberty. All the rest of Sunday and all day Monday, I endured the "cutting away." I was sick to my stomach and sick in my soul. At church Sunday night, I was extremely quiet and several people came up to me after church to say, "What's wrong, you don't look so good." My husband said, "Are you getting depressed again? Please don't get depressed again."

I stayed "in the camp," that place of spiritual rest, until I was healed on Tuesday, October 2nd, and then the Holy Spirit began to speak to me about the experience. He told me, *"Yes, Rosanne, you personally failed and the Church corporately failed. But I, your God, did not fail. And today, because you presented yourself (your soul) and endured the cutting away, I insist on rolling away your reproach, all your guilt and shame associated with your failure, along with the Church's failure. Today, I'm rolling away your reproach. I agree you are guilty, and I still insist on rolling away your reproach. I am the One who can do this. Today, Rosanne, if you choose to carry the shame and reproach, if you choose to live out the consequences of your wrong decisions and the corporate wrong decisions of the*

Church, you will—but you do not have to. Today, I have rolled away the reproach and shame off of you and the Church."

He told me that this was a type of me having to present my most private, intimate, and sensitive places in my soul to Him, the place that no one could see but me and then endure the "cutting away." We're ashamed to have the private parts of our souls exposed, the places we keep covered and don't discuss openly. I presented the most sensitive area of my soul life—my questions and guilt and shame about Sharon—and endured the cutting away. That day God rolled away the reproach from me. I could not do this for myself; nor could my church or Sharon's church.

God said, *"The children of Israel were already my chosen people when I did this for them. But, they could not 'possess' the new land (the kingdom of God) until the old way of thinking, believing, and doing was cut away."*

He couldn't let them go into the Promised Land living out the consequences of decisions and choices from the past. God was saying to me that I was born again and He had provided for me there in the wilderness of my disobedience, but it was manna, not the bread of life. He provides even in our disobedience, but God was forced (by my choice) to sustain my soul life with "lite" soul food. As Psalm 106:15 (*NKJV*) says, *"God gave them their request; but sent leanness into their soul."*

Liberty, I have experienced leanness of soul. Every day, just like David talked to his soul, I now talk to mine. Every time my soul tries to run another set of facts to process concerning Sharon or the Church, I remind my soul, "Hey, that might even be true, but Sunday, September 30th, 2001, God rolled away my reproach. Soul, God rolled away all the conditions of shame, disgrace, and all the pain associated with my failure. What a deal, soul! Since God says I'm not guilty, then I say you are not guilty, either. Accept your pardon." Then I back my soul down with the Word of God and the word of my testimony.

I know that because I have persistently prayed the binding and loosing prayers for breaking the power of my unsurrendered soul, I heard God when He spoke to me and said, *"Today, Rosanne."* I admired what you said about how God could remove the sting of painful memories and emotions without the facts of the traumatic event being changed. Now I know it is true, and although I still have to back my soul down sometimes, somehow God has taken the sting away. Thank you, Liberty. Rosanne

Your teaching, pure and simple, has made the surrender of the soul a reality. Something "doable." You have taken an obscure spiritual truth and made it practical for those people who will submit to the fierce soul inventory. The only way we can know Christ like Tommy Tenney is talking about in *The God Chasers* is through confession, repenting, and restoration. I believe that successful God-chasing is the result of a surrendered soul. Instead of the other drives coming up out of an unsurrendered soul, the drive coming out of a surrendered soul will be constantly and continually pushing to know Christ.

The Holy Spirit woke me several weeks ago with a very strong word. He said that I needed to actively, actively, actively choose the Gift of Life every day. He said that for those who didn't, it was death by default.

Previously, I didn't know how to speak "life" words into a person or into a situation. As a RESULT of the ongoing process of surrendering my soul and learning to pray in God's will, the "life" words came out of my mouth in a very serious situation recently. My still surrendering soul did what it is designed and created by God to do.

The Holy Spirit said that if I am not actively choosing the Gift of Life, then I am by default choosing death. He also said that life overpowers death only as long as I choose it. I thought the Holy Spirit was talking and teaching me about Sharon and how we need to make life choices. I thought and thought about the words and began to practice using them in my own binding and loosing prayers. Then I received a phone call from a close relative who was in a health crisis in the hospital. She said, "Rosanne, pray for me right now."

I listened to her and then said, "This is not God's will that you should die. Do you understand that? We don't know everything about God's will, but we know that whenever He is involved, there is life, not death. He came to give us life." I told her that she needed to choose life. We prayed together to bring her spirit, soul, and physical body into agreement with God's will, God's Word, and God's plans and purpose and destiny for her. I kept repeating to her what the Holy Spirit had said that we must actively choose the Gift of Life. God said He set before us life and death; therefore choose life that you may live.

In those moments of praying with her, I saw that when something is coming to threaten and to steal life, *we must actively choose life*. We must affirm it, confirm it, and agree with God. She exercised her will to choose life against all the common-sense testimony of the medical experts that was being spoken around her. All that week her life hung in the balance. On Sunday I was in church asking for prayer, and the head surgeon of her trauma team was in his church asking for prayer for her.

On Monday, she regained consciousness and called me. She said, "During the night someone put up a nativity scene at eye level on the glass door of the intensive care unit. The first thing I saw when I opened my eyes this morning was the Son shining through. I saw the Gift of Life, and I knew I was going to live." God is so good, Rosanne

I see now that I was building my own version of the Kingdom of God in my soul. I was allowing my soul to choose what I wanted and expected in the spiritual realm. I would then look for evidence in God's Word to support the decision I had already made. I was remaking my soul in the image I wanted and using Scripture to support my wrong choices. As a result of praying for the will of God to be done, I can now make a distinction between " soul talk" and the life-giving instructions of the Holy Spirit to my human spirit. Thank you, Rosanne

Liberty, I belong to an awesome Bible-teaching church, and spiritual salvation in my church is ongoing—sometimes 300 people are saved in a three-month period. We celebrate as they walk back down the aisle as born-again Christians. At this point in the process, I'm thinking, "Wow, we really should celebrate because this is the only spiritual experience we can't get wrong." My question now is where are they now? They are not in our church, where are they? If all the people who were born again just last year suddenly started coming to church we would have to build a new building.

Many of them will never go on to the salvation of the soul. They will continue to try to walk the Christian walk, burdened with unmet needs, unhealed hurts, and unresolved issues — all three of which have so destructively contributed to their unrenewed minds, their unsurrendered wills, and their unhealed emotions. This is how they were sent out even though a spiritual leader took them to a little room and gave them a Bible and a little booklet about "What Happens Next." Why don't you write a book about "What Really Happens Next? The Salvation of the Soul." Perhaps it could be something like my words below:

"God has already done what only He can do. Fortunately for you, God has not allowed man to be involved in the salvation of your human spirit. That is strictly a God thing. The covenant you made today is between your human spirit and God. From this moment on, no matter what anyone says to you, you are forever spiritually connected to God. Along with the salvation of your spirit, God has given you the right and privilege to hear His life instructions at all times. This spiritual covenant or contract also includes eternal life for your human spirit (spiritual salvation).

"Let's talk about the salvation of your soul and physical body. The human spirit, soul, and body were involved in the original fall of man. To address that problem, God has a really great plan for the salvation of man in the same order that he fell. Salvation of the human spirit, which you just experienced, then the salvation of the soul, and finally the physical body. Spirit, soul, and body, in that order.

"If I could take your regenerated human spirit right now and put it into a fully-surrendered, God-functioning soul and physical body, your soul would automatically translate the revelations of God to your words, actions, and behaviors, thereby manifesting His love and power to all who were around you. The life words would flow from God to your human spirit to your soul and out through your earth suit. You would function just like God originally created you to function. Spirit, soul, and body in alignment with His will, His Word, and His ways.

"Now, let's talk about God's dilemma with the condition of the human soul after His salvation of the spirit. God's Word contains the power of salvation for your soul, too, but it doesn't want it for the most part. Your human soul is most likely scared silly by the salvation of your human spirit. Your human soul is not desiring to partake any of your spirit's newly acquired ability to hear God's life instructions, nor is it impressed with God's written or spoken Word. Are you beginning to see any problems you might have with God's plan for the salvation of your soul?

"By the time you walk out to the parking lot, your anxious soul will begin to tell you how this spirit salvation is going to work out in your 'real life,' and it won't be pretty! Your soul will tell you that you're going to have to give up this, you're going to lose your right to do that, and you're going to have to pray all the time and read some dusty old King James Bible for hours. That's just the beginning of the lies the soul whispers. It will tell you that your 'real life' is, always has been, and always will be, in the soul. The soul says, 'I have been running your real life just fine, I don't need any help.'

"God says, '*As of today, tomorrow, and forever, your real life is in the spirit. It is your right and privilege to expect to hear my life instructions through your spirit and then pass them on into the soul.*' If you are unaware of God's intended purpose for the soul, you might hear the soul's voice and accept its lies as truth. You have been listening to the voice of your human soul for so long that you are used to it.

"Don't panic. God has a way to restore the damaged soul so that you will be able to hear His life-sustaining, life-giving instructions. Just as your spirit's salvation required a decision, the salvation of the soul requires a decision—only this decision will be ongoing, sometimes with challenges every day. You will have to choose His life-giving workings in your soul every day. God will not break apart the self-sustained, self-defense systems of your soul, He will not smash into its secret hiding places to fix and restore you. You are going to have to choose to give Him permission to do His work in you.

"He asks us to voluntarily take down our self-defense systems (ineffective and pitiful as they are) and voluntarily expose our innermost wounds and needs to Him for healing and answers. This is what the soul has been calling your 'real life,' its frantic attempts to hide the unhealed hurts, unmet needs, and unresolved issues you have accumulated over your whole life. Just as you said what we call a sinner's prayer, giving God permission to covenant with your human spirit, you can say a prayer giving God permission to start the salvation of the soul process. Here, let's pray these binding and loosing prayers and start it right now.

"**Father, I bind my will to your will. I bind my mind to your mind, Jesus. I bind my emotions to your healing balance, Holy Ghost. I bind myself to the truth of your Word. I want to obey your commandments and I ask you to help me do so.**

"**I loose all walls of stronghold thinking, I loose all of the effects and influences of wrong agreements I have made, and I loose all of the layers of self-image, self-understanding, self-reliance, and whatever else my soul has piled up over my unmet needs, unhealed hurts, and unresolved issues. I loose all of the enemy's hindrances and devices that he is using to try to confuse and deceive me.**

"**Thank you, Lord, for giving me the Keys of the Kingdom to surrender all that I have and all that I am to you. Please heal me and help me to hear your every word to me. Amen.**"

Liberty, I'm sure you will recognize some of your words in the above. But why couldn't this appeal to new Christians in the Church? To me, it's the salvation of the soul or it's the waste-howling wilderness. Only those two choices. The waste-howling wilderness is in the Bible, you know, Deuteronomy 32:10, (*KJV*). When I found it, I said, "Wow, something that God said thousands of years ago describes where Sharon and I went."

Most of the believers I have talked to and given *Shattering Your Strongholds* to are still waiting for God to do what needs to be done in their lives. Just as Sharon and I were. Everyone gets all religious on me when I say your books, teachings, and ministry are the "how to" for soul restoration and getting the spirit, soul, and body aligned and connected to God. Am I the only one who thinks the Bible is a "how to really live" book? All the religious folks say to me, "Don't you know that you can't just reduce God to a formula, a certain way of praying—a step-by-step system?" Well, I think that we can work within God's step-by-step system of surrendering our souls to Him.

Thank you, thank you, thank you for your amazing patience with this sister. Love, Rosanne

Hi, Liberty. During my relative's recent medical emergency and intensive care stay, I observed the nurses were giving her blood transfusions almost continually. I watched the tubes and bags as the blood all drained out. She would respond to the blood transfusions, life seeming to seep back to the surface, and she would regain consciousness. Then, because they were unable to stop her internal bleeding, she would slip into unconsciousness and ultimately to a life-support system.

A friend who has read your books and is practicing the binding and loosing prayers was talking to me one day about her husband and their relationship. The Holy Spirit spoke to me as she was speaking, and He said, *"He's dying, he's hemorrhaging, his life is hemorrhaging."* I told her what the Holy Spirit was saying to me. She said, "Yes, he is hemorrhaging life and what he is using for his transfusion isn't Christ's Life is it? He regains 'consciousness' for a while but with no real life change. Then he must go back to his life-support system of wrong behaviors, wrong habits, wrong attitudes, and thought patterns." I remembered what you wrote about our memories being kept alive by means of the artificial life-support systems of the soul. We prayed for him. I'm learning how to pray right now. Love, Rosanne

As long as I am in this physical body, every area in my soul that I yield, surrender, or die to becomes part of the new creation in Christ. Christ wants to move into my entire soul and set up His house. When He can, His image and His characteristics will be manifested out through my physical body to speak God's words of life. My real life in the Spirit is functioning, but it is hidden with Christ in God.

It helped my concrete thinking to understand that being "in Christ" is actually a condition, a position, and it takes place in my surrendered soul. I didn't know that before. My human spirit knows it is possible to know Christ and it has deep, deep longings and desires to know Him in oneness of spirit, soul, and body. My human spirit knows that the capacity also exists in the surrendered soul to know Christ. But this capacity is guarded by strongholds. Stronghold thinking raised up against the true knowledge of Jesus Christ, how dumb is that?

Last Sunday morning at church we celebrated the recently born-again and recently rescued dropouts from other churches, attending a two-hour class, receiving a certificate, and signing a card about volunteering to work in our church. Our attitude was one of acceptance. It feels good to be recognized like that, and it helps our church grow.

It is right for us to celebrate, but we were wrong to equate attending a two-hour class, getting a certificate, and signing a helps pledge card with true spiritual growth and maturity. We're wrong to equate religious behavior with knowing Christ. Our initial salvation of our spirit means that we know Him as Savior, but we don't know Him as Lord of our soul life, yet. I'm really, really in Christ. Rosanne

Hi, me again. Two weeks ago I had a dream that I call the Lego dream, which I've had two more times since. In the dream I am talking to Jesus about how others helped me become a spiritual birth defect. I was rationalizing and justifying how I was taught wrong in the Church. The Church should have taught me about the soul, the Church should have recognized that I didn't know Christ like I should, and so on.

In my dream, Jesus basically said, *"You don't even know you."* He proceeded to show me a picture of my identity in Christ—the identity He had planned ahead of time for me. I saw a huge wall made of Legos in front of my identity. I guess this was the medium

He chose because I often play with them with my grandchildren. They have Lego tables with large blocks, and they have hundreds of those tiny Lego pieces that you step on in the dark.

Jesus showed me that every time I made a stubborn, rebellious choice, I was putting a Lego piece in front of my new identity in Christ. This was very painful because I had been calling this the "little stuff," "the who cares anyway stuff"—the "God couldn't possibly mean that stuff." I was blocking out the new creation I was designed to be by putting up this Lego wall of my wrong decisions and free will choices.

I recently read this line in a book, "There is a God we want, and there is a God who is. They are not the same God. The turning point of our lives is when we stop seeking the God we want and start seeking the God who is." Wow, our task is not to reinvent God in our imagination but to discover the God who is already there. That is when we want to know His will and be all He wants us to be, isn't it? Love, Rosanne

Dear Liberty: I have been talking to my daughter (the buck-up queen) about the brain's capacity to build more pain receptors to accommodate more pain. I had migraine headaches for over twenty years. Using your teaching and prayers on healing for the physical body, I began to pray differently. I loosed the wrong agreements I had come into with doctors about the sources of migraines. Even though I couldn't get others to agree with me, I began loosing the pain receptors my brain had been building for years. I also loosed some word curses I had spoken, such as, "This body doesn't know how to have just a headache, it has to have a migraine."

I began talking to my body about not "needing" to express inner pain this way, about not needing to come into alignment with emotional pain any longer. I have since had several "normal" headaches, none requiring injections. The frequency of migraines is way down and some of my fear has left about the power these migraines were able to exert over my life.

The Holy Spirit also told me that I should say, *"Jesus, your name is greater than migraine in this body."* I had been lifting up the name of migraine in my body, He said. I think there might be a spiritual principle working here for us believers. I told my daughter, "Hey, I was willing to learn how to give myself injections to stop the pain. How hard could it be for me to learn to talk to my body? I was already talking to it with a needle."

After Sharon's death I clearly saw that I had been poised to walk the same path of depression and hopelessness into death as she did, and would have without some kind of intervention. I'm a living example that the chart you call X-Ray of the Unsurrendered Soul can be a life-saving tool. I'm not sure why it had to take me so long, but I recognized that the surrender of the soul was a life and death choice when I read your books.

I haven't had a lot of success yet with trying to convince depressed and discouraged people that this is the answer. But I know from reading all the testimonies on your web site and in your newsletter that there are many people who have recognized this truth. That continues to be a source of encouragement to me and reason enough to continue on. I'm learning to leave the results to God, to be obedient, and to try not to make it my personal responsibility to rescue, heal, deliver, and save every individual who dares to talk to me about depression and suicide.

I continue to give your books away and encourage each person to call or e-mail me, and then to check out your web site. I know as I hand them a book that I am giving them a life-saving tool, a spiritual weapon they can use to get to the truth that will set them free to know Jesus Christ. He not only knows the answers to life, He is The Answer!

These are some of the symptoms of healing and retraining in my soul. I don't experience this every day, but it is happening more days than before. This has come three years after Sharon's death and a year and a half of praying the binding and loosing prayers, reading and studying, and attending some of your meetings. There is within me a new ability and desire to enjoy each moment. There is within me a tendency to think and act more spontaneously, rather than acting based on fear of painful memories and experiences that I cannot bear to remember, but do not dare forget.

I'm also experiencing a loss of interest in interpreting the actions of others and judging other people. A loss of interest in conflict. A loss of the ability to worry. And, I am experiencing frequent, overwhelming episodes of appreciation. Isn't that cool! I have contented feelings of being connected with others and nature. And get this: I'm having frequent attacks of smiling!

I have an increased susceptibility to the love extended by others as well as having my own desire or urge to extend it. What I have discovered this past year and a half is this feeling of being in control, like my mind is my own. I no longer have these strung-out periods of thought and contemplation—useless conversations with my unsurrendered soul. My mind simply feels quieted; it's really a strange feeling. My emotions have become more stable; and I haven't felt depressed for longer periods of time.

I feel like my will is mine. I feel like I have the ability to choose life, to embrace the Gift of Life each day. I am beginning to understand for the first time what it means to have my life hidden with Christ in God. Scripture seems different; I actually understand what it is saying. I feel connected to God each morning when I awake. For the first time I think I understand what it actually means to be a Christian.

I have the freedom to quickly identify negative, non-life producing thoughts and the desire to make them bow their knee to the Umpire of my soul. I feel capable of helping people, but not driven, and I feel capable of helping myself. I was co-dependent for years with Sharon, but this last year I haven't felt the need to be dependent on anyone except God.

I guess I am describing what it is like to be at peace. I feel this quiet, soft joy in my soul. I miss Sharon terribly, but I am capable of celebrating her life in Christ. I'm no longer tormented and taunted by an unsurrendered soul filled with grief, condemnation, guilt, and shame.

I am friendlier with strangers and more comfortable. I have begun to actively participate in life, instead of just passively yet critically watching it. My capacity and ability to hear and respond quickly to the Holy Spirit's teaching and correction in my life has greatly increased, and as a result of that many of my responses to life have become less painful.

I don't know what I'm going to be when I "grow up," and my marriage and relationship with my husband has become a rather urgent issue. He laid down his life and covered mine while I walked through this valley of the shadow of Sharon's death. He doesn't know me now since I'm not Sharon's mother in mourning. I think we're going to become really acquainted finally. I'm not afraid of the future as I continue to bind my will to God's will and my husband's will to God's will. Blessings to you, Liberty, and to your staff. Your friend, Rosanne

Dear Liberty. Over a year and a half ago you reached into the waste-howling wilderness of my unsurrendered soul and shared the Keys of the Kingdom spiritual principles with me. Desperate and alone, I grasped the keys and walked out of the valley of the shadow of death. As if that wasn't enough, as a bonus I found out I didn't know Christ as Lord. I thought I ought to write a book about that. Imagine my surprise when I went to the Christian bookstore and noticed that Philip Yancey had "taken" my book title and already used it. The name of his book is: *Soul Survivor, How My Relationship With Christ Survived The Church.*

I was in another city recently watching my son coach baseball. Although he was a champion player, wrote his own ticket through college, played professional for several years and traveled the world, he didn't find his real gift until he was 40 years old and his right shoulder was worn out and inoperable. He has a love for the game and he loves coaching both boys and girls in it. As I was watching him, the Holy Spirit spoke to me, He said, *"See, Rosanne, that's you. You have a love of the Gift of Life and you're a coach in it."*

He told me to watch my son. He was "in" the game, not just sitting on the bench calling out plays. Each boy and girl was the recipient of his teaching and encouragement. Even when they made errors, it was a teaching moment. He corrected, instructed, and encouraged them. He invented "tools" to teach skills with, and if they couldn't get it one way, he tried another. Every kid played, and every kid was valuable. Each year he produces one or two champions; a boy or girl who probably wouldn't have had the opportunity will get a scholarship to college.

I agree with the Holy Spirit; I am a coach. I want to help others learn how to be champions for God's team. I believe He will help me do it, because He loves me. There is an old song by the singing group called Bread that I changed into a spiritual song. The line said, "When my love for life was running dry, You come and poured yourself on me." Thank you, Liberty, for helping me to receive that from Him. In Christ, Rosanne

Rosanne's and Sharon's stories have been hard to tell and perhaps hard to read. However, Rosanne now walks in victory because of her stubborn belief that the Keys of the Kingdom prayers would help her surrender her soul and its mind-numbing grief to her heavenly Father. I, too, have felt the victory in helping this story to be told. This victory will be all the more sweet if these words and the following prayers help those who are in deep pain listen to their spirits' cries to Choose Life! This chapter closes with two prayers, one being for the person who is struggling with overwhelming discouragement and hopelessness which is called the *I Want To Choose Life Prayer*. The second prayer is for all of us to pray for our friends and family members who are too discouraged to pray for themselves. We can stand in the gap for them, holding onto their wounded, desperate souls with these powerful keys. This second prayer is called the *Let Them Choose Life Prayer*.

I have been ministering online to a man, "Victor," who is struggling with giving up on life because he feels so helpless and hopeless. Please remember "Victor" in your prayers, along with the many others you may know who are slowly sinking into hopelessness. He has given me permission to use portions of the suicide letter left behind by his brother, Wayne, who committed suicide. Victor said the following about his brother:

"My brother, Wayne, committed suicide. He claimed to be a born-again Christian, but didn't go to church and had no friends. He was a hateful, sarcastic, jealous, and sometimes violent person.

There seemed to be no love in him and, regardless of his claims, he was a miserable person for most of his 39 years. He got along with no one. That is why we were shocked when he left behind this note."

To My Family: There is no way you will ever know all that I have done in trying to control my thoughts and moods, as I was very private about it. I knew that bringing my family into it would not provide a cure, but only cause everyone to be more distressed. My belief in a loving God is very strong, thanks to being brought up by loving parents in a loving family. Please don't think that my actions are an indication that I had a miserable life. Most of my life was very happy and fulfilling, with only periods of gloom, but the gloom was something that was beginning to take over and prevent me from seeing the possibility of things ever getting better. One thing is certain; I had absolutely no control whatsoever over my moods or my outlook. It did not seem to matter what I did to try to counter it, my negativity always won out. I have come to believe that this is something very much like a disease—like cancer or diabetes. A disease that can be controlled in ninety percent of the cases, but not all cases. I believe in Jesus Christ as my Savior. I don't pretend to understand His ways, but I know He is my hope for the next life, if not for this one. I hope and pray that every member of my family will accept Him as their Savior so that we will all be together again someday in heaven. I know I am not setting a good example for Christianity, and I don't know what to say to this. I am completely at a loss for an explanation as to why this seemed to be the only way for me. I don't blame God for my fate; I just don't understand why He seemed to not answer my plea. But I know He is not responsible. The first thing I hope to ask Him when I get to heaven is where I went wrong. I have no clue what the answer might be. Wayne

This tragic letter, more than anything I can write, reveals the incredible web of deception and denial that a wounded soul is capable of creating to convince a human being that death is the only way to stop the pain. Wayne obviously was in terrible pain, yet he believed that he had kept it hidden from others. This denial of his struggle and hopelessness somehow kept him from reaching out to someone to help him. I cannot even begin to understand what Wayne was feeling. But I do know that once the cycle of such negative thoughts begins, they seem to etch trails in the mind that become like deep ruts. If we are not affirming life, if we are not constantly choosing life (as Rosanne said) then death takes over by default. If those people who are locked into their own prison of pain do not reach out to God and to other people for help, then we must begin to reach in to them. Use these prayers to help someone—perhaps to help yourself.

I Want To Choose Life Prayer

Lord, help me! I don't think I can hear my born-again spirit crying, "Choose life! Choose life!" any more. The pain in my soul/heart keeps trying to drown out my spirit's words. Can I still choose life? I need your hope in me, God, so that I can believe that I still have this choice that I can make. Your Word says you found your people, your inheritance, in a barren and howling wasteland. Lord, that sounds like where I am now. Your Word also says that when you found them there, you shielded them and cared for them, guarding them as the apple of your eye in that place. Guard me and keep me as the apple of your eye, Lord, and bring me out of this barren and howling wasteland.

All of my soul/heart's ways have brought me down lower and lower, but the Word says that Jesus left me the Keys of the Kingdom to use here on earth. So I bind my will to your will, Lord, so that you can stabilize and steady me as you hold me. I bind my mind to the mind of Christ so that I can hear His thoughts instead of the dark thoughts of my own soul/heart. I bind my emotions to you, Holy Spirit; I need your comfort so much. I bind myself to an awareness of your blood, Jesus, that you shed for me that I could live. I want to want to live.

Teach me your way, O LORD; give me an undivided soul/heart that will strain to get to you instead of always trying to back up into the darkness. I loose, smash, crush, and destroy all of the wrong thought patterns, wrong beliefs, and wrong ideas that my soul/heart is embracing right now and I CHOOSE LIFE! I loose, smash, crush, and destroy every effect and influence of all wrong agreements made about me, over me, and those that I took part in myself and I CHOOSE LIFE.

Forgive me, Lord, for my part in any wrong agreement and set me free from those influences. Have mercy upon me and strengthen me TO CHOOSE LIFE. I bind myself to your truth, and your truth says that you will never leave me or forsake me. You are a God who can only speak truth, so I choose to believe this and I CHOOSE LIFE. You know where I am, you know how I feel, and you know my soul/heart wants to give up. I loose the deception and denial that my soul keeps trying to shroud my spirit with. I bind every divided part of my soul/heart back to you, Lord. Thank you for fixing the broken parts of my soul/heart so that I CAN CHOOSE LIFE AND LIVE. I surrender myself to you, Lord, and I believe you will help me come out of this valley of despair. I long to feel free and to walk on the high places with you. Thank you, my God, for doing this for me. Amen.

Let Them Choose Life Prayer

Lord, help me to be a light, a hand outstretched, an intercessor for those who can no longer hear their born-again spirits crying, "Choose life! Choose life!" Help me speak life into the orphaned souls of those who do not yet know that Jesus died for them that they could CHOOSE

LIFE. Help these souls, believers and not-yet-believers alike, to hear your voice encouraging them to surrender to you and come out of the barren and howling wasteland they are in right now. Those who have lost their hope, their courage, their faith, and those who have no faith yet, please shield them, care for them, and guard them.

Those whose heads are bowed with pain, I bind their wills to your will, Lord, so that each one can be stabilized and steadied as they are held by you. I bind their tossed and torn minds to the mind of Christ so that they can hear His thoughts instead of the dark thoughts of their own soul/ hearts. I bind their battered and negative emotions to you, Holy Spirit; they need your comfort so much. I bind them, believers and yet-to-be-believers alike, to an awareness of your blood, Jesus, that you shed for them that they could live. I want them to want to live.

Teach these sad souls your way, O LORD, give them undivided soul/hearts that will strain to get to you instead of always trying to back into the darkness. I loose, smash, crush, and destroy all of the wrong thought patterns, wrong beliefs, and wrong ideas that their soul/hearts are embracing right now. I ask that you would cause them to think these words, to hear these words, and to see these words — CHOOSE LIFE, CHOOSE LIFE, CHOOSE LIFE! I loose, smash, crush, and destroy every effect and influence of all wrong agreements ever made about each one of them, over them, and including those wrong agreements they took part in themselves. I ask that you pour LIFE into their soul/hearts to refresh and to encourage them. Forgive them, Lord, for their part in any wrong agreement and please set them free from those influences. Have mercy upon them, shower them with your love and strengthen them that their choice will be to CHOOSE LIFE.

I bind these wounded soul/hearts to your truth, which says that you will never leave them or forsake them. You are a God who can only speak truth, so I choose to believe that they will let me speak these words to them, or they will hear or read them and CHOOSE LIFE. You know right where they are, you know how they feel, and you know the soul/hearts who are the most desperate, even wanting to give up. I loose the deception and denial that their soul/hearts keep trying to shroud their spirits with. I bind every divided part of their soul/hearts back to you, Lord. I thank you for fixing the broken parts of these soul/hearts and I ask you to keep speaking these words to them: CHOOSE LIFE AND LIVE! Help them come out of the valley of despair they are in so they can feel free to walk on the high places with you. Thank you, my great and gracious God, for doing this for them. Amen.

eight

Obedience and Surrender

"As the Father has loved me, so have I loved you. Now remain in my love. If you obey my commands, you will remain in my love, just as I have obeyed my Father's commands and remain in his love. I have told you this so that my joy may be in you and that your joy may be complete ... You did not choose me, but I chose you and appointed you to go and bear fruit— fruit that will last. Then the Father will give you whatever you ask in my name" (John 15:9-11, 16, *NIV*).

These verses tell us that if we obey His commands, we will remain in His love. Another verse says He knows that we love Him when we obey His commands. Our Lord seems to place a great deal of importance upon the act of obedience.

Obedience does not always mean that you won't feel conflicted about what you know you must do. Obedience does not mean you will never feel uneasy, frustrated, or overwhelmed. Obedience means that you will simply do what you know you should. You will not be sidelined by your human emotions, and you will respond to your spirit's desire to do the will of God.

There is an interesting story in the Book of Acts about a disciple named Ananias who was afraid to obey God.

Reluctant Obedience

"In Damascus there was a disciple named Ananias. The Lord called to him in a vision, 'Ananias!' 'Yes, Lord,' he answered. The Lord told him, 'Go to the house of Judas on Straight Street and ask for a man from Tarsus named Saul, for he is praying. In a vision he has seen a man named Ananias come and place his hands on him to restore his sight.' 'Lord,' Ananias answered, 'I have heard many reports about this man and all the harm he has done to your saints in Jerusalem. And he has come here with authority from the chief priests to arrest all who call on your name.' But the Lord said to Ananias, 'Go! This man is my chosen instrument to carry my name before the Gentiles and their kings and before the people of Israel. I will show him how much he must suffer for my name.' Then Ananias went to the house and entered it. Placing his hands on Saul, he said, 'Brother Saul, the Lord Jesus, who appeared to you on the road as you were coming here—has sent me so that you may see again and be filled with the Holy Spirit.' Immediately, something like scales fell from Saul's eyes, and he could see again. He got up and was baptized, and after taking some food, he regained his strength." (Acts 9:10-19, *NIV*).

Ananias was very frightened of this task that Jesus Christ was asking of him. He nervously reminded Jesus just exactly who this Saul of Tarsus was and what he had been doing to the believers. How often we feel that the Lord may be out of touch with our reality, or that perhaps He has forgotten the circumstances by which we find ourselves surrounded. So we anxiously remind Him of what we have been through, what has been done to us, and how impossible our lives already seem right now!

Jesus reassured Ananias that Saul was now a believer by telling him that Saul could be found at a certain house praying. This man, who had just a few days prior been breathing out threatenings and slaughter against those who would follow this Jesus Christ, was now praying to God (Christ's Father) for answers.

A Christian has no rights that are in conflict with the Word of God. While it is a natural human desire to want attention paid to our negative emotions such as fear, God is more interested in what is right for everyone involved in situations than He is with our self-perceived rights.

"Do everything readily and cheerfully—no bickering, no second-guessing allowed! Go out into the world uncorrupted, a breath of fresh air in this squalid and polluted society. Provide people with a glimpse of good living and of the living God" (Philippians 2:14-15, *The Message*).

Some people think that God's will is multiple choice. I have actually tried to convince God of this, myself, and I've certainly heard others do it, too. "Well, God, here is how I see this problem. I would like you to answer this way (A), I could also handle it if you answered this way (B), and I suppose I could manage to live with answer (C) if you absolutely just have to do it that way. All right, God! I'm sure we're in agreement here. Now which one is your will?"

I think God answers, "(D) *None of the above!*" God's will, His ways, and His thoughts are not our ways and our thoughts. Isaiah 55:8-11 (*KJV*) tells us that God says, *"For my thoughts are not your thoughts, neither are your ways my ways, saith the Lord. For as the heavens are higher than the earth, so are my ways higher than your ways, and my thoughts than your thoughts. For as the rain cometh down, and the snow from heaven, and returneth not thither, but watereth the earth, and maketh it bring forth and bud, that it may give seed to the sower and bread to the eater: so shall my word be that goeth forth out of my mouth; it shall not return unto me void, but it shall accomplish that which I please, and it shall prosper in the thing whereto I sent it."*

We need to obey God's Word, doing what He wants instead of believing the interpretations of His Word that our souls spin.

I once heard a true funny story about a man, his prize strawberries, and a three-year old toddler. This man carefully tended his strawberry plants, waiting with anticipation as the berries turned red and swelled with juice. Every morning he would walk out in his back yard and pick the biggest and juiciest of the berries that he had watched ripening for days, slicing them up for a fine breakfast treat.

One morning he went out to get the berries he knew would be ready and found that they were gone! His whole morning was ruined and he angrily stomped back into the house where he found his three-year old son, covered with red juice stains and stuffing the last purloined berry into his mouth. "Donny," he said with a raised voice, "you *cannot* pick Daddy's strawberries. I have juice for you, bananas and oranges for you, and all kinds of other things. Those strawberries are not for you to pick. Do you understand me? You are not to pick another strawberry off those plants out there or Daddy will be very angry. Do you understand me?"

Donny's eyes got very big and he nodded yes vigorously. Don't pick the strawberries off the plants, or Daddy will get very angry.

The following morning, the man went eagerly outside to check one huge, prize berry that would surely be ripe for picking that morning. Yes, it was still nestled in its leafy green spot, waiting for him. The man carefully picked the strawberry and turned it over to admire it. The entire back of the huge berry had been eaten by someone leaving small teeth marks. The man stormed back into the house and called his son to come immediately. He showed Donny the half-eaten berry.

As Donny's eyes filled up with tears, he said, "You said not to pick the strawberries off the plants. You didn't say anything about eating them on the plants."

When God tells us not to do something, *we need to just not do it.* Too often we try to figure out how to reinterpret His meaning so we are more comfortable with it. "Well, God only said I shouldn't go to the horse races. He didn't say I shouldn't go to the casino." Or, "God said I shouldn't get a divorce, but He didn't say I couldn't find myself a companion." Or, "God said that He wanted me to stop watching television so much, but do you think that means not watching videos and DVDs, too?"

How Do We Begin to Obey?

You begin by believing you are part of the beloved Bride of Christ. You don't have to understand what that means, anymore than you need to understand how your brain processes electrical impulses and messages from your nervous system. You just are and it just does.

There are some things that you just have to accept and go on with your life secure in the knowledge that there is Someone who is making it so, and He knows what He is doing.

As part of the family of God, part of the Bride of Christ, you are known for your love one for another. So begin your journey of obedience by seeking to know and understand the love of God poured out upon all of us.

The Message translates Jesus' words in John 14:15, *"If you love me, show it by doing what I've told you."* It is very clear that Jesus is saying that the proof of our true love for Him is not in our words, but it is in obedience to what He has told us to do. Obedience is the fruit of *our love towards Christ*. If we are not obeying what He has told us to do, then we are not showing the fruit of love.

Truth does not exist just in words; truth must have corresponding actions to verify that it is present. The Father has made it quite clear that the performance of truth is *"trustworthy, straightforward correspondence between deeds and words"* (Isaiah 45:19, *Amplified Bible*). Truth has a straightforward relationship with our actions and what we say.

After hearing Jesus reasoning together with some Pharisees, Herodians, and Sadducees, one scribe asked Jesus what the first commandment of all was. Jesus answered him:

> *"The first of all the commandments is: 'Hear, O Israel, the LORD our God, the LORD is one. And you shall love the LORD your God with all your heart, with all your soul, with all your mind, and with all your strength.' This is the first commandment. And the second, like it, is this: 'You shall love your neighbor as yourself.' There is no other commandment greater than these"* (Mark 12:29-32, *NKJV*).

Making Right Choices

Many people have said, following tragedies and loss of life, "Why didn't God stop the people from making those choices?" I have wondered how these people would feel if God suddenly said to them, *"You will no longer have any choices. You will stop doing what you are doing, and you will do what I say or else!"*

Forcing people to make right choices is not how God has set up His New Testament covenant with those who believe in Christ Jesus. I do believe that just as the grumbling, mumbling Israelites stumbled around the desert, some of us just take years to walk out of our deserts, too. God keeps putting obstacles in our wrong paths and nudging us toward right doors of opportunity. Some people, such as the Apostle Paul, may get a turbocharged nudge into their destinies.

In Acts 26:14, Jesus told Paul that resisting God's will was a hard way to go. He said, *"It is hard to kick against the goads."* The *Living Bible* says, *"You are only hurting yourself."* Goads (or pricks) are sharp, pointed iron rods used to jab oxen to motivate them to move. After Jesus knocked Paul off his horse on the road to Damascus, He then said to him:

> *"Now get up and stand on your feet. I have appeared to you to appoint you as a servant and as a witness of what you have seen of me and what I will show you"* (Acts 26:16, *NIV*).

Jesus didn't ask Paul if this was all right with him, or if he would agree to it. Jesus just told him that he was going to be His servant and His witness. Jesus did not consult Paul to see if he was okay with that. Christians love to say that God will not cross their will, but Jesus actually crossed Paul's will so hard He knocked him off his horse and struck him blind. It is pretty obvious that He meant to get Paul's attention focused on what He was about to tell him.

We have come up with the deception that we have a spiritual right to exercise our own wills to choose things that have nothing to do with what God wants. Don't make Jesus poke you with a sharp stick, knock you off a horse, and strike you blind to get your attention! Pray for a turbocharged nudge into your destiny! Give God permission to take off the velvet gloves in dealing with you and push you into your place in the race where you fit best. If you are afraid to pray and commit yourself to that, then you need to examine your own faith and beliefs, as you really don't trust God's plans for you.

One of the meanings of the word "bind" is to put oneself under obligation to another. When you bind your will to the will of God, you are putting yourself under obligation to Him and whatever He wants to do with you. We need to speak the Word, act on the Word, and obey our God in perfect agreement with His will and His plans. There is something about agreeing with God and acting upon His Word that brings us into prospering.

Christians' wills really only have four choices. Number one and two are that we can choose life or death. Deuteronomy 30:19-20 tells us that God told His people, *"I call heaven and earth as witnesses today against you, that I have set before you life and death, blessing and cursing; therefore choose life, that both you and your descendants may live; that you may love the LORD your God, that you may obey His voice, and that you may cling to Him, for He is your life and the length of your days; and that you may dwell in the land which the LORD swore to your fathers, to Abraham, Isaac, and Jacob, to give them"* (NKJV).

Numbers three and four are: "Will you obey or disobey the Word of the Lord?" The Lord said,

> *"See, I am setting before you today a blessing and a curse —* **the blessing if you obey the commands of the LORD your God** *that I am giving you today;* **the curse if you disobey the commands of the LORD your God** *and turn from the way that I command you today by following other gods, which you have not known"* (Deuteronomy 11:26-28, NIV).

Each one of us has the capacity to make wrong choices or to make godly choices. Which choices will you make? Life or death — obey or disobey?

Get Serious

> *"If you're serious about living this new resurrection life with Christ, act like it. Pursue the things over which Christ presides. Don't shuffle along, eyes to the ground, absorbed with the things right in front of you. Look up, and be alert to what is going on around Christ — that's where the action is. See things from his perspective"* (Colossians 3:1-2, The Message).

One woman who had been raised in a Christian home her whole life came into our weekly prayer meeting one night. She seemed upset and unhappy, so I asked her why.

She said, "I just had to stop at my bank and get some cash so I could pick up something to eat on my way here. There was this man begging for money for food outside my bank. I wish the bank would do something to keep those panhandlers away from their parking lot so I don't have to see them. They always upset me so much!"

When I asked her why she didn't just buy him some food and bring it back to him, she was taken back, replying, "I guess I didn't think of that." She was telling the truth; the thought had never occurred to her.

This is exactly the kind of self-absorbed mentality that the above Scripture is addressing: *"Don't shuffle along, eyes to the ground, absorbed with the things right in front of you. Look up, and be alert to what is going on around Christ—that's where the action is. See things from his perspective."*

The binding and loosing prayer principles address this very issue. When you bind your will to the will of God and your mind to the mind of Christ, you are taking the first step to being alert to what is going on around Christ, instead of being focused on how everything relates to you. You can begin seeing things from His perspective. When you loose stronghold thinking that protects your soul's self-absorbed thought patterns, you are taking the next step to receiving revelation understanding *on the spot* as to what you need to know from Him. He will speak when He sees you doing what you can to be able to hear His voice.

One of the most wonderful things about setting your will to align with His will is that you position yourself to receive not only guidance but divine power to accomplish His will. God is such a good God! He knows our frame, He knows we are made of dust, and He does not expect us to accomplish His divine plans and purposes in our own strength. He does, however, expect us to understand that our motives and intents must be clean and focused on Him before He will strengthen us with His power.

Every time we open the Bible, we must always aim at finding some spiritual benefit, some word of love to strengthen our relationship with Christ, and some truth we have not yet chewed upon. The Word of God is not a collection of sayings to ritualistically read each day to say you have had devotions. It is a chance to peek into the very heart of God, an opportunity to know Him better. Just reading the Scriptures to find an intellectual agreement with your beliefs will not lead to life and light in Jesus Christ.

The Apostle Paul told the Roman Christians that the Word of God would bring hope, saying,

"For whatever things were written before were written for our learning, that we through the patience and comfort of the Scriptures might have hope" (Romans 15:4, *NKJV*).

Paul encouraged the one he called "his son," Timothy, with these words:

"But you must continue in the things which you have learned and been assured of, knowing from whom you have learned them, and that from childhood you have known the Holy Scriptures, which are able to make you wise for salvation through faith which is in Christ Jesus. All Scripture is given by inspiration of God, and is profitable for doctrine, for reproof, for correction, for instruction in righteousness, that the man of God may be complete, thoroughly equipped for every good work" (2 Timothy 3:14-17, *NKJV*).

In Ephesians 2:10, *Amplified Bible*, we read of the wonderful, glorious plans and purposes God has for us: "*For we are God's [own] handiwork [His workmanship] recreated in Christ Jesus, [born anew] that we may do those good works which God predestined (planned beforehand) for us, (taking paths which He prepared ahead of time) that we should walk in them—living the good life which He prearranged and made ready for us to live.*"

These are not works, paths, and a good life for us to embrace unto ourselves alone. These are all for the greater purpose of recognizing that we are all one body, filled with many members working together:

"... speaking the truth in love, (that we) may grow up in all things into Him who is the head—Christ—from whom the whole body, joined and knit together by what every joint supplies, according to the effective working by which every part

does its share, causes growth of the body for the edifying of itself in love" (Ephesians 4:15-16, *NKJV*).

Racial Prejudice and Class Structure in the Church

In Ephesians 2:13-16, (*Amplified Bible*) Paul tell us, *"But now in Christ Jesus, you who once were [so] far away, through (by, in) the blood of Christ have been brought near. For He is [Himself] our peace—our bond of unity and harmony. He has made us both [Jew and Gentile] one (body), and has broken down (destroyed, abolished) the hostile dividing wall between us, by abolishing in His [own crucified] flesh the enmity [caused by] the Law with its decrees and ordinances—which He annulled; that He from the two might create in Himself one new man— one new quality of humanity out of the two—so making peace. And [He Designed] to reconcile to God both [Jew and Gentile, united] in a single body by means of His cross; thereby killing the mutual enmity and bringing the feud to an end."*

The enemy has worked hard in the souls of the members of Christ's body so that we would find ourselves today faced with a class structure, with racial bigotry, and with gender prejudice within the Church. There was also great enmity between the Jews and the Gentiles when Jesus walked into His public ministry. The above Scripture clearly tells us that Christ's death on the cross was designed to reconcile the Jew and Gentile into a single body, thereby bringing the feud to an end.

God must look at us and ask Himself, *"There is not one of them who does not come from either a Jewish background or from a Gentile background. What part of Ephesians 2:13-16 don't they get? I sent my Son to die on a cross to abolish all the enmity and division between my people. Why don't they see that?"*

When that "one new man," created by the sacrificial death of Christ Jesus, renewed by the Spirit of God and reconciled to itself chooses to segregate itself, division and death follows. Matthew, Mark, and Luke all quoted the same words of Jesus, *"If a house is divided against itself, that house cannot stand"* (Mark 3:25, *NKJV*). A body divided against itself cannot stand, either. There is a form of crippling arthritis that occurs when the body turns on itself and begins to attack its own cells. I am sure there are several other deadly diseases that bring about the same self-destructive patterns when the body divides against itself.

When spasms and palsy affect the limbs of a human being because they can no longer receive the right signals from the brain, that body is out of control. When we allow bigotry, prejudice, and favoritism to thrive in the Church, the body of Christ is sick and unable to follow direction from its Head. It is crippled and out of control.

God's will is aimed so much higher than for just our own personal blessing. God's will is that we should love one another, for this is how the world will recognize us. Read with care the following commands of our Lord:

"A new command I give you: Love one another. As I have loved you, so you must love one another. By this all men will know that you are my disciples, if you love one another" (John 13:34-35, *NIV*).

Jesus was saying here that the way the world will really know we are disciples of Christ is not by our works with the poor and the homeless—not by our works when there is a disaster. When the events of September 11, 2001, brought down the World Trade Center buildings, non-believers, atheists, and backsliders all came together to try to help and comfort one another. You are not known to be a disciple of Christ because you do good works for others. You are known as a Christian because you love one another. The only way the world will know that we are His is when they see us—His followers—loving one another and forgiving one another.

"Now that you have purified yourselves by obeying the truth so that you have sincere love for your brothers, love one another deeply, from the heart" (1 Peter 1:22, *NIV*).

The word "heart" as used here is *kardia*, which is used in the verse to mean the fountain and seat of the thoughts, passions, desires, appetites, affections, purposes, and endeavors—the soul. Love is received from God, incredible divine love, but it must also be allowed to pour out of the born-again spirit to be deposited and to grow within the mind, the will, and the emotions. This is another reason for making sure that we have emptied our soul of its grudges, bitterness, wrong attitudes, and anger through loosing prayers.

"This is how we know who the children of God are and who the children of the devil are: Anyone who does not do what is right is not a child of God; nor is anyone who does not love his brother. This is the message you heard from the beginning: that we should love one another" (1 John 3:10-11, *NIV*).

This passage clearly states that if we do not sincerely, truly love our brother, we are not a child of God. As you are struggling with trying to learn to love those you don't feel like loving, you will not be cast out from God. But you will surely be sent again and again to the "end of the line," or the "back of the room," if you remain in a state of not loving because of rebelliousness to the many commands to love.

And finally:

*"If someone says, 'I love God,' and **hates** his brother, he is a liar; for he who does not love his brother whom he has seen, how can he love God whom he has not seen? And this commandment we have from Him: that he who loves God must love his brother also"* (1 John 4:20-21, *NKJV*).

Hate is a very strong word and it can mean to "detest and loathe." But according to many biblical scholars (including *Thayer's Greek-English Lexicon*), "hate" also means the following:

- to love less,
- to postpone esteem,
- to slight,
- to disregard, and
- to be indifferent towards.

Ouch! Who has not felt this way about difficult people, particularly difficult relatives—both spiritual and natural? This particular word study brought me up short as I realized that I had worked hard to bring my soul to a place of forgiveness with one particularly difficult person who had caused me a great deal of grief.

I became aware that while I had forgiven this person, I had no feelings of esteem or value for this person, yet I would say with vigor that I loved God.

This verse says that I really don't, that I'm lying if I cannot assign some sort of value to this person who is one of God's children. This is what I call those little "spiritual checkups" that the Holy Spirit runs on us when we will allow Him the room in our souls to do so.

In Luke 14:26, Jesus said, *"If anyone comes to me and does not hate his father and mother, his wife and children, his brothers and sisters—yes, even his own life—he cannot be my disciple"* (*NIV*).

This requirement of Christ that we are to hate father and mother, wife and children, does not mean that we are to despise them and even ourselves. It means that all earthly ties to them and our love for them must be secondary to our love for Christ. We are to love them less than we love Him. We must always be ready to be there for them, but willing to place them second if we are directed to do so following one of His commands.

The commandments of the Law are wrapped up in the new commandment that Jesus Christ said He gave to the people of God. The Law was fulfilled in Christ; He made it come together in a new covenant of love. John 13:34-35 gives us the words of our Savior himself: *"A new commandment I give to you, that you love one another; as I have loved you, that you also love one another. By this all will know that you are My disciples, if you have love for one another"* (*NKJV*).

We must always rely upon and expect the Lord to empower His Word when it is presented in truth. First Thessalonians 2:13 (*Amplified Bible*) says this: *"We also [especially] thank God continually for this, that when you received the message of God [which you heard] from us, you welcomed it not as a word of [mere] men but as what it truly is, the Word of God, which is effectually at work in you who believe— exercising its [superhuman] power in those who adhere to and trust in and rely on it."* This means one thing to me: I must be all over the Word as if it had Super Glue on it—adhering to it permanently!

The Power in the Word

When I was a new Christian, I was so often confused by people saying, "Well, bless your heart, you can't claim that Scripture! That verse was for the Jews or the Romans or the king." I struggled to understand what part of the Bible was for me—a mixed-up Gentile of Scottish, Irish, English, German-Dutch, and Cherokee descent. There didn't seem to be any verses specifically appointed to that combined racial lineage. Fortunately, I hung on to my belief that the Bible was written for me anyway. I ultimately decided that I would claim and stand upon and hold close any verse of the Bible that encouraged me, strengthened me, or caused me to feel the love of God.

If you have ever struggled with that same issue as to what part of the Bible is yours to claim, read this:

"Therefore, remember that formerly you who are Gentiles by birth and called 'uncircumcised' by those who call themselves 'the circumcision' (that done in the body by the hands of men) … you are no longer foreigners and aliens, but fellow citizens with God's people and members of God's household, built on the foundation of the apostles and prophets, with Christ Jesus himself as the chief cornerstone. In him the whole building is joined together and rises to become a holy temple in the Lord … through the gospel the Gentiles are heirs together with Israel, members together of one body, and sharers together in the promise in Christ Jesus" (Ephesians 2:11, 19-21; 3:6, *NIV*).

Now, that's encouraging!

First Thessalonians 1:5, *The Message*, records Paul telling the Thessalonian Christians, *"When the Message we preached came to you, it wasn't just words. Something happened in you. The Holy Spirit put steel in your convictions."* The King James Version says that the Gospel came to us in power, in the Holy Ghost, and in much assurance. That word *assurance* in this verse means "complete confidence."

Our own words have power, too. We must always consider what impression our words are making on others. *"Watch the way you talk. Let nothing foul or dirty come out of your mouth. Say only what helps, each word a gift"* (Ephesians 4:29, *The Message*). Being able to speak does not give us the right to say anything we want to. There are so many people today who feel that freedom of speech means that they have the right to spew words of perversion, violence, and hatred into the minds of others through the internet, music, movies, television, rallies rooted in racial hatred, and magazines and books.

It is a sin for believers to speak words that tear down and discourage. We should be speaking only what helps, making sure that each one of our words is a gift to those who are struggling, discouraged, and depressed. In 1 Thessalonians 1:8, Paul commends the Thessalonian Christians, saying, *"The news of your faith in God is out. We don't even have to say anything anymore—you're the message!"* (*The Message*).

Forgetting What Is Behind

Expectancy for your future can be deflated by old memorials you have built to your past. You cannot embrace God and His Son, Jesus Christ, while still holding onto everything you are still nurturing from your past, your old life. In Philippians 3:12-14, Paul says, *"I press on to take hold of that for which Christ Jesus took hold of me. Brothers, I do not consider myself yet to have taken hold of it. But one thing I do: Forgetting what is behind and straining toward what is ahead, I press on toward the goal to win the prize for which God has called me heavenward in Christ Jesus"* (*NIV*). The word *forgetting* as used in this verse (*Thayer's Greek-English Lexicon*) means, "to neglect, to no longer take care of it." In other words, stop tending it, stop nurturing it, stop fertilizing it, and stop giving those old "things" artificial life support.

When a person suffers some type of trauma growing up but never allows God to heal their memories of it, this person can stop growing mentally and emotionally right at that point. This same person will usually have a lower threshold for dealing with stress and disappointment than others, causing him or her to be overwhelmed more by people and situations that other people might. Depression can come when your soul is on overload because of stress and disappointment in your life.

Second Corinthians 13:5 (*The Message*) tells us this: *"Test yourselves to make sure you are solid in the faith. Don't drift along taking everything for granted. Give yourselves regular checkups. You need firsthand evidence, not mere hearsay, that Jesus Christ is in you. Test it out. If you fail the test, do something about it."*

When you are praying the binding and loosing prayers with conviction and purpose, you are testing yourself to see whether or not you are solid in the faith. You are giving yourself a checkup to see if you need to make changes in your life. When you are reading the Word regularly, forcing yourself to see the hope and expectation that it speaks of, you are testing to see if your belief system is true. Hopelessness, which is believing that one has no future, also contributes to depression. You must remember that Christ in you is the hope of glory. How could such a partnership have no future?

Prove to yourself and to others that He is in you. How do you do that? Find a verse that speaks of His love for you, and take some step of faith to prove that you believe that to be true. For example, Philippians 4:13, *"I can do all things through Christ who strengthens me"* (*NKJV*). Paul said this to mean that we also could do anything *God wants us to do* through Christ who strengthens us. Think of something that you have wanted to do for God, but you have been afraid that you couldn't do it. If you are intimidated or feel that there is no place for you in the outreach ministries of your own church, there are small churches in every town that welcome volunteers. You do not have to leave your church to give a few hours during the week to help another church out. You just might be needed more in the little church. Call some small churches and ask if you could help out in some way during the week when you are not involved in your own church.

Appropriating His Promises

Second Peter 1:2-4, *Amplified Bible*, tells us that mighty things are waiting and ready to be multiplied unto us.

"May grace (God's favor) and peace, (which is perfect well-being, all necessary good, all spiritual prosperity and freedom from fears and agitating passions and moral conflicts) be multiplied to you in (the full, personal, precise and correct)

knowledge of God and of Jesus our Lord. For His divine power has bestowed upon us all things that [are requisite and suited] to life and godliness, through the (full, personal) knowledge of Him Who called us by and to His own glory and excellence (virtue). By means of these He has bestowed on us His precious and exceedingly great promises, so that through them you may escape (by flight) from the moral decay (rottenness and corruption) that is in the world because of covetousness (lust and greed), and become sharers (partakers) of the divine nature."

This sounds wonderful, but it is fairly abstract as to how we escape through His promises. After so much frustration and resentment of the abstract promises that I heard preached the first ten years I was a Christian, I became dedicated to searching out how to turn God's seemingly abstract faith promises into reality through concrete cooperation on my part.

Second Peter 1:5-8, *Amplified Bible*, gives us some very good information on what we are to do to appropriate these promises that we might escape the corruption of this world.

"For this very reason, adding your diligence [to the divine promises], employ every effort: in exercising your faith to develop virtue (excellence, resolution, Christian energy),
- *and in [exercising] virtue [develop] knowledge (intelligence),*
- *and in [exercising] knowledge [develop] self-control;*
- *and in [exercising] self-control [develop] steadfastness (patience, endurance),*
- *and in [exercising] steadfastness [develop] godliness (piety),*
- *and in [exercising] godliness [develop] brotherly affection,*
- *and in [exercising] brotherly affection [develop] Christian love.*

For as these qualities are yours and increasingly abound in you, they will keep [you] from being idle or unfruitful unto the (full personal) knowledge of our Lord Jesus Christ, the Messiah, the Anointed One."

Diligence comes from the Greek word *spoude* (spoo-day'), which means to eagerly, earnestly, and *speedily* take care of business. Speed is definitely implied in this original Greek word. Do what needs to be done and do it now! Do you need to forgive? Do it now! Do you need to ask someone to forgive you? Do it now! Do you need to help someone? Do it now! Do you need to give up a wrong habit, do it now! Has God asked you to perform a special task? Do it now! A lot of our struggles would be passed over if we just quit thinking about what we need to do and just begin doing it.

We are to add our diligence to God's divine promises. He has promised that He will never leave us or forsake us; that is an established promise. We must diligently act like He is with us in all things, everywhere we go and in whatever we do.

When we exercise our faith in this manner, we develop virtue, which means moral vigor. As we are exercising our moral vigor, we begin to get understanding and knowledge of how to exercise self-control. Moral vigor and self-control require an agreement between the body, soul, and spirit. The body and soul must continually be made to practice moral vigor and self-control. How do you become a great tennis player, or an Olympic skater? You practice, practice, practice. As Christians today we do not understand the concept of practicing the Word of God. The Word tells us to love our enemies. You practice this verse by doing something kind for an enemy, by speaking well of an enemy to another person, by recommending an enemy for a job. Practice helps us learn patience and endurance as we act in a godly manner towards our brothers and sisters. We also need to practice loving people who are not that obviously lovable.

God's Word above says that we have these great qualities within us, which I would say are resident within our born-again spirits. Practice, practice, practice will help them abound in us. As these qualities abound in us, the above Word of God says that they will keep us from being unfruitful!

How do you first exercise your faith? First of all, you need to know what the original words used in most verses as *faith* meant. Faith is "trust and confidence in the goodness and power of God towards you." What do you know about the goodness of God? What do you know about God's power? You will have a problem having genuine trust and confidence in Him if you don't know why you should. Again, the very words *trust*, *confidence*, and even *goodness* are comforting but abstract. Trust in something means that you can lean on it, you can be supported by it, and you can rely upon it. Following are only a few of God's promises to us that we can lean on and be supported by:

"Know therefore that the LORD your God is God; he is the faithful God, keeping his covenant of love to a thousand generations of those who love him and keep his commands" (Deuteronomy 7:9, *NIV*).

"Those who know your name will trust in you, for you, LORD, have never forsaken those who seek you" (Psalm 9:10, *NIV*).

"Now I know that the LORD saves his anointed; he answers him from his holy heaven with the saving power of his right hand. Some trust in chariots and some in horses, but we trust in the name of the LORD our God. They are brought to their knees and fall, but we rise up and stand firm" (Psalm 20:6-8, *NIV*).

"You will keep in perfect peace him whose mind is steadfast, because he trusts in you. Trust in the LORD forever, for the LORD, the LORD, is the Rock eternal" (Isaiah 26:3-4, *NIV*).

In some verses with the same root word as *trust*, we find that *trust* has been translated as "believe": *"Let not your heart be troubled; you believe in God, believe also in Me"* (John 14:1, *NKJV*). To believe, in the New Testament Greek, means to be aligned in deed, thought, and purpose with the will of God. Paul quoted the Old Testament to the Roman Christians (Romans 4:3), as did James (James 2:23): that Abraham believed and it was accounted to him as righteousness. The word *believed* in this verse means Abraham put his trust in God. This word also means he had confidence in God. This trust and confidence in God is faith in action.

"Isn't it obvious that God-talk without God-acts is outrageous nonsense? ... Faith and works, works and faith, fit together hand in glove. Do I hear you professing to believe in

the one and only God, but then observe you complacently sitting back as if you had done something wonderful? That's just great. Demons do that, but what good does it do them? Use your heads! Do you suppose for a minute that you can cut faith and works in two and not end up with a corpse on your hands? Wasn't our ancestor Abraham 'made right with God by works' when he placed his son Isaac on the sacrificial altar? Isn't it obvious that faith and works are yoked partners, that faith expresses itself in works? That the works are 'works of faith'? The full meaning of 'believe' in the Scripture sentence, 'Abraham believed God and was set right with God,' includes his action. It's that mesh of believing and acting that got Abraham named 'God's friend' ... The very moment you separate body and spirit, you end up with a corpse. Separate faith and works and you get the same thing: a corpse" (James 2:17-25, *The Message*).

Cooperating With The Word

Ephesians 4:22-27 in the *Amplified Bible* gives us eight important points to consider with regard to obeying God. All of these points can be cooperated with by using the binding and loosing prayers:

"Strip yourselves of your former nature—put off and discard your old unrenewed self—which characterized your previous manner of life and becomes corrupt through lusts and desires that spring from delusion; and be constantly renewed in the spirit of your mind—having a fresh mental and spiritual attitude; and put on the new nature (the regenerate self) created in God's image, (Godlike) in true righteousness and holiness. Therefore, rejecting all falsity and done now with it, let every one express the truth with his neighbor, for we are all parts of one body and members one of another.

"When angry, do not sin; do not ever let your wrath—your exasperation, your fury or indignation—last until the sun goes down.

"Leave no [such] room or foothold for the devil—give no opportunity to him."

In Colossians 1:28, *NKJV*, Paul said that he was and we should be preaching Jesus while we were *"warning every man and teaching every man in all wisdom, that we may present every man perfect in Christ Jesus" (NKJV)*. Too often spiritual leaders do not fulfill that verse, only warning others of the pitfalls of walking away from Christ. This book is my attempt to not only warn, but to teach others how to walk away and stay in the paths that have been ordained for them to walk!

In *The Message*, Colossians 2:16-19, the Apostle Paul says,

"Don't put up with anyone pressuring you in details of diet, worship services, or holy days. All those things are mere shadows cast before what was to come; the substance is Christ. Don't tolerate people who try to run your life, ordering you to bow and scrape, insisting that you join their obsession with angels and that you seek out visions. They're a lot of hot air, that's all they are. They're completely out of touch with the source of life, Christ, who puts us together in one piece, whose very breath and blood flow through us. He is the Head and we are the body. We can grow up healthy in God only as he nourishes us."

We grow as we surrender and submit to our Lord. We don't grow because we obey religious rules and regulations, because we pay our tithes, or because we haven't missed Sunday school in three years. There are commandments in the Bible that we should follow, we should pay our tithes, and we learn from the teaching and fellowship of one another in Sunday school. But WE GROW in God because He nourishes us when we are obedient and surrendered to Him. All we have to do is obey Him and surrender to Him. When we get that right, we will grow and flourish in all ways, finally moving into the abundance He promises in the Word.

This sounds simple because it is. Our unsurrendered souls have so tried to complicate our walk with God. The human soul automatically resists God's ways from the very beginning.

Our Conscience

Thayer's Greek-English Lexicon says the conscience means "joint knowledge," a joint knowing with the Holy Spirit. One interlinear

191

Bible says that conscience means co-perception, or moral consciousness. Vine says that it is that faculty by which we apprehend the will of God. *Nelson's Bible Dictionary* says that the conscience is our inner awareness of when we are conforming to the will of God (a sense of approval) or departing from it (a sense of disapproval).

The conscience always tries to give input into the choices that man's will decides to make. This is when the soul begins to rationalize and justify the choices that appeal to it. The will is actually like the enforcer of the soul. The mind determines that something would be good to do or to have. The emotions kick in with feelings and yearnings. Then the will enforces the choice. A conscience that has been properly exercised has some muscle and can override the will and determine a right choice. A neglected or ignored conscience is flabby and easily overcome.

A seared conscience—scarred and deadened—is a fearful thing. A deadening comes over all of the emotions, patterns of thinking, and the will. Such a deadened conscience must surely exist in the mind of one who will kill, rape, and torture other human beings without a second thought.

Could the conscience be part of the soul? Can we care for and nurture our own conscience? The Apostle Paul said several things about how he tended his conscience. *"This being so, I myself always strive to have a conscience without offense toward God and men"* (Acts 24:16, *NKJV*).

If your conscience is troubled, there are no sacrifices you can make, no good deeds, no willing yourself to a new behavior that can purge your sense of guilt. You can actually force yourself to deny the guilt and to shove it away, the beginning steps towards searing your conscience so that you can't feel anything from it ever again.

The purifying of our consciences comes only by the washing of the blood of Jesus.

*"The blood of goats and bulls and the ashes of a heifer sprinkled on those who are ceremonially unclean sanctify them so that they are outwardly clean. **How much more, then, will the blood of Christ, who through the eternal Spirit offered himself unblemished to God, cleanse our consciences from acts that lead to death, so that we may serve the living God!** For*

this reason Christ is the mediator of a new covenant, that those who are called may receive the promised eternal inheritance—now that he has died as a ransom to set them free from the sins committed under the first covenant" (Hebrews 9:13-15, *NIV*).

Matthew Henry says this about Hebrews 9:8-14: "What the efficacy (Author's note: effectiveness, value) of Christ's blood is; it is very great. For, first, It is sufficient to purge the conscience from dead works, it reaches to the very soul and conscience, the defiled soul, defiled with sin, which is a dead work, proceeds from spiritual death, and tends to death eternal. As the touching of a dead body gave a **legal uncleanness, so meddling with sin gives a moral and real defilement, fixes it in the very soul;** but the blood of Christ has efficacy to purge it out. Secondly, it is sufficient to enable us to serve the living God, not only by purging away that guilt which separates between God and sinners, but by sanctifying and renewing the soul through the gracious influences of the Holy Spirit, purchased by Christ for this purpose, that we might be enabled to serve the living God in a lively manner." (From *Matthew Henry's Commentary on the Whole Bible*: New Modern Edition, Electronic Database © 1991 by Hendrickson Publishers, Inc.)

That certainly is a mouthful, but Matthew Henry is onto something here. He reminds us that the blood of Jesus can purge the conscience from dead works and the soul from the defilement of sin. The born-again human spirit, no longer an orphan but connected to the Spirit of its Creator, cannot be defiled with sin. Sin operates through and in the unsurrendered soul. Matthew Henry also says that meddling with sin fixes defilement in the soul, and only the blood of Jesus can purge it out.

"Jesus, I bind my mind, will, and emotions to you. I repent of this thing I have done (or for my feelings about what was done to me), please forgive me. I loose all thoughts of guilt and depression, and as I release their hold on my soul, please take them away. Please purge and purify my conscience with your precious blood, Jesus. Please cleanse my conscience and make it fresh and new.

"I do not want any hardening of my conscience, any searing or cauterizing that would make it scarred and insensitive. Jesus, please heighten my sensitivity to right and wrong. Forgive me for having dulled my senses by exposure to things that would have shocked me ten years ago. Lord, please don't ever let me become complacent about the world's doings in these days. I love you and I thank you, Amen."

Do we have the power to affect other peoples' consciences? It certainly seems so according to Paul,

"For if anyone sees you who have knowledge eating in an idol's temple, will not the conscience of him who is weak be emboldened to eat those things offered to idols? And because of your knowledge shall the weak brother perish, for whom Christ died? But when you thus sin against the brethren, and wound their weak conscience, you sin against Christ. Therefore, if food makes my brother stumble, I will never again eat meat, lest I make my brother stumble" 1 Corinthians 8:10-13, (*NKJV*).

Those who have ears, let him hear.

God's Operating Manual

Most biblical understanding is the opposite of what we, as human beings, would come up with. If we understood all truth just by our own common sense, then what point would there have been for God to have the Bible written? He knew that there were many things that we could not possibly learn in our own experiences, so He gave everyone on Earth the opportunity to have a Master Operating Manual for Abundant Life—the Word of God. No one has to go without this Manual anymore.

I read an interesting article on the Australian Outback that parallels why we need to accept the Word of God as truth and obey it whether we understand it or not. One important rule of survival in the harsh Australian Outback is that you never leave your vehicle if it breaks down. No options, no alternative choices, just that fact. Stay with your disabled vehicle regardless of the situation.

Consider this situation: Your vehicle conks out, you have no way to send word that you need help, you may not see another human for weeks, and your water supply can keep you alive for only a few days. Trying to walk to where help might be found can seem to be a good idea, considering your circumstances. The hard and fast rule still is: stay with your disabled vehicle.

Many unfortunate souls have died in the Australian Outback because of disregarding that rule, even though those who issue warnings all say that it is easier to find a lost vehicle than it is to find a wandering human who may be near complete dehydration and sunstroke. *Those unfortunate people died because they tried to save themselves.* Had they trusted that they would be saved, obeyed the rules and stayed put, they would probably have lived. This is the interesting parallel to our lack of regard for God's rules and commands that make no sense to us: The people who perished in the Outback disobeyed the rules that would have saved their lives because *such rules only make sense to people who can believe they will be saved in time.*

The Word of God tells us if we stand on His promises, obey His commands, have trust and confidence in Him performing His Word, He will come to our rescue. In fact, He has placed His whole reputation upon the truth of whether or not He will keep His Word. If God wants to be proven trustworthy, why do we always try to come up with ways to not trust Him? What is our problem with trusting Him? Is it because we do not really know what He has promised to us in His Word? How can you trust and obey when you don't know His way?

It is easy to become so familiar with the words of Scripture and respect for the Word of God, and still not recognize the life or death importance of actually practicing it in our own lives. The truth and guidance in God's Word is rarely similar to what our human minds think up. Think about these truths and commands: God's strength is made perfect in our weakness. Love your enemies. Whoever believes in Me will never die. Cast your bread upon the water and it will come back to you. Life comes out of death. These phrases do not seem logical to the natural mind, yet they are true and they do bring good consequences when heeded. So just accept that you are not going to always understand what God is telling you to do. Just do it anyway!

Better Than Fighting the Devil and Disease

I remember when I first went to work for a church after becoming a Christian, taking a very large cut in pay from my management job in a commercial photography studio. I was stunned at the lower salary offer, but felt I was doing what God was asking me to do. Different people in the church who knew of my salary cut said to me, "Well, don't worry. God will have to make up for that. He will." I became assured that because I had done my part, now God was bound to having to make it up to me.

I had heard from God and obeyed Him, but my daughter and I often had little to eat and I nearly lost my car believing that God owed me because I had obeyed Him. I had to learn several more lessons about what God did and didn't have to do when I obeyed Him. God is not bound to doing anything we expect Him to do in response to an action we take. This is an area that can get very abstract when you are trying to explain it.

We have the promise of God that all things work together for good to those who love Him and are called according to His purpose (Romans 8:28). The word "called" in this verse means those who have been invited to partake of God's offer of salvation in the Kingdom through Christ Jesus. Many are called, invited, but few step up to surrender their soul and obey God's commandments in order to walk in the Kingdom. I'm focused on stepping up to that invitation; I'm focused on surrendering and obeying the One who loved me first.

Only God can take a job in a church, a loss in income, and the near loss of a car and work them together for good for one He has invited into His Kingdom purposes. God used that instance in my life in many different ways. I found out that I had an overblown perception of the importance of money, that I was embarrassed by not having any, and that I was too proud of my ability to care for myself. I finally did learn to understand that these were things that God was working out in me, and I accepted and grew from them.

I became very dependent upon that church as my provision and my source of covering and protection. I felt that the church leaders would never let me get into severe need, and I believed that I would be at that church forever. Imagine my shock when I was let go from my job at that church four years later, along with several other people, due to a church split over a new pastor. I was devastated for I felt I had given up so much to work for that church.

God was again refining and redirecting my understanding that the church was not my source, nor was it my covering or my protection, nor was He working in my life based upon what I had given up to obey Him. Those are things you cannot read in a textbook or even always understand from reading the Word. Sometimes the Word in you works together with the life experiences God uses to teach you what you must know so that you can turn away from death-producing beliefs and mindsets.

After several lean weeks on unemployment and some odd manuscript jobs, I was offered a job in another church as an administrative assistant to the senior pastor. Aha, my soul said, this is even more security. After nearly three years, I was again let go by the church and replaced with a volunteer because of church finances. I was beginning to believe that this church work had been a mistake from the beginning. But I learned so many things about leadership, administration, ministry, and even making mistakes while working in those two churches. I learned that God takes us through different phases of learning that we could not get anywhere else, and we don't recognize that until much later.

When I left the second church, they took up an offering for me to buy a computer to start my writing career. With that love offering, I purchased one of the original Macintosh computers and loved it dearly. I named him Max. Max and I began to write and I learned that I was not yet through being humbled. While working temp jobs and writing, I had my electricity turned off twice, and I had my phone turned off once. My soul would rage, "Doesn't God want His Christians to be good stewards? Why would He let me be put in these situations? He doesn't really care, does He?" But, again, I was learning to refocus on who my source was and it was taking some hard things to get it through to me.

I was still making some mistakes, but I was learning important things in the school of life. God doesn't care whether we are a secretary, a ditch digger, a dishwasher, or an academic professor—He will use whatever is at hand to train us for future purposes He has planned for us to fulfill.

Because of obedience on my part, I have received many healings in my body. I needed to learn that healing is often a cooperative effort on God's part and mine. There is such a thing as passively waiting to be healed and aggressively waiting to be healed. When I am aggressively waiting to be healed, I keep checking myself for open doors that have allowed the enemy to send demonic attacks, natural viruses and infections of the world, or accidents my way. I go through, as Rosanne put it in her story about Sharon, a fierce soul inventory.

For those who have read *Breaking the Power*, you will already know that over a period of several years I was in five rear-end automobile accidents, each time sitting at the end of a line of cars at a traffic light. That was an interesting learning curve to go through regarding nursing grudges and offenses! I was very glad to get on with new things after that.

I was also learning that the more I surrendered and submitted to God, the more healing I seemed to get. I was aggressively cooperating with His healing every time I bound every cell in my body to His will and plans and purposes for my life, and every time I loosed unforgiving thoughts, wrong attitudes, angry or bitter thoughts, and grudges and frustrations I had with other people. Unforgiveness, attitudes, anger, bitterness, and grudges are opportunities for attacks from the enemy. Demonic opportunity because of rebellion in the soul can end up causing serious damage to the body.

There is such a connection between the soul and the body that the body is always affected by any distress in the soul. Regardless of what kind of façade a person may put up to hide anxiety, anger, or bitterness in their minds, wills, and emotions—the body will reveal it. Nervous tics, indigestion, headaches, insomnia, and an impaired immune system that is prey for colds, flu, allergies, and more; all become manifested in the body when the soul is upset.

I had no desire to be a victim of demonic attacks on my body. I worked aggressively to keep from opening doors to my mind, will, and emotions, and I believed my body would hang close to my constantly being scrubbed soul. For the last three years or so, my ministry has taken some giant leaps. My books are doing well, my internet ministry is growing and responding with scriptural and prayer counsel, and my bills are being paid on time.

Hallelujah! But I have developed some painful problems with one knee and hip. For a long time, I was able to just "walk through" the pain that fluctuated from almost fine to almost crippled. That has always been my answer to pain, just to ignore it and "walk through" it. That is, unless it was in childbirth or the dentist's chair! Then I was hollering for more shots and more pills and more of anything that would stop that pain.

I was diagnosed by one doctor after a fall in an airport as having serious arthritis in my knee and hip. I was told by another doctor that I didn't have any arthritis; I just need more exercise and a trip to the chiropractor. I was prayed for constantly, because it seemed at times as if the whole world was concerned about my limping. Everyone wanted to pray for me. Usually I am always happy to receive prayer for healing, but this time something strange was going on.

The more anointing on the person praying, the more my knee and leg would start hurting. I have had the leaders of major healing ministries pray for my knee and my leg and I would feel horrible shooting pains like electricity in my knee and hip. I began to wonder if the pain was from a spiritual problem, and I searched and pummeled my soul to see if there was something I was unaware of going on inside of my mind and my emotions.

One night, after speaking in a team ministry conference, a pastor wanted to pray for my knee and I let him. The usual pain increased in my leg. I was thanking him, smiling at his wife, and trying not to wince in pain all at the same time. Then another pastor stepped up to me and said softly, "That pain in your leg isn't a physical thing, it is a spiritual thing. There is something that God wants you to understand from it, and then it will go away." I felt an immediate response to his word from deep inside and I began to cry with relief. Someone had confirmed to me what I had been suspecting for some time.

I became quite prayer-shy. I would squirm out of peoples' requests to pray for me with any reasonable excuse I could think of. I knew that this was not a good thing for a minister who emphasizes teaching people to pray. I was becoming aware that I was going to learn something new, because prayer as usual wasn't solving this problem. I was aware that the pain would definitely increase just before and after going out on the road to teach in new areas. During the times of teaching and preaching, when I was under the anointing, I would not feel any pain at all. But later, I really did.

I began having very bad nights, having so much pain in my leg that I couldn't sleep. I would awake suddenly, biting back a scream, because my knee seemed frozen and on fire at the same time. The sleepless nights were beginning to wreak havoc with my energy and mental abilities. Then one night, I awoke crying out, locked in such pain that I couldn't move and I yelled out loud, "God, what is this? God, please show me what is causing this!"

Instantly I saw a man's large face and he was chanting something towards me in the darkness of my bedroom. Because of all of the binding and loosing prayers I have prayed for so many years, the following prayer burst out of me:

"Lord, I bind every cell of my body to your will and purposes for my life. I bind my mind to your mind, Jesus, and I need you to speak to me. I loose, smash, crush, and destroy every effect and influence of word curses being directed towards me. I loose the effects and influences of any witchcraft, voodoo, incantations, and any calling upon demonic forces to attack me. I loose, smash, crush, and destroy any hexes or curses or wrong prayers that have been directed at me. Thank you, Father."

The pain instantly ebbed and almost ceased. I got out of bed, walked around the room, and lay back down. As the pain began to try to come back, I remembered Psalm 64 where David was praying for God to turn on His enemies:

"Hear me, O God, as I voice my complaint; protect my life from the threat of the enemy. Hide me from the conspiracy of the wicked, from that noisy crowd of evildoers. They sharpen their tongues like swords and aim their words like deadly arrows. They shoot from ambush at the innocent man; they shoot at him suddenly, without fear ... But God will shoot them with

*arrows; suddenly they will be struck down. **He will turn their own tongues against them and bring them to ruin*** (Psalm 64:1-4, 7-8, *NIV*).

Remembering the above verses in part, now I prayed,

"Lord, I bind every cell of my body to your will and purposes for my life. I bind my mind to your mind, Jesus, and I need you to speak to me. I loose, smash, crush, and destroy every effect and influence of word curses being directed towards me, of any witchcraft or voodoo being directed towards me, and of any calling upon demonic forces to attack me. I loose, smash, crush, and destroy any hexes or curses or wrong prayers that have been directed at me. Hear me, O God, and turn the words of their own tongues back on them and bring them to ruin. Amen"

The pain stopped, and I slept the night through. It comes back from time to time, but I pray, remembering to ask God to turn wrong words back upon whoever would speak evil towards me and my family and my staff. I'm sure that those who have been deceived by Satan are cursing many leaders who are impacting his onslaught of darkness. These deceived people, whether practicing witchcraft, voodoo, or others forms of demonic incantations, are calling upon demonic forces to stop spiritual leaders who are teaching people how to surrender to God. I believe we should all pray for ourselves in this manner and for other leaders as well.

No More Division Between Spirit and Soul

The human spirit and soul are designed to work closely together, and when they are divided one again each other—the person becomes unstable.

"If any of you lacks wisdom, let him ask of God, who gives to all liberally and without reproach, and it will be given to him. But let him ask in faith, with no doubting, for he who doubts is like a wave of the sea driven and tossed by the wind. For let not that man suppose that he will receive anything from

the Lord; he is a double-minded man, unstable in all his ways" (James 1:5-8, *NKJV*).

To be double-minded means to both think with the thoughts of the born-again spirit and with the thoughts of the unsurrendered soul. Those who do this (the majority of the body of Christ today!) do not have an unshakable stability. I remember once hearing something said by a woman who had been a Christian for over twenty years, "I don't know why God lets these things come against me to tear my faith apart. When things go right, my faith is just fine. Doesn't He know that?"

He does know that and He's trying to fix that very problem in each one of us. Glory to God, let's tell Him that we want everything He has for us, and we'll let Him work it out in us however He sees fit. We just obey and let Him take care of the details.

nine

Power Leadership—Surrendered Souls with Servant Attitudes

So You Want To Lead?

We live in complex times with many issues pulling and tearing at spiritual leaders today. I recently attended a Ministry CEO Conference where we were told that pastors in America leave the ministry at the rate of nearly 1,600 a month. This figure does not even include the attrition rate of the different ministers and spiritual leaders who are not actually pastoring a church. These pastors and leaders have fallen away from their first love, having become overwhelmed in the magnitude of the expectations of them and their ministries.

The sadness of these figures is multiplied hundreds of times over when you realize the number of people those pastors could have helped if they, themselves, had only known how to come out from under their souls' dominion and moved into their new creatures' spiritual life.

Leaders whose relationships with Jesus are ever deepening will always have access to the Father's wisdom and revelation understanding on any issue that confronts the Church. Many of the issues that are splitting and dividing the Church today—ordination of women, speaking in tongues, "once saved always saved," denominations, religious politics—are more issues of the human soul's interpretation of the Scriptures than issues of God's heart. We must all turn to God's heartbeat to hear what He is saying about these things. We cannot think our way through these things as leaders, because our souls will be giving self-agenda input into everything our tired little brains try to come up with.

As leaders, we do not have to be perfect, we do not have to be spectacular, and we do not have to be affirmed and praised. Spiritual leaders need to examine themselves to be certain that they are not trying to meet their own unmet needs for approval, acceptance, and love that they did not experience as children, young adults, or even older. Ministering and leading that flows out of knowing the love of the heart of God can so warm the heart of the leader that no praise of man is necessary to feel affirmed and approved.

"Lord, if I am leading others because I have unmet needs that I don't know how to surrender to you, please show me. I want to open those things up to you and right now! I bind my soul to you, Jesus, with a full desire that the Holy Spirit would search me and try my ways. I loose all the layers of self-importance and self-agendas that my soul has used to try to compensate for my unmet needs. I will make a way for you to get into my soul's deepest recesses where my needs are buried. I need you to meet them that I might lead with clean hands and a pure heart. I need you to refine my motivations for being a leader, Lord. I surrender my plans and purposes to you. Amen"

Servant Leaders

Servant leaders know they must be led by the Spirit of God in everything they do. This requires an emptying out of natural desires and personal goals to make room to receive God's destiny purposes. All spiritual leaders should loose preconceived ideas and personal agendas that their souls are protecting regarding what they want to do for God. Never forget that Jesus emptied himself of all His divine attributes to become as we are. As spiritual leaders, we must do likewise.

Servant leaders for Christ are not leaders who are unable to make decisions and provide guidance, being helplessly pushed about by those who want to use their authority. True servant leaders for Christ lead from a position of humility strengthened by love and grounded in God's truth. True servant leaders lead from a position of being filled with God's richest spiritual treasures of wisdom and understanding. These are leaders who know that spending time with God is not the time they are supposed to be getting messages for others or researching a new book. It is time to get to know Him better.

"By wisdom a house is built, and through understanding it is established; through knowledge its rooms are filled with rare and beautiful treasures" (Proverbs 24:3-5, *NIV*).

Servant leaders for Christ do not worry about money or power.

"A devout life does bring wealth, but it's the rich simplicity of being yourself before God. Since we entered the world penniless and will leave it penniless, if we have bread on the table and shoes on our feet, that's enough. But if it's only money these leaders are after, they'll self-destruct in no time. Lust for money brings trouble and nothing but trouble. Going down that path, some lose their footing in the faith completely and live to regret it bitterly ever after" (1 Timothy 6:6-10, *The Message*).

Paul explains God's divine plans and purposes for spiritual leaders in the following words to the Ephesian Christians:

"And he gave some, apostles; and some, prophets; and some, evangelists; and some, pastors and teachers; **for the perfecting of the saints, for the work of the ministry, for the edifying of the body of Christ: till we all come in the unity of the faith, and of the knowledge of the Son of God, unto a perfect man, unto the measure of the stature of the fullness of Christ: that we henceforth be no more children,** *tossed to and fro, and carried about with every wind of doctrine, by the sleight of men, and cunning craftiness, whereby they lie in wait to deceive"* (Ephesians 4:11-14, *KJV*).

Spiritual leaders should edify, instruct, and guide saints to the perfecting of their faith and growth in the knowledge of Christ so that they would mature and fulfill their destinies. If God has given you a capacity and a responsibility to influence others to follow you towards accomplishing God's purposes for their lives, you have the makings of a spiritual leader.

You will have to genuinely like and love people to do this, for they will balk, buck, and boo hoo as you try to lead them past their souls' unresolved issues and excuses. If you can, nothing is more rewarding than seeing people stand up and walk out of their current circumstances and head towards their destiny purposes in God. A leader who doesn't both like and love people, who doesn't want to see them succeed in their walk with God as much as he wants to succeed in his, should resign from leadership and find something else to do for God.

Always remember this: However many people you can help is the same number of people you can hurt or hinder! No one should be preparing sermons and teachings that they are not practicing and having victory with in their own daily lives. A leader must be experienced in being real to teach someone else how to be real.

I recently read that the original meaning of the word theology was "union with God in prayer." How far have we come from that definition? Many of today's theologians are more interested in the academic discipline of the Word than they are in prayer. The Word of God was not written for theologians to study as much as it was written for us to know God's love and to receive life that we might change and become more like His Son, Jesus Christ.

God will do what He needs to do to encourage humility and meekness in His greatest of leaders. Think about what He said to Paul who kept praying for a "thorn in his flesh" to be taken away.

"To keep me from becoming conceited because of these surpassingly great revelations, there was given me a thorn in my flesh, a messenger of Satan, to torment me. Three times I pleaded with the Lord to take it away from me. But he said to me, 'My grace is sufficient for you, for my power is made perfect in weakness.' Therefore I will boast all the more gladly about my weaknesses, so that Christ's power may rest on me. That is why, for Christ's sake, I delight in weaknesses, in insults, in hardships, in persecutions, in difficulties. For when I am weak, then I am strong" (2 Corinthians 12:7-10, *NIV*).

Soulish Leadership

Pretend with me that three spiritual leaders in Northern California all felt "led" to swim about 100 miles down the mighty Sacramento River to the San Francisco Bay. All three swam for ten miles and the first leader gave up and drowned. About ten miles further the second leader gave up and drowned. The third leader swam twenty-five more miles before giving up and drowning.

Was the third leader the strongest leader? That is the wrong question. The question really should be: Which one made it to their goal? The answer is: none of them. They all ended up as catfish kibble!

As a leader, your unsurrendered soul will try very hard to convince you that you have not only done more than others have, but that you have done all that you could be expected to do for God. I have known many spiritual leaders since I was saved in early 1972, leaders who were very powerful and impressive. When I was new in the Lord, I was quite awestruck by their spiritual abilities. I could not imagine how I could ever understand the Word of God like they did. Most of them are still working in the fields of the harvest and some have gone on to their heavenly reward, but not all of them

One strong leader fell to moral temptation when I had been saved about two years. Another leader I loved very much burned out and began operating a service station about five years later. A third leader who had taught me so much about Christian truths left the ministry about ten years after that and became a salesman because of being weary of struggling with financial need.

Which one of these leaders fulfilled the purposes that God had ordained? It would appear that all of them fell short of reaching the goals He had for them. These former leaders are restored to God now and I know I'll see them in heaven, but none of them sought to be restored to the callings in which they once moved so powerfully. I wonder if they regret their loss. I wonder if they recognize that they lost what they had because they had been ministering out of the finite strength of their own souls.

Your unsurrendered soul cannot sustain a true course through times of personal struggle, temptation, and difficulties in leadership. It will always be weighing the right thing to do against what it wants to do and can rationalize as accepted. Spiritual leaders come back to the same fork in the road over and over which is marked by one sign pointing left which says:

and one sign pointing to the right which says:

This fork in the road of the leader will come again and again. If the unsurrendered soul is allowed to weigh in on the subject, then the civil war starts all over again each time. Often, it just seems easier to go towards the soulishly acceptable thing and try to control any sinful tendencies that might crop up. Eventually, the right choice becomes harder and harder to make, causing stress and exhaustion to the leader.

The term "spiritual burnout" is not a true description of why some leaders fall away from their callings. The born-again, washed in the blood, forgiven human spirit *cannot burn out*. Every born-again human spirit becomes attached to the Spirit of its Creator by way of the blood of Jesus Christ with access to all of the infinite spiritual gifts its Creator has for it.

The unsurrendered human soul, on the other hand, has finite limits to its abilities. The unrenewed mind, the unsurrendered will, and unhealed emotions are finite in their carnal state (not being surrendered to or governed by God). Finite attributes and abilities have an end. Infinite attributes and abilities, such as our Creator's, have no ending.

As if it wasn't restrictive enough to have finite abilities to work with, humans generally are not using but perhaps a tenth of their natural abilities. This is probably a good thing, as man has only become more and more wickedly creative as his opportunities to think about sin have increased. The Christian leader who tries to accomplish great and mighty things for God in his or her own power will eventually burn out, some even going down in flames—but it won't be spiritual burn out, it will be soul burnout. The Bible records Paul's words regarding laboring for his Lord:

*"Now I rejoice in what was suffered for you, and I fill up in my flesh what is still lacking in regard to Christ's afflictions, for the sake of his body, which is the church. I have become its servant by the commission God gave me to present to you the word of God in its fullness—the mystery that has been kept hidden for ages and generations, but is now disclosed to the saints. To them God has chosen to make known among the Gentiles the glorious riches of this mystery, **which is Christ in you, the hope of glory**. We proclaim him, admonishing and teaching everyone with all wisdom, so that we may present everyone perfect in Christ. **To this end I labor, struggling with all his energy, which so powerfully works in me**"* (Colossians 1:24-29, NIV).

When you are not trying to fulfill your destiny through the power of Christ's life and energy in you, you can struggle yourself right into soulish and physical burnout. That leads to compromise, cutting corners, recycling methods and messages, as well as learning how to use and even abuse those who want to help in whatever way they can.

Spiritual Abuse

Being a spiritual leader is about helping people. Most positions of leadership are sought because they give concerned men and women opportunities to help people with complex problems, to offer His peace to confused emotions, and to calm anxious minds. While the majority of spiritual leaders minister successfully to many of these concerns, the ability to do so should never be the prime reason for wanting to be in ministry.

When your satisfaction in doing what you are called to do is based solely upon your ability to be the one who knows how to help people, you are drawing upon a finite source of validation. Regardless of the validation received, the souls of leaders can become very tired of dealing with complex situations, intense emotions, and anxious people. You can reach a point where you feel that you are hitting the wall with too many people you cannot help to change. There is a deeper reason for being a spiritual leader and only that reason can hold you steady when things continually seem to be falling apart instead of turning out how you had hoped.

You must be dedicated to obeying God because you love Him which means loving His people, as well. Whatever position or fivefold office you may hold, your calling is not to just be a problem solver. Your calling as a leader must be to love, to encourage, and to teach people how to increase their love for God and each other. You must never create a wounded following of people who are dependent upon you. Paul told the Corinthian Christians,

> *"We're not in charge of how you live out the faith, looking over your shoulders, suspiciously critical. We're partners, working alongside you, joyfully expectant. I know that you stand by your own faith, not ours"* (2 Corinthians 1:24, *The Message*).

A godly spiritual leader can never just be charismatic, dynamic, and persuasive. Many charismatic, dynamic, and persuasive "spiritual" people have led others in a powerful manner—such as Koresh (Waco, Texas), Jones (Guyana in South America), and Applewhite (Santa Barbara, California). Both David Koresh and Jim Jones came from Christian backgrounds. Somehow these two men, and countless others, lost their understanding of how to follow God's guidance in their own lives. Then they led countless others away from His guidance as well.

There is always a temptation to consider authority, power, and control as necessary to being a strong leader. Because of such thinking, the Crusades were held, Indians were beaten by monks until they would confess Christ, holy jihads have been launched, and many other cruel and tortuous things have been done to people in the name of God and the "Church." We must remember that as spiritual leaders, our job is to lead souls into maturity in Christ. Power and authority is very appealing to the unsurrendered soul, while loving people into following Christ holds no appeal for it.

Expecting grace to get you out of a situation in your own life after deliberately acting on a soulish temptation can be a fearful thing. The human soul is extremely good at convincing us that there are certain self-willed decisions we can make or some ungodly things we want that can be adjusted and prayed into alignment with God's will. I've heard people say, "I know I shouldn't, but I'll repent later." I think God looks upon such presumptuous acts with strong displeasure. To presumptuously displease God, counting on grace to get you out of it after acting on your temptation, is a fearful thing.

Aaron was the first priest God commanded Moses to consecrate unto Him. He told Moses to also consecrate Aaron's four sons to serve as priests. Read about two of Aaron's sons, chosen and consecrated by God, who presumptuously fulfilled their priestly duties "their way."

> "And Nadab and Abihu, the sons of Aaron, each took his censer and put fire in it, and put incense on it, **and offered strange and unholy fire before the Lord, as he had not commanded them.** And there came forth fire from before the Lord and killed them, and they died before the Lord. Then Moses said to Aaron, 'This is what the Lord meant when He said, I (and My will, not their own) will be acknowledged as hallowed by those who come near Me, and before all the people I will be honored. And Aaron said nothing." (Leviticus 10:1-3, Amplified Bible).

God had very specific rules and regulations for His priests, His spiritual leaders, under the Old Testament. They were responsible for doing exactly what they had been told to do, and they were held responsible to not do what they had not been told. In other words, they were not to be presumptuous about adding anything to what God had told them.

His priests were to perform the duties He had meticulously laid out, recorded in different passages in the Old Testament Scriptures. The Old Testament priest was to represent the people before God. God also has some very specific rules and regulations about how we, as New Testament Christians and spiritual leaders, are to walk in our roles as well.

We can read an interesting type of Aaron's will being in alignment with the will of God. God said that the Urim and the Thummim were to be sewn into the breastpiece he was to wear whenever he went into the presence of God.

"Whenever Aaron enters the Holy Place, he will bear the names of the sons of Israel over his heart on the breastpiece of decision as a continuing memorial before the LORD. Also put the Urim and the Thummim in the breastpiece, so they may be over Aaron's heart whenever he enters the presence of the LORD. Thus Aaron will always bear the means of making decisions for the Israelites over his heart before the LORD" (Exodus 28:29-30, *NIV*).

The Urim represents light and the Thummim represents truth. Any time Christians have to make choices, light and truth should always be the guiding straightedge for their decisions. This is one very good reason to bind your will to the will of God and to bind your mind to the mind of Christ every day. Jesus is light and God is truth.

Aaron's four sons knew the rules of the priesthood, but Nadab and Abihu took upon themselves to take common fire from an unconsecrated source and they most likely took common incense rather than consecrated incense to the altar. They must have been sure that their *assigned roles as priests* would protect them from any problems over these "small" changes to the rules of God. They offered incense their way without any regard for God's way. Their sin was trying to do God's work their way instead of His way. This sin cost them a terrible death—they were consumed by fire.

Soul Power Control

God has created leadership structure within the social structure of mankind. He has instituted certain positions of authority in the home, in the Church, and in government. But human authority is always horizontal—it is never vertical. Any leader's authority over you should never usurp your right to hear from God in your own spirit, which then conveys the spiritual information to your soul. Your spirit's success at actually getting the information through to your mind, will, and emotions is based upon how surrendered your soul is. That is why it is so important to have your soul cleansed of all misconceptions and preconceived ideas about God's plans.

Watchman Nee said that our biggest concern about our unsurrendered souls' power is their ability to mimic the directing of the Holy Spirit. I've been there, I admit it, and I earnestly tell you that I don't ever want to go there again! Some spiritual leaders do use soul power to control those who are following them. There are the truly self-focused leaders who care little for the success and growth of anything other than their own position of power and popularity. They use people as easily as others use paper towels to wipe up a spill. God's leaders are not gods and should never elevate themselves to that status. Always remember that God's anointing on your public ministry will correspond 100 percent to your personal life. Treat people right, pay your bills, and be a person of your word. Do not say that the Lord has told you to do something if you are not going to do it.

On the other side of soulishness, leaders should be aware that very needy people often try to ingratiate themselves with the leader for wrong reasons. Some of the worst possible candidates for positions that need filling in your church or your ministry can look like answers from heaven if you are easily affected by soul power. Such a person can seem to be the perfect answer when he or she wants to fill a position of help to you that you have been most anxious to fill. Your own soul power or unmet needs can definitely be involved in responding to the needy person's soul power. This can cause you to tune out warning signals from your spirit.

Binding your will to the will of God, your mind to the mind of Christ, and yourself to the truth as you loose all wrong motives, agendas, and desires can help clear the part of your soul that would want to take advantage of a needy person in order to get a need of the church or your organization answered. Soul ties come out of such things.

Soul ties are the products of wrong agreements made out of soulish need, soulish opinions, and soulish agendas that perceive a benefit in doing so. These wrong agreements are made between human souls seeking human support, attention, and help. There is usually an inappropriate type of acceptance that your soul feels when another Christian wants to enter into a soulish prayer agreement with you. This can seem to give a kind of spiritual covering over a very wrong agreement.

One of my staff members, Marian Johnson, had a vision from God of how power can be made perfect in weakness. She said that after praying about Paul's statement that God had said His power was made perfect in Paul's weakness, God showed her a weather map. He showed her that wherever there was low pressure in the earth's atmosphere, it became like a magnet for high-pressure systems to move into the area. When we acknowledge that we are weak in our own strength, that is like a magnet to God's strength.

When we move in our ideas of power and authority, we puff ourselves up with far more importance than we deserve. When we do that, God often lets us move without His power and strength. It is a frightening thing when a self-important "minister" is actually ministering with signs and wonders following him and God is not involved in any of them. Human beings cannot perform signs and wonders on their own, so whose power does that leave?

When you pray with the keys of binding and loosing, you will also be able to discern whether there is a human soul, a demonic spirit, or the Holy Spirit's influence upon behaviors, actions, or word ministry given to you.

As I have prayed in this manner, when I read the Word of God (which I have been reading since 1972) I find hidden nuggets of incredible insight that I cannot believe I have missed for so many years. When you pray in this manner, you will also find yourself perceiving God's hidden truths in situations that occur during your times of leadership or ministry, rather than just relying upon the apparent and often erroneous "facts" that your natural mind perceives. Our fine minds are so pitiful when it is necessary that we discern what spirit may be in operation during a leadership moment that requires a direct word from God. You cannot trust yourself to think your way out of spiritual problems that arise, but you can trust God when you surrender to His Spirit and obey your way out.

If these principles of prayer do not appeal to your soul and you choose to just continue to do what you've always done, know that you will receive the same results you have always received. If that is satisfactory to you, then I ask God to bless you and lead you into even greater opportunities. But binding and loosing prayers can put you in a position to give up some deadwood in your soul. To be more fruitful in ministry and leadership, we all need pruning, we all need growth, we all need some opposition, and we sometimes even need rejection to get rid of our deadwood in our souls.

We are probably going to have to accept the fact that we will have to put up with smelly, poopy sheep leaving messes everywhere and stepping all over our toes while we keep trying to lead them the best we can!

Leading Can Be Hard Work

Our pride is the greatest objector to the releasing of our passion, and genuine passion is a valuable quality in a leader. Genuine passion is exciting. If you think you are just not a passionate person, let me ask you to reconsider. God has given a measure of passion to each of us, because without passion we just sort of float along with the currents of whatever wind is blowing. The good news is that you have about a 99.9 percent chance of having some real passion inside your soul somewhere.

That passion may have been a trial to your parents, your teachers, or some other authority figure in your life because you had no idea how to channel it. Do you remember being told, "Quiet down! Stop asking so many questions. Put that down! Can't you be still for five minutes? Don't touch that. No, you can't have friends over for the night! No, you can't run the movie projector!"? You had a passion for everything you saw and touched and wanted. If your parents misunderstood this energy and enthusiasm, they probably continually tried to get you to be quiet and be still. Some people allow that kind of squelching to slowly bury their passion, because they are repeatedly led to believe that it is not acceptable. How do you uncover that burial? Pray like this:

"Lord, I don't feel very passionate, and I want to be. I want to take risks for you, I want to convince people that you're the greatest! I want to go where you want me to go, speak to whoever you want me to speak to, and have people ask me what it is that makes me so excited and different.

"I bind myself to you, I bind every fiber of my being to your will and purposes for me. I loose every word curse that was ever spoken to me about my enthusiasm and energy, whether it was meant to be cruel or it was just thoughtless. I loose all wrong beliefs I have formed about being excited. I loose all wrong mindsets and patterns of thinking I have about not wanting to have people wondering if there is something wrong with me.

"I loose all deceptions and lies that the enemy has caused my soul to form about being embarrassed. I loose all negative labels from myself: I am not foolish, I am not stupid, I am not out of order, and I am not a mistake! I bind myself to your truth because I am going to be passionate and excited for you and people are going to ask me why. Lord, give me exciting things to say back to them. I want them to get excited, too. I want to be a whirlwind and a dynamo for you—but I want to be passionate with godly character. Help me to know where I am lacking in your character and I will passionately do something about that! Thank you, God; I'm getting excited already. Amen."

Also remember that passion alone is sometimes a little dangerous to those around you. Passion must be linked to consistency, accountability, truthfulness, morality, and love for others. When passion is not blended with these characteristics, it can become soulishness. Our passion has to override our own sense of self-possession and presumed dignity. Can passion be taught? I don't think it can be taught, but I think you can learn from seeing godly passion in action. It can help spur the hunger to release your own passion within.

The Complete Leader

For far too long, the Church has had a split personality. Its earthly leaders cannot decide if the Church should be super-spiritual and lost in God with no need for earthly endeavors; or if the Church should be socially acceptable and user-friendly, which usually results in a controlled interaction with God. More churches need to balance both the spiritual needs and the natural needs of mankind, adequately touching both realms of the human spirit and the human soul.

Perhaps it is possible to bring that Church concept down to you and me as individuals. Jesus walked this earth fully touching both the realm of the human spirit and the realm of the human soul and body in all those He interacted with. He knew when the people who had flocked to hear Him preach were tired and hungry and He fed them. He knew when He needed to lie down as sleep, and He did.

Paul was an Apostle of the highest calling, yet he was deeply concerned about the lives of the men on the ship during the terrible storm we read about in Acts. He was concerned about the health of Timothy's stomach. Paul said that he had worked hard with his own hands to provide for his own needs and those of his companions, so that others would see that they should help each other, too. Paul often sought the help of the different churches for believers who were poor in material things.

I'm not sure about John the Baptist having much concern for the practical and natural realm of human life, for he seemed driven to preach almost exclusively on man's spiritual need. But John the Baptist was a specialist for a special time. Stephen was a specialist for a special time, too. Be careful that you do not decide that you are a specialist unless God clearly reveals that you are.

The Word of God says that the life of God's leaders should be walked on a higher road. Spiritual leaders only need to read the New Testament passages about the disciples and the apostles to know that their lives were not easy, not prosperous in worldly ways, and not filled with man's approval. I worry about the lifestyles of some of today's more successful Christian ministers. This is not because I think that God doesn't have enough money to help the dying and the lost if His ministers own big homes and luxury possessions. I worry because the luxuries of this world have a built-in lure and hook waiting for those who become accustomed to them.

Just as wild animals that are fed by humans lose their fear of humans, they also lose their natural drive to forage for their own food and they become dependent on the handouts of people. These wild animals become used to an environment that is not natural to them, making them more dangerous once they have lost their fear of the world's civilization. Christians are not of this world, though they walk in it. The success methods and luxuries of the world are not the Christian's natural environment. If you want to weaken or even kill something, take it out of its natural environment. In other words, put a fish in a birdcage, or put the bird in the fish tank.

Spiritual leaders grow through trials and tribulations, and God does give them tests to both strengthen them as well as show them what they don't have. I had a spiritual father who used to say, "Hard circumstances are not to show you what you have; they're to show you what you don't have." Paul told the Thessalonians Christians this in 1 Thessalonians 2:3-6 (*The Message*), "*God tested us thoroughly to make sure we were qualified to be trusted with this Message. Be assured that when we speak to you we're not after crowd approval— only God approval. Since we've been put through that battery of tests, you're guaranteed that both we and the Message are free of error, mixed motives, or hidden agendas.*"

Discipline in the Church

The same Paul who has proclaimed his great love for the believers and who prayed for unity, wisdom, and growth in the body of Christ also enacted discipline in the Church. In his first letter to the Corinthian church, Paul has used his authority as a spiritual leader, an Apostle, to excommunicate a church member:

"*It is actually reported that there is sexual immorality among you, and of a kind that does not occur even among pagans: A man has his father's wife. And you are proud! Shouldn't you rather have been filled with grief and have put out of your fellowship the man who did this? Even though I am not physically present, I am with you in spirit. And I have already passed judgment on the one who did this, just as if I were present. When you are assembled in the name of our Lord Jesus and I am with you in spirit, and the power of our Lord Jesus is present, hand this man over to Satan, so that the sinful nature may be destroyed and his spirit saved on the day of the Lord"* (1 Corinthians 5:1-5, *NIV*)

In his second letter to the Corinthian church regarding this same man, he said,

"The focus of my letter wasn't on punishing the offender but on getting you to take responsibility for the health of the church. *So if you forgive him, I forgive him. Don't think I'm carrying around a list of personal grudges. The fact is that I'm joining in with your forgiveness, as Christ is with us, guiding us. After all, we don't want to unwittingly give Satan an opening for yet more mischief—we're not oblivious to his sly ways"* (2 Corinthians 2:9-11, *The Message*).

Any time sin is ignored in a church, whether it is incest or unforgiveness, Satan has an opening to work in the souls of the church members. It is not a kind and loving thing to ignore believers who are walking in sin, disobedience, and rebellion. Such ignorance leaves these believers standing alone in their vulnerability to the works of Satan.

Many years ago I watched church leadership try to "save" a leader and his ministry by a cover-up. This man had become sexually involved with a woman in the church. The staff and directors of that church agreed to keep quiet about the affair, wanting to avoid public censure and chastisement. Having little experience in such things, I thought the leaders must be doing the right thing. It seemed right to forgive and give him another chance. Yet I knew, somehow, that it wasn't right to try to cover up the situation.

For many years I and countless others have prayed for the ensuing leaders of that church as its attendance and finances slowly dwindle each year. The leaders did not do what was needed to be done to *keep the church healthy,* as Paul states above. We have many unhealthy churches and ministries today. Healthy, strong Christians focused on their destiny purposes will not be raised up in such churches. But healthy and strong Christians who are raised up already can begin to pray and encourage other leaders in these situations.

Today we find that there are moral failings in major churches all over our nation—pastors divorcing their wives to marry women in their churches, spiritual leaders involved in homosexual relationships, and leaders who have misappropriated God's funds. Lee Grady, editor of *Charisma* magazine, said in a recent Charisma editorial entitled *Sin in the Camp*, "Restoring a person into ministry after a moral failure is not that simple. We're supposed to give people time to heal. But the truth is that when it comes to marital breakdown or sexual sin, we charismatics are way too eager to grant immediate pardons … Apparently what is important to us today is hype, not holiness. I guess what we want are ministers who can move a crowd to swoon and to write big checks. What we need are broken men and women who can move us to repentance."

God Himself uses severe discipline at times to show His love for those believers in His Son who are wobbling off their destiny paths.

"For whom the Lord loves He chastens, and scourges every son whom He receives. If you endure chastening, God deals with you as with sons; for what son is there whom a father does not chasten? But if you are without chastening, of which all have become partakers, then you are illegitimate and not sons. Furthermore, we have had human fathers who corrected us, and we paid them respect. Shall we not much more readily be in subjection to the Father of spirits and live? For they indeed for a few days chastened us as seemed best to them, but He for our profit, that we may be partakers of His holiness. Now no chastening seems to be joyful for the present, but painful; nevertheless, afterward it yields the peaceable fruit of righteousness to those who have been trained by it" (Hebrews 12:5-11, *NKJV*).

Leaders must be willing to address moral failings in the body of Christ. Correction, instruction, and healing must be prayed about, monitored carefully, and always ministered with love. Otherwise, we will all share responsibility for the sheep who learn to believe that sin isn't such a bad thing; in fact, sometimes it seems to work out pretty good.

Missing The Point

I usually delete all general e-mails that are not from one of my internet prayer or question and answer addresses, but just the other day I did happen to open an e-mail with a "story" about a man who was visited in his cabin one night by the Lord Himself. This happened right after all of my staff and I had been praying together about the fact that we keep ministering and doing what we feel we have been told to do, and the pressures upon us—especially financial—just seem to go on and on. I was feeling a little down that day, but back to the story.

The "story" said that the Lord told this man that He wanted him to push as hard as he could on the big rock out in the middle of his front yard. He wanted him to do this every day.

The man faithfully pushed on that big rock day in and day out, month after month, and year after year. The rock never budged an inch. Finally, the man became discouraged, questioning as to whether or not all of his obedience had been in vain. Sensing his chance, Satan quickly stepped up to agree with the man's discouragement. "Yes, you are a failure, you know. You have not been able to move that rock an inch. Are you sure you really heard from God? The past years of your life have been a great big waste of time."

The man trudged back into his cabin and knelt beside his bed. He could hardly lift his voice to pray, "Lord, how have I failed you so badly in what you asked me to do? I've just wasted all these years without accomplishing anything."

The Lord replied, *"Who told you that you failed? I did not ask you to move the rock, now did I? I just asked you to keep pushing on it. You think you have wasted those years with no results? Look at the thickness of your powerful arms, the width of your strong back, and the muscles in your legs. Now you are prepared for the great opportunity that I have been waiting to give to you."*

I thought all day long about that story and wondered how the pressures that we were feeling might be coming down on us because we felt responsible to accomplish things that we had not been asked to accomplish. God has never told me that I needed to create my own speaking engagements, and I've never forgotten that. God has never told me that I needed to become famous and powerful, and I've never forgotten that. But I had forgotten that He also had never told me I have to raise my own finances. All I have ever heard Him ask me to do is to teach what He tells me to teach and write what He wants me to write. I feel a prayer coming on:

"Lord, I need to get my orders clarified from you. What exactly have you asked me to do? What have I gotten mixed up about that? I bind my will to your will, Father, and I choose to obligate myself to your desires alone. If you want me to serve at the soup kitchen, just say so. If you want me to build houses for families who cannot afford them, just say so. If you want me to preach on a street corner, just say so. If you want me to open a Christian business, just say so. I choose to do what you want.

"I also need to be reminded of what you have not asked me to do. Lord, help me come out of agreement with doing things that you did not assign to me to do. Help me to stop responding and reacting to feelings of guilt over the fact (insert your own statements below):

- *That I am not evangelizing if you have called me teach.*
- *That I am not pastoring a local church if you have called me to travel and speak in other churches.*
- *That I am not singing if you have called me to write.*
- *That I am not a missionary if you called me to train others to teach.*

"Help me, Lord, to be so sensitive to your direction. I bind my mind to the mind of Christ that I will hear the thoughts of Jesus' mind. I bind my feet to the paths you have ordained for me to walk. I bind my hands to the work that you have called me to do. I loose all feelings of guilt and all soulish desires to do works that belong to others. I loose all hindrances and devices of the enemy from the paths you have called me to walk. I choose to be who you created me to be. Thank you, Lord. Amen."

Ministry Finances

Following the extreme drop off of giving to the Church and its ministries after 9/11/2001, I spoke with many ministries across the nation that were struggling to stay afloat. In the final three months of 2001, our financial situation also became very intense. Not only did the giving drop off, but we found ourselves having to cancel two of our major schools because people were unable or unwilling to fly to our Training Center in Northern California after 9/11.

Everywhere we turned, we found ourselves losing income. Our donations plummeted, our orders dried up, and our meeting invitations dwindled. All we could hold onto was the fact that God was not surprised nor at a loss as to what was happening to us and all of His ministries.

We did weather the storm with intense prayer meetings, reading of the Word of God, and the prophetic words we heard. One particularly comforting word sent to our ministry from South Africa was that we should not view the hard things that we were going through as negative, rather to view them as advanced training for rising to a new level. This word said that the hardships were God-ordained to teach us new things. I held on to that, and we did come through.

At the worst time of our financial struggle, we felt we had done all we knew to do—both spiritually and in the natural realm. We had carefully checked ourselves to see if we had any areas we were not addressing individually, and we searched our motives and methods in the ministry. We did quite a bit of territorial warfare against the principalities and strongholds over the area where we live. We used the Daniel 9 prayer, which is not a prayer of national or local repentance, but a prayer of confession of sin and an asking of forgiveness and healing for our area and our state. I elaborate on this prayer in Chapter 9 of *Producing the Promise*.

As I spoke with other struggling ministries, I encouraged them to remember that God knew exactly what was going on, and that they needed strength of character and trust and confidence in His love and wisdom to wait out His answers. I did not encourage them to hold on because they had a great blessing coming financially, because I felt they needed the blessing of understanding more.

During our LSM year-end Board Meeting, one of my Directors, Michael Lenhart, heard out my concerns about the other pressures we were feeling, as well as the heavy financial pressure. He asked me if I could tell God what I wanted and He would do it, what would I say to Him. I thought for a minute and said, "I would tell Him to heal my parents, give me good health, and send me enough money to pay off my debts."

Michael cut right to the last part of my statement with regard to enough money to pay off my debts, saying, "That would just lift you up out of the swamp you're sitting in now and dry you off for a bit, but you would be right back in that swamp by the end of next year if you don't figure out why you got there in the first place." He was absolutely right. We needed understanding more than we needed money.

Financial blessings can be consumed by debts and bills. Then you are right back where you started. Blessings of understanding continue to give and give if they are received and believed. We began to pray regularly for understanding and we were blessed with some unexpected miracles.

Another pressure we deal with at LSM is never having enough time to get everything done. As I was sitting one day, fading under the pressure of all the things I knew I could not get done, I turned to the Word for encouragement. I was hoping that I would be empowered by reading the Word, having great strength to forge on and accomplish everything I had committed myself to doing. I was surprised and a little embarrassed by what I read. This is an example of the power of the Word to point right to the problem that neither I nor anyone else was addressing.

Acts 6:1-7, tells us this about Paul's days of pressure and stress:

"Now in those days, when the number of the disciples was multiplying, there arose a complaint against the Hebrews by the Hellenists, because their widows were neglected in the daily distribution. Then the twelve [apostles] summoned the multitude of the disciples and said, 'It is not desirable that we should leave the word of God and serve tables. Therefore, brethren, seek out from among you seven men of good reputation, full of the Holy Spirit and wisdom, whom we may appoint over this business;

but we will give ourselves continually to prayer and to the ministry of the word.'

"And the saying pleased the whole multitude. And they chose Stephen, a man full of faith and the Holy Spirit, and Philip, Prochorus, Nicanor, Timon, Parmenas, and Nicolas, a proselyte from Antioch, whom they set before the apostles; and when they had prayed, they laid hands on them. Then the word of God spread, and the number of the disciples multiplied greatly in Jerusalem, and a great many of the priests were obedient to the faith" (NKJV).

There are times when I pray and bind my will to the will of God, bind my mind to the mind of Christ, and bind every cell of my body to God's will and plans and purposes for my life, and I feel like Super Christian! I am ready to shout, *"I can do all things through Christ Jesus, which strengthens me!"* as I charge off to engage myself in another project, another council, another conference, another meeting. After I have somehow managed to accomplish most of them, I crawl home to my teal green recliner and wilt.

The above verses spoke to me very clearly. I might be doing twenty-five things pretty well, but what if there were just five things I was supposed to do very, very well? I began to assess my life with a rather critical eye. Wasn't I always busy for God? Didn't I often work on messages and new books and my e-mail ministry of questions and answers seven days a week? You can't do much more than that, can you?

I heard from Michael Lenhart, my Board Director, again— Michael, the one who wades right into my life where others fear to tread. He said, "You can't do everything you're trying to do and still have the time you need to have with the Lord. Something is going to suffer." I began to think about how many times I hurry through my reading of the Word to get to work because there are so many things to do "for God." I began to think about how often I find myself praying while I'm driving to utilize my time productively, rather than just sitting down and talking to God. Ouch, that hurts to reread that confession.

All ministers should ask themselves, "Has my ministry helped me get closer to God? Or, do I have less time to spend with Him and less time to pray because I am too busy fulfilling my ministry?" Often, the work of the ministry leads to leaders praying less, isolating themselves more, and pursuing causes. Even though everyone tells the minister that he or she is doing great and wonderful things, *success and affirmation in the ministry can strengthen your soul's resistance to surrendering that attention to God.*

Perhaps we should all stop and pray this prayer from time to time:

"Lord, am I really doing what you want me to do? Do I rely upon you every day to help me make decisions, or am I making decisions based upon my prior successful experiences? I bind my will to your will, Lord, and I bind my mind to the mind of Christ. I loose all of my soul's desires to be on top of everything. If I need a reminder that I must rely on you for everything, then put me into circumstances and situations where I do not know what to do, where I do not have any prior experiences to call upon. Put me into circumstances where no one cares or is impressed by my credentials, my licenses, my accomplishments, or my personal style—put me into circumstances where my self-confidence is severely shaken.

"I must be confident only in having you in me, Jesus. Make me need your guidance once again. Help me rediscover who I am in you and who You are to me before returning me to circumstances where I can use my skills, experience, and natural abilities. Thank you, Lord. Amen."

Could You Not Tarry?

Last summer I went to a beautiful ministers' retreat center in Oregon with a woman pastor who is a close friend of mine. We spent hours in our own cabins trying to hear from God. It took me nearly three days to decompress and get over the fact that I couldn't use my cell phone (no signal out in these woods), I didn't have a normal phone line and couldn't access my e-mail or my website, and I didn't have any radio or television or morning newspaper to keep up on the news. I was stuck, alone, in the woods, with GOD.

By the end of the third day I was beginning to understand just how far I had come from the concept of tarrying. I began to realize that I was only going to receive new revelation understanding from God at this time in proportion to my passionate pursuit of more of Him. Passionate pursuit of Him? I was sitting sulking in the middle of my cabin because I couldn't get in touch with the "world"!

I tarried painfully for the next three days. To tarry means to prefer. In other words, tarrying means that you prefer to spend time with God. God did meet me and blessed me with a revelation vision about a new phase of my ministry. I was quite overwhelmed by what He said and what has been unfolding since that special time.

You need a personal plan of action to get back in touch with tarrying, yourself. Take three days to go away, fast, and pray. Leave your cell phone locked in your trunk, or you'll keep running outside to see if the clouds have moved and you can get a signal if you're out in the woods.

Take your God-given missions statement along with you. If you don't have a God-given missions statement, that's a problem right there. You may be trying to complete your own missions plans. Lay your God-given missions statement out before the Lord and ask Him to speak to you about it. "You gave me this, Lord, so I am asking you to talk to me about where I am in this plan. I'm ready to listen to what you want to tell me about where we go from here."

Write down the rhema words that God has given you over the years. Write out the prophetic words, the memorials, and each thing that has sustained you this far. Write out all of the big things and the little things that you have held onto for years. Recount the history of your ministry and write it all out; document where you and God have come from. Be sure to write out the supernatural happenings that you and He have met together in the middle of. Put this all into one book—call it YOUR BOOK of God's Words To You.

Write out the significant teachings that He has taught you. Ask Him, "How am I doing now—personally—today, Father? What do I need to learn now?" Tell Him, "Lord, you've been telling me to do these things, now tell me how am I doing? What are you telling me that I need to do now? On a scale of 1-10, Lord, how did I do? On a scale of 1-10, how do my plans for the future look?"

Make a list of the significant things about your relationship with Him, and list what you wish could happen in this relationship. Talk to the Lord about the future. Michelangelo said, "I saw the angel in the marble and I chiseled until I set it free." Ask God to show you yourself in the marble. Then begin to chisel with the binding and loosing prayers until you get free to be who He wants you to be.

Diligent Disciples

Matthew 25:14-30 contains the parable of the talents committed to three servants, a wonderful story of ministers who were aware of the necessity of investing their spiritual gifts in others.

"It's also like a man going off on an extended trip. He called his servants together and delegated responsibilities. To one he gave five thousand dollars, to another two thousand, to a third one thousand, depending on their abilities. Then he left. Right off, the first servant went to work and doubled his master's investment. The second did the same. But the man with the single thousand dug a hole and carefully buried his master's money.

"After a long absence, the master of those three servants came back and settled up with them. The one given five thousand dollars showed him how he had doubled his investment. His master commended him: 'Good work! You did your job well. From now on be my partner.' The servant with the two thousand showed how he also had doubled his master's investment. His master commended him: 'Good work! You did your job well. From now on be my partner.'

"The servant given one thousand said, 'Master, I know you have high standards and hate careless ways, that you demand the best and make no allowances for error. I was afraid I might disappoint you, so I found a good hiding place and secured your money. Here it is, safe and sound down to the last cent.'

"The master was furious. 'That's a terrible way to live! It's criminal to live cautiously like that! If you knew I was after the best, why did you do less than the least? The least you could

have done would have been to invest the sum with the bankers, where at least I would have gotten a little interest. Take the thousand and give it to the one who risked the most. And get rid of this "play-it-safe" who won't go out on a limb. Throw him into utter darkness'" (The Message).

In this parable, we can assume that the Master is Christ and the servants are Christians. In reading Matthew Henry, it was interesting to note that he believes that these particular Christian servants were probably spiritual leaders. Jesus Christ always intended for His spiritual leaders, His servants, to be about their Father's business as He had been when He walked on this earth. To provide for this work of the Father's business, He prepares us and gives us resources to do what He left for us to do after He went away. He Himself is back at the side of the Father interceding for us.

Everything Jesus Christ has ever done for us, taught us, and given to us relates directly to our purposes in His body while we are still here on earth. First Corinthians 12:7 tells us that all of these many gifts that are given to us by the Holy Spirit are given for this reason: *"The manifestation of the Spirit is given to each one for the profit of all"* (NKJV). Do not ever create a band of survivors who keep coming back to you or your meetings to get a "fix." Instead, lead in a manner that might cultivate a band of disciples who are passionate to do the Father' s will. Survivors are not free and they are not overcomers; they have only survived. Surviving is not winning!

The Master was going to travel far away to another country. When Jesus left earth to return to the Father in heaven, He made sure that everyone still here had an appropriate share of gifts to use until He returned. The parable actually says that the Master gave these three servants talents, which appear to have monetary value in the parable. But we need to consider them as being valuable gifts. The parable says that the Master gave to one Christian servant five talents, to another two, to another one; to every one according to his several ability.

In the parable, two servants were both diligent and faithful. Faithfulness to our destiny as spiritual leaders requires that we be diligent. Without diligence, our faith may never have any action—or works. James asks and answers the following question:

"Do you want evidence that faith without deeds is useless? Was not our ancestor Abraham considered righteous for what he did when he offered his son Isaac on the altar? You see that his faith and his actions were working together, and his faith was made complete by what he did. And the scripture was fulfilled that says, 'Abraham believed God, and it was credited to him as righteousness,' and he was called God's friend. You see that a person is justified by what he does and not by faith alone. In the same way, was not even Rahab the prostitute considered righteous for what she did when she gave lodging to the spies and sent them off in a different direction? As the body without the spirit is dead, so faith without deeds is dead" (James 2:20-26, *NIV*).

The first two servants were diligent in investing their gifts in others. Diligent means to be: steady, earnest, energetic, untiring, zealous, persistent. They had extremely successful servant attitudes. They went forth and used or invested their gifts in helping others. A successful servant is not one who passively stands by until the Master finally gives a direct command. This is one attitude that the Body of Christ needs to get over! A successful servant's attitude about everything in life is steady, earnest, energetic, untiring, zealous, and persistent—alert and ready to obey whatever the Master desires. I remember how blown away I was by Tommy Tenney's imagery in the opening pages of his book, *The God Chaser*. Coming from a family of former hunters, as a child I remember trailing around through fields and thickets after my father and my uncle and their hunting dogs. When Tommy Tenney spoke of a true God-chaser as being like a hunting dog, straining at the leash, clawing at the ground, panting, even drooling, totally focused on pursuing the object of the hunt, I knew exactly what he was saying. A true God-chaser should be avidly chasing after God with the same earnest, energetic, untiring, zealous persistence.

The first two (spiritual leader) servants, one with five talents and one with ten talents, used their leadership ability to make good investments in others. A good investor usually works hard to learn his trade, often shaping his life around the gain that he expects to receive. Our only value to invest is that which Christ has gifted us with. Everything our souls accomplish for God is accomplished through the investing of those gifts.

It appears that the Master expected a return from His investment in these spiritual leaders of at least a return of one for one. The servant who received five talents was expected to return an investment gain of at least five more. The servant with the two talents was only expected to gain at least two more.

This should be an encouragement to those who feel overwhelmed to raise their investments to the spiritual level of perhaps a Billy Graham. Each servant is only expected to gain a return in proportion to the gifts he has been given. He may gain more than a one-to-one return after investing his gift through diligence born out of love for the Master, but if he does not, he has still met his Master's loving expectations. The greater the gifts that each one of us has received, the more obligation we have to dutifully invest them often and well in the only market that appears to matter to God: human souls.

The third servant completely failed his Master's expectations. He buried his Master's spiritual resource gift. He did not see any way to invest his single talent to a good return, so he not only neglected what he had been given—he buried it. Spiritual leaders and ministers who have been given great gifts and opportunities for doing good, but do not stir up the gift or gifts within them, make a sad statement of their love for the Lord.

When the Master returned from His long journey to another "country," He said, *"Well done, good and faithful servant,"* to those who had put their gifts to good use. It is important that we realize that our labors to put our spiritual gifts to use may not bring us any praise or recognition from man. That should mean nothing to us if we have done our best to fulfill our destiny purposes for God. We should long to hear Jesus Christ saying to us, *"Well done, good and faithful servant. You took my gift to you and you used it wisely; you invested it in others that their souls might be saved."*

In this parable, we read what the Master said to His two wise servants.

"The man who had received the five talents brought the other five. 'Master,' he said, 'you entrusted me with five talents. See, I have gained five more.' His master replied, 'Well done, good and faithful servant! You have been faithful with a few things; I will put you in charge of many things. Come and share your master's happiness!' The man with the two talents also came. 'Master,' he said, 'you entrusted me with two talents; see, I have gained two more.' His master replied, 'Well done, good and faithful servant! You have been faithful with a few things; I will put you in charge of many things. Come and share your master's happiness!'" (Matthew 25:20-23, *NIV*).

Then the Master said of the servant who had failed, *"Take the talent from him and give it to the one who has the ten talents. For everyone who has will be given more, and he will have an abundance. Whoever does not have, even what he has will be taken from him"* (Matthew 25:28-29, *NIV*). This hopeless servant had received the least of all, but that was the only gift he was called to account for. He was not confronted for not having five talents' or two talents' gain, only for lacking a one-talent gain. He almost seemed to be expecting praise for the fact that he had carefully hidden his Master's talent and not taken any risks with it. The Word says, *"Like clouds and wind without rain is a man who boasts of gifts he does not give"* (Proverbs 25:14, *NIV*). We must stir our gifts up, increasing them by investing them in others.

Disunity Among Leaders

Along the way there are fences that need to be repaired. The places that are repaired are much stronger usually than the rest of the fence. This has been proven over and over in my own life in terms of broken or damaged relationships. At some point, we have to quit prophesying and quit praying and quit quoting the Bible and just go and reconcile with someone.

While attending a Jack Hayford conference on leadership a year ago, I wrote down some notes that touched my heart. I would recommend that any leader try to attend at least one of these annual conferences. Jack Hayford asked, "How does humility behave in spiritual leadership?" Then he began to give a long list of humility's attributes. Below I have recaptured the flavor of some of ten of them.

- Never slight someone who cannot help your ministry in favor of another person who might.
- Treat everyone with respect, whether you like them or not.
- Be willing to admit you need prayer.
- Always try to encourage others' efforts.
- Recognize that some will make mistakes just like you did when you first started out.
- Always forgive quickly and be hard to offend.
- Always be thankful and never really sure why God wants to use you.
- Let whatever God does for you always amaze you.

I heard a preacher once say, "God is nosy. He wants to be involved in every jot and tittle of your life." He has a reason to be, you know, because of the wealth of the deposit of gifts He has invested within you. He is only checking up on His portfolio of investments. How well are you doing with His investment? Will He be pleased with the performance of your stock?

In closing, please remember to pray both for and with those who have been called to help you lead. I spoke recently with a large, well-known ministry and I was asked to pray for the staff because of great turmoil and dissension. I asked the person if the staff members and workers were all praying together. She immediately replied, "Oh, yes, all of us have good prayer lives." Again I asked if they all prayed together—with each other. She replied, "No, but we all pray separately every day." I urged this woman to get the staff to begin praying together in agreement that God's will would be done in each of their lives and in the ministry. A good leader must pray together with the ones who help him or her to lead. There is a power in right agreement that transcends the cumulative individual prayers of people. The resulting power is greater than the sum of all the separate prayers.

And finally, leaders, you must learn to see those who are working with you as jewels God has entrusted to you to train, to encourage, to polish, and to help grow. If you have employees and workers who are not doing a good job, you need to take a long, hard look at yourself before you decide to replace them. It is your job to see that they succeed at what they are trying to do to help your ministry put out God's Word. God doesn't always send His leaders finished products. He usually sends leaders "works-in-progress." Why? So you can be His instrument in training them, encouraging them, polishing them, and helping them grow. If you would invest more of your experience and your abilities in your workers to train them, He might send you a finished product or two to help train, encourage, polish, and grow up more workers. Invest your experience and understanding in your own people. God will see that your investment grows and pays great dividends!

Whoever has the heart desire and feels called to work with you, find a place for them. Consider such a person a jewel that God has just blessed you with. The work of the ministry of the Kingdom of God must never value skill and ability above loyalty, faithfulness, and desire. As you begin to train these individuals, ultimately training some of them to train others, teach all of them to turn every failure into a teaching moment. To turn every mistake into a celebration of impending growth. Polish your people with love, encouragement, and instruction to enhance their beauty in God's Kingdom work.

ten

Agree with God and Just Do It!

Someone recently said to me, "Why do we ask others if they are Christians and then act as if a reply of yes is "the" ultimate good answer? Why aren't we asking them, 'Do you really know the heart of God? Do you sense His forgiveness, His caring, His healing? Do you know that His heart has no suspicion, no vindictiveness, and no bitterness in it? Are you receiving daily infusions of trust, love, consolation, and hope from Him every day?' Wouldn't that be more important than just saying 'praise God' because they said they were a Christian?" Now those are heavy questions, aren't they?

I know so many Christians who can say all the right things, quote all the right verses, and pray beautiful prayers, but are they receiving infusions of love, consolation, and hope from the heart of God every day? Probably not. If you scratch most Christians' façades, they will bleed some form of pain, fear, and anxiety.

I pray every day to have opportunities to teach believers that those feelings are not from God. Pain, fear, anxiety, loneliness, and hopelessness all come from a wounded, unsurrendered soul that does not understand God's unconditional love. This is the human mind, will, and emotions that do not comprehend the magnitude of being loved first by God. The Apostle John wrote such sweet words that should assure us of this, *"So you see, our love for him comes as a result of his loving us first"* (1 John 4:29, *TLB*).

Our souls base their understanding of love upon their experiences with human love. Our understanding of human "love" is often based upon receiving affirmation, praise, sympathy, and support from those who are important to us. Unfortunately, when we only believe that we are loved because of such demonstrations and expressions from others, there is always the chance of rejection, betrayal, withdrawal, and punishment as well. These negative expressions of the other side of the human form of "love" cause unmet needs, unhealed hurts, and unresolved issues which come from betrayal, rejection, lack of nurturing, little love, abuse, and generational bondage thinking.

Human love is a totally inferior and invalid standard to judge God's love by. Human love is only a shattered mirror's reflection of God's love. When you bind your mind to the mind of Christ, when you bind your soul to the heart of God, and you begin to receive a glimpse of the power of His love, something begins to happen. The desire to be important and successful begins to fade, and it is replaced with a desire to communicate to others, "Do you know that you are loved? Did you know that God created you to love you?"

Some people have fussed and complained about the many written binding and loosing prayers in all of my books, which I encourage people to pray on a regular basis. One of the Scriptures that comes up is out of the words of Jesus' teaching found in Matthew 6:6-10. *"And when you pray, do not use vain repetitions as the heathen do. For they think that they will be heard for their many words. Therefore do not be like them. For your Father knows the things you have need of before you ask Him. In this manner, therefore, pray: Our Father in heaven, Hallowed be Your name. Your kingdom come. Your will be done on earth as it is in heaven"* (NKJV).

The word vain means full of folly, manipulative, and attempting to squeeze. Jesus was really saying to us today, *"Don't pray foolish, manipulative prayers trying to squeeze God into a corner. And, for heaven's sake, don't pray such foolish prayers over and over. Instead pray that God's will would be done on earth as He has already established it in heaven."*

Right after Jesus tells us how not to pray, He begins telling us how we should pray with the opening lines of the Lord's Prayer. These opening lines are the basis of the purpose of the binding and loosing prayers from Matthew 16:19. *"Our Father in heaven, hallowed be Your name. Your kingdom come. Your will be done on earth as it is in heaven."* These prayers are to steady you and give you stability in God with the binding key while you use the loosing key to cut away your own ideas and beliefs, your own bondage thinking, and your own preconceived ideas about what God wants from you and what you want from Him.

Prayer is the great equalizer in the Body of Christ. Your prayers, my prayers, and Billy Graham's prayers all have equal access to the ear of God. But I think that "right prayers" come in with red lights flashing and angelic choruses in the background. The Word of God says this about wrong prayers, soulish prayers, *"When you ask, you do not receive, because you ask with wrong motives, that you may spend what you get on your pleasures"* (James 4:3, *NIV*). Right prayers are always directed to wanting God's will to be done, wanting Jesus' work to be finished, and wanting to fulfill the reason that you were born into this time and place in history.

The Apostle John tells us that Jesus said,

"The person who trusts me will not only do what I'm doing but even greater things, because I, on my way to the Father, am giving you the same work to do that I've been doing. You can count on it. From now on, whatever you request along the lines of who I am and what I am doing, I'll do it. That's how the Father will be seen for who he is in the Son. I mean it. Whatever you request in this way, I'll do" (John 14:12-14, *The Message*).

We can see the divine wisdom in God's use of right agreements to manifest His works and purposes here on earth. God has always sought agreement with Himself and individuals, as well as He has called His people to come into right agreement collectively with Him. There is a reason that He wants us to reach agreements on what He has said. *The Message* translates Matthew's record of the words of Jesus to say,

"Take this most seriously: A yes on earth is yes in heaven; a no on earth is no in heaven. What you say to one another is eternal. I mean this. When two of you get together on anything at all on earth and make a prayer of it, my Father in heaven goes into action. And when two or three of you are together because of me, you can be sure that I'll be there" (Matthew 18:18-20, *The Message*).

So many people have misinterpreted this verse to mean that all you have to do is agree with someone in the name of Jesus, and God has to do what you have asked—whether you had agreed that the pastor of your church would quit, that God would see to it that you would win the lottery, or that someone would offer you a recording contract. This is not the true meaning of these Scriptures! These words, as well as the words above in John 14, are telling us that when we come together and agree in prayer about who Jesus is, what Jesus wants us to do to complete the works He left for us, and what God wants us to know and have so that we can do it—IT WILL BE DONE!

The other side of agreement is that when you are gathered together to think, say, or do wrong, you are gathered together with demonic forces. Gathered together because of Jesus, He is there. Gathered together to agree, say, or do wrong, Satan or his representatives are there.

If We Just Had the Faith

If we just had the faith to recognize what God wants to do and send our way if we would just get ready to receive it, it would be more exciting and incredible than anything we could think up to pray for. When we get together to pray and *agree in* faith that God's will should be done, it is easy for others to see that God honors love, harmony, cooperation, and agreement between the brethren.

In Hebrews 11, the ancient saints in this Hall of Faith were not commended for their accomplishments, nor for their talent, nor for their virtuous lives. They were commended for their faith. Faith means trust and confidence in the goodness of God towards you. That means trust and confidence in the goodness of God's love, grace, mercy, and healing directed towards you.

The Christian relationship with God is the only "religion" where the concept of mercy and grace exists. All other religions are based upon performance or sacrifices to satisfy or appease false gods. The god of the Taliban and the Muslim religion requires people to send their sons to die for their "holy" wars. The God of Abraham, Isaac, and Jacob sent His own Son to die for holy peace and restoration of those who were lost to Him.

When we are not walking in faith, we constantly miss what God is doing. I heard someone tell a story about the survivor of a shipwreck who was washed up on an uninhabited island. He prayed fervently with faith for God to rescue him, and every day he scanned the horizon for help, but none came. Discouraged and exhausted, he eventually managed to build a little hut out of driftwood to protect himself from the elements, and to store his few possessions. But one day, after scavenging for food, he arrived home to find his little hut in flames with the smoke rolling up to the sky. The worst had happened; everything was lost. He was stunned with grief and anger.

"God, how could you do this to me!" he cried. He was so deeply hurt that he turned his back on God as he lay down in the open to cry himself to sleep. He was awakened early the next morning by the sound of a ship approaching the island. It had come to rescue him. "How did you know I was here?" asked the weary man of his rescuers. "We saw your smoke signal," they replied.

This is a great example of how angry we can become when our pitiful attempts to take care of ourselves fall apart, and God uses that breakdown of our own resources to produce a permanent answer. We must change our way of seeing things in the natural.

One woman wrote to our office, saying, "After binding my will to the will of God and loosing my own wrong thinking, I can see clearly now that the abundant life that Jesus promised me is really obtainable. I am persuaded that I can do all things through Christ. I'm finally ready to confront my greatest contender, me. I now know that when change is necessary, to change in accordance with God's will is doable. To not change is to be self-destructive."

Working Out The Salvation Of Our Souls

Philippians 2:12 tells us that we are to work out our own salvation—the salvation of our souls—with fear and trembling. This means that the renewal of our minds by the washing of the Word, the surrendering of our wills to the supreme will of the Father, and the submitting to the work of the Spirit for the healing of our emotions is very important. Paul told the Roman Christians, *Do not be conformed to this world, but be transformed by the renewing of your* mind, that you may prove what is that good and acceptable and perfect will of God" (Romans 12:2, NKJV).

The Word of God affects the renewing of our minds. Hebrews 4:12 tells us that Paul said:

"The word of God is living and active. Sharper than any double-edged sword, it penetrates even to dividing soul and spirit, joints and marrow; it judges the thoughts and attitudes of the heart" (NIV).

We can ask Him to teach us how to cooperate with His will. That does not mean we can then just sit in front of an altar and He will pour His will over us and into us. Desiring to be taught His will means that as we read His Word so that it can penetrate and divide our soul and spirit, He will make plain to us what He wants. God does not want us forever trying to find out what His will is; He wants to show us so that we can begin to walk in it. It is the clutter and residue of the world that is still in us that keeps us from clearly hearing His Word. But just ask Him, *"Teach me to do your will, for you are my God; may your good Spirit lead me on level ground"* (Psalm 143:9-10, NIV). Then begin to act on what He reveals to you. Pray like this:

"Lord, I bind my will to your will, because I desire to put my soul under obligation to your plans and purposes for my life. I now choose to bind my mind to the mind of Christ as I loose all old patterns of thinking and reasoning from it. I thank you for a fine mind, but I am choosing to want it renewed and cleansed of all its own soulish patterns of self-rationalization and self-justification.

"You are my God and I am your child. I need your Holy Spirit to lead me to the paths you want me to walk, the paths you pre-determined for me since before I was born. Thank you for helping me. I choose to rejoice always, pray without ceasing, and in everything give thanks to you; for this is your will. I am confident that you will help me and I will press towards your promises. I will do good so that others may see I love and honor you. Amen."

Surrendering and Submitting to His Will

We make the choice to cooperate with submitting our wills to His will, but the energy to do so comes from God. *The Message* puts it beautifully,

"... Be energetic in your life of salvation, reverent and sensitive before God. That energy is God's energy, an energy deep within you, God himself willing and working at what will give him the most pleasure" (Philippians 2:12-13).

This is a work from the inside out. Paul spoke to the Ephesian Christians, telling them:

"We do not have the excuse of ignorance, Everything—and I do mean everything—connected with that old way of life has to go. It's rotten through and through. Get rid of it! And then take on an entirely new way of life—a God-fashioned life, a life renewed from the inside and working itself into your conduct as God accurately reproduces his character in you" (Ephesians 4:21-24, *The Message*).

The Lord God told the prophet Jeremiah:

"Stand in the ways and see, and ask for the old paths, where the good way is, and walk in it; then you will find rest for your souls. But they said, 'We will not walk in it.' Also, I set watchmen over you, saying, 'Listen to the sound of the trumpet!' But they said, 'We will not listen.' Therefore hear, you nations, and know, O congregation, what is among them. Hear, O earth! Behold, I will certainly bring calamity on this people—the fruit of their thoughts, because they have not heeded My words, nor My law, but rejected it" (Jeremiah 6:16-19, *NKJV*).

To stand in the way is to stand at the crossroads of choosing which road or path you will follow—your way or His way. Jeremiah tells us that the Lord said if we stop, look, and then walk the paths which have been carefully recorded in the Word of the Lord for us to walk in, then we will find rest for our souls.

"Go through, go through the gates! Prepare the way for the people; build up, build up the highway! Take out the stones, Lift up a banner for the peoples!" (Isaiah 62:10, *NKJV*).

While this verse refers to the deliverance of the Jews coming out of the bondage they experienced—coming out though the gates of Babylon—it is also a prophetic type of the redemption the Christian receives. As Christians, we are called to come out of the bondage of our pasts and the bondage of our daily routines and rituals. Then we are to help those who are trying to come out behind us.

This verse tells us who come out that we have an obligation to tell others about the Good News and we are to raise up a banner—our own lives—for them to follow. We are also called to take care to lay down a trail, a highway even, for them. We are to work at removing the stones and obstacles such as strongholds so they can follow us to Him. It is a hard thing to clear the way of stones and boulders and strongholds so that others can understand that God is for them and not against them when you are burdened down with stones and boulders and strongholds yourself.

Not all wrong paths are strewn with boulders and obstacles. Sometimes they are quite level and close and cozy, just like a rut. From time to time, I think about a dream that I had prior to the early days of my ministry, about the late '70s. In this dream, I was a sheep in a seemingly unending line of sheep. We were all plodding, single file, nose to tail, along a narrow path between eight-foot, grass-topped walls of earth on either side. There was a fence near the top of each side of our "rut."

All of the sheep's heads were drooping low, and their hooves were raising little clouds of dust, which turned into mud and caked around their eyes, ears, and mouths. This seemed to impair all of the sheep's ability to see anything but the ground in front of them, to hear anything but their own muffled steps, and perhaps even to communicate any of their feelings of being in a deep rut with no apparent way out.

I felt a great sense of hopelessness and despair, yet I continued to plod along with them. Then I heard the words, *"Come up here!"* I looked up the dirt bank to my left and I saw that there was a small path to the top leading to a break in the fence. I hurried up the path, and reaching the top, I saw a beautiful grassy valley on the other side of the wall with a sparkling brook running through it. The Voice said, *"Come and eat, drink, bathe, and rest."*

I hurried down into the valley, looking around with delight and joy at the rich, lush grass and the gurgling brook. Then I looked back to see who else had come with me, and only a few had come out of the long line of plodding sheep. I said, "Why didn't more come out?"

The Voice replied, *"They did not hear Me call."* The called ones did not hear His call. How puzzling that is. The word "called" means those who have been invited to partake of all that the salvation of the Lord offers to them. The Word of God says that many are called, but few are chosen (Matthew 22:14). To be called means you are invited to the abundant life, but you must submit and surrender your ways, your life, your choices, to be chosen to actually partake of its fullness.

You Are Being Watched

When we use the principles of binding and loosing as we pray for God's will to be done, we are being prepared as the Bride of Christ to walk the ancient pathways once again. In Hebrews 12:12-13, *NASU*, we read, *"Therefore, strengthen the hands that are weak and the knees that are feeble and make straight paths for your feet so that the limb which is lame may not be put out of joint, but rather be healed."* This speaks first to us as individuals needing encouragement, so that we might better run our spiritual race.

It speaks secondly to us to know that this is the attitude and purpose with which we are to go forth so that we encourage others who are attentively watching how we walk. Christians often focus on what they are going through as if they were the only ones being affected. We must always remember that the world is ever watching us, trying to see if there is truth, if there is a reality, to our profession of faith in a God who can get us through anything in victory.

As our minds become renewed daily by the Word of God and by praying the Keys of the Kingdom prayers, we can better understand the words of Paul when he said he was *forgetting* what was behind and pressing—even straining—forward towards the prize of the high calling in Jesus Christ. That word "forgetting" as used in this verse actually means stop watering and fertilizing those weeds that are sucking all the life out of your soul! Loose them, pull them up by the roots and let good things be planted in the soil of your heart instead.

We have to let go of what our souls have so carefully collected and protected before we can have what Jesus Christ has prepared for us. It is really pretty simple: give up your bad stuff to get His good stuff. Don't let your fine mind, your intellect and your will, convince you that this is not so. Be simple about it. Mark Twain once that said, "It is strange the way the simple so often succeed where the intellectually informed fail."

Will these truths keep you from ever experiencing disappointments? No, of course not. We are all going to have disappointments in life, but sometimes an answer that has not materialized is only awaiting timing and an attitude change on your part.

While some disappointments can be very hard, some other smaller ones can turn out to be for the best. I'm not sure, but the bigger ones may function the same way if we can just hold tight to our faith that God works everything together for our good. Just the other night, I was disappointed to miss my preferred turn into the best parking lot for our seat numbers at a very large arena to watch my own beloved Sacramento Kings versus the Los Angeles Lakers (go Kings!). I knew the exact lot I wanted to park in so I could avoid walking forever, as I was having some serious discomfort in one of my knees that night. Somehow I drove right past that particular entrance and ended up in another parking lot that was about as far away from the arena entrance that we wanted as you could get—really far. I just knew my knee was going to be very unhappy all night!

I murmured, "Oh well, Lord, I bind myself to your will and I'm thrilled to be able to go to this game, so let's get going." As my friends and I began walking, a special motor cart pulled up to us and the lady said, "I'm really supposed to be watching for anyone who is disabled, but I don't have any passengers right now. I see you are limping, so would you like a ride right up to the front door? Your friends can ride, too, unless I see a disabled passenger I need to pick up."

This was a case of where a small disappointment over a planned parking spot turned into a blessing not only for me—but for those who were with me as well. We need to realize that blessings that come to us can also bless those around us, blessings that have come because of our right attitudes and expectations of a good God who loves us. I'm a firm believer that if I had really been out of sorts and grumpy about missing the right turn, that lady might not have seen me. We miss a lot of small blessings because our attitudes do not position us to receive them.

Another simple yet special little blessing came to me recently after an all-day seminar that I taught at a Bible College in Atlanta, Georgia. This was at the end of nearly two weeks of being on the road in Alabama, with thunder and lightning, torrential downpours of rain, and tornadoes lurking all around us every step we took. The evening after the seminar in Atlanta, as I was driving the rental car back to the house where Linda Cady and I were staying some 30 miles above Atlanta, I happened to reach over and turn on the car radio. I immediately heard an announcer say, "How about those Sacramento Kings! They're hot tonight in this first game of the second round of the NBA playoffs."

There I was, doing what God had laid out for me to do some 3,000 miles away from home during the NBA playoffs, which I hated to miss. And God blessed me with a car radio tuned to this precise station that was broadcasting the playoff game between the Sacramento Kings and the Dallas Mavericks—while I was driving on the Georgia 400 freeway! That is a sweet little blessing that only my God can set up in such a special way. The Kings won, too!

It is amazing how often those who have survived disappointments both small and large (those who did not let the big disappointments break them) say that they wound up where they knew they were ultimately intended to be. Even when our disappointments seem to end up for the worse, however, we can recover and grow from them.

God Equips His Servants

What we can accomplish on our own is hardly noteworthy. We try our best, but the results aren't exactly graceful flowing music. Remember, God doesn't call the already perfect and equipped; He equips the servants He calls. He'll always be there to love and guide you on to greater and greater things. All you have to do is agree with

Him and submit to His plans. Be sure that you are not trying to achieve something that you simply are not destined to fulfill. Your destiny will be so perfectly tailored for you, that you will excel when you finally get on track with it.

Another wonderful thing about working with God is that being God's messenger is one career that has absolutely no age limits. You're never too old for this race! And speed isn't an advantage here, either. Remember that the snails were on Noah's ark along with the cheetahs, and they both got back on dry land at the same time. Isn't that great?

"Lord, thank you for the age I am today. You must have had a wonderful plan in mind to make me as young or as old as I am, in this place, on this day. I bind my feet to the paths that you have ordained for me to walk today. I bind my hands to the work that you have ordained them to accomplish this day. Open my eyes to see where I am needed this day.

"I bind my thoughts to your thoughts, Jesus, that I might hear your guiding words. I loose all preconceived ideas that I might have regarding the limitations of what I can do. I loose all the effects and influences of wrong words that I have agreed with about myself. I am not who others say I am, I'm a child of God who can do all things through Christ. You will equip me and provide what I need to do whatever you designed for me to do this day. Thank you, Lord, for such special and precious plans for my life. Amen."

Every single member of the body of Christ should read this copy of a letter from someone's father who was dying. The man's son sent this letter to me. The older man had very recently accepted Christ as his Savior. As he lay dying, he said, "I am sad that I've fought all my life for things that I now realize are worthless. The one true and valuable thing that I now know I have—I have no time left to share it with anyone." How distracted we can get in life, pursuing the gold ring on the merry-go-round, chasing the carrot, and reaching for all we can get "because we only go around once." This is the philosophy of the world, and it is promoted as expedient regardless of who gets knocked out of the way.

Napoleon Bonaparte got it right as he was awaiting his death. It is recorded that he told his assistant the following words. "Charlemagne and Alexander and I conquered nations by force. Jesus Christ conquered millions by love, and many of those would be willing to die for Him right now." I think he had an understanding of where he had gone wrong. Perhaps he asked Jesus to help him face eternity.

Reminders In His Word

It is easy to get discouraged when things are going bad. But we shouldn't lose heart, because God is at work in our lives, even in the midst of the pain. Remember that next time your little hut is burning to the ground—it just may be a smoke signal to summon the grace of God. In 1 Chronicles 28:20 we read that David said to his son Solomon, *"Be strong and of good courage, and do it; do not fear nor be dismayed, for the LORD God—my God* (author's note: and your God)*—will be with you. He will not leave you nor forsake you, until you have finished all the work for the service of the house of the LORD"* (NKJV).

Read, memorize, and even sing the following promises from God's Word:

The LORD your God will bless you as he has promised (Deuteronomy 15:6, *NIV*).

The LORD my God will enlighten my darkness (Psalm 18:28, *NKJV*).

My God will hear me (Micah 7:7, *NKJV*).

My God will meet all your needs (Philippians 4:19, *NIV*).

Agree that God's will shall be done on earth as He has established it in heaven. Remember that God knows every thing that has happened, is happening, and is going to happen. God has said that if His people would humble themselves, turn from their own wicked ways (Hebrew: stop inflicting hurt and emotional and mental pain upon others, stop causing dissension), then He would hear from heaven and heal our land.

If we choose not to hear God's true Word, our self-wills may set our feet on paths that will force us to have to walk out difficult consequences. If you have areas in your life that you would like God to help you overcome, pray now and bind your will to His will, connect your every thought and wish and hope to Him. Loose and let go of those things that are holding you down. God is waiting for you to take the step and break away from those things that you know are wrong. He promises to help you overcome the obstacles you are facing.

Remember that Enoch didn't build an ark, he didn't lead millions through the wilderness, he didn't write a book of the Bible, he didn't call fire down out of heaven, he didn't slay a giant; he just walked with God. That pleased God tremendously. It doesn't matter whether we are rich or beautiful or strong or intellectual or not! Every one of us, tall or small, young or old, slender or stout, any level of intelligence, any type of personality, any age, can surrender our souls and walk with God and please Him.

Teaching Others About the Keys

So You Want To Teach?

A good teacher always has a passion to communicate something he or she passionately believes in! No amount of research, personality, intellect, or perfect teaching methodology can compensate for a life that has no passion in it. A good teacher is also a good learner and never assumes that he or she has learned all there is to know. With regard to this message, you can hear it taught, practice it, and then turn around after a few months and get new inspiration from it. How you formerly perceived the message has changed and you are ready to change with it. If you are always learning, you will always apply your store of knowledge in different ways as time goes on.

When people hear good information that they recognize can change their lives, they will often make a mental assent with that information. "Yes, I agree with this, it makes sense. I should do it." Here is where the biggest gap in learning occurs—between assenting to the information's worth and actually doing what it says to do! If you never apply what you have learned, then it becomes an exercise in futility to bother to learn it. Only when you have learned how to apply the knowledge you have learned, can you truly teach it to others. You have no credibility to teach on something you know only in theory.

Good teaching requires a fairly thorough understanding of and personal experience with the concepts and principles of a message or a subject. Good teaching of the binding and loosing principles of prayer requires personal, hands-on usage of the concepts together with understanding of the cause-and-effect relationship of such praying.

When we were taking our Teaching Certification Training on the road to certify people in teaching this message, I repeatedly ran into a situation that dumbfounded me. One of the requirements of our Teaching Certification Training is that students have to read all three books in the Keys of the Kingdom Trilogy: *Shattering Your Strongholds* (I), *Breaking the Power* (II), and *Producing the Promise* (III) at least once, preferably twice. It is also mandatory that they are studiously applying the principles of binding and loosing prayers in their own prayer lives. At least one of the people who signed up for each Teaching Certification complained, even balked, at reading all of the books. Some of them then reported they had stayed up all night the last two nights before the school to do so.

The students who had not studied the principles, applied them in their lives and walked out the circumstances that came, were often the very ones who went into meltdown during the school. Even the ones who had dutifully read the books and prayed the prayers for a few months were admitting that what they thought they knew about the Keys of the Kingdom principles was a long way from what they learned at the school. You need to know your subject with firsthand experience and put the principles into practice—then you will be a life-changer!

Five keys to successful teaching—Pray, Pray, Pray—Prepare, Prepare, Prepare—Practice, Practice, Practice—Pray Some More—Now Teach. Let's break them down.

Pray, Pray, Pray

Whether teaching from the original Keys of the Kingdom Trilogy, or the other binding and loosing prayer books, I always recommend much prayer on your part. Pray, pray, pray to have a life-changer's heart. Practice the principles daily in your own life. This is an absolute prerequisite to effectively teaching this information.

Prayer accomplishes good things on several levels. One level is to bring your mind, will, and emotions into alignment with the Father. Another level is to pray for empowerment and the Holy Spirit's help, pray for the people you will teach, and pray to destroy the influences of territorial spirits.

1. Pray for yourself.
2. Pray for divine empowerment and the Holy Spirit's help.
3. Pray for the people you will teach.
4. Pray to destroy the influences of territorial spirits.

POINT 1

"Lord, I desire to teach your Word to others. I bind my will to your will, Father, so that I will be steady and stabilized as I teach for life change in my hearers. Remind me often, Lord, that I am only teaching so others might receive life-changing information. I am not to be a Bible wired for sound! I loose all preconceived ideas, wrong expectations, and misconceptions that I have believed about how to teach.

"I bind my mind to your mind, Jesus, that I will hear your thoughts and purposes while I am teaching. I loose all wrong attitudes and mindsets that my soul has developed. I seek your direction and your guidance, as I only want to say what you want said. Help me to develop understanding from your Holy Scriptures, help me make my message relevant and understandable, and help me to remember that I am only a vessel. It is your truth that must transcend my words. Amen."

POINT 2

An excellent scriptural way to pray for divine empowerment and the Holy Spirit's help is to pray from the following verses. The Apostle Paul's words to the Corinthian church regarding his teaching ability and style were these:

"And I passed into a state of weakness and was in fear (dread) and great trembling [after I had come] among you. And my language and my message were not set forth in persuasive

251

(enticing and plausible) words of wisdom, but they were in demonstration of the (Holy) Spirit and power [that is, a proof by the Spirit and power of God, operating on me and stirring the minds of my hearers the most holy emotions and thus persuading them], so that your faith might not rest in the wisdom of men (human philosophy), but in the power of God" (1 Corinthians 2:3-5, *Amplified Bible*).

POINT 3

"Lord, I bind myself to you, placing myself under obligation to your will and purposes for the people I will be teaching. I desire to help others learn how to surrender their wounded, fearful souls to you. I bind their wills to your will, Father, that their souls will begin to line up with you before they even come to this meeting. I bind their minds to your mind, Jesus, that their thoughts will be in alignment with the will of the Father. I loose all preconceived ideas they might have about you, Jesus, about this message, and even about me. Give me great wisdom to address any issues that will help take down any stronghold thinking in their souls. Amen."

POINT 4

"Father God, I believe this meeting will change lives. I believe the people will receive new understanding to surrender their souls to you. I bind them to your will, and I ask you to steady and stabilize them, keeping their feet on the paths you have ordained for them to walk at this time. I loose all hindrances and devices of the enemy from myself and from each one of them. I loose the effects and influences of all wrong agreements that have been made in this area, that have been made about these people, and that have been made regarding you, Jesus. I loose, smash, crush, and destroy all residue from any wrong agreements ever made about these people, over these people, and by these people. I loose and rip up the wrong agreements that territorial spirits have been feeding from here. I loose, smash, and destroy their so-called "right" to be in this area because of wrong agreements that have been spoken. Lord, tonight I am asking for open lines to heaven as we gather in your name. Thank you, Lord."

Prepare, Prepare, Prepare

Content, Style, and Structure

After prayer, there are three things to consider when preparing a teaching: content, style, and structure. Content is the meat of your subject. Your message content should ensure that your audience understands the three-part makeup of man (body, soul, spirit) and the three-part makeup of the human soul (mind, will, emotions). Also be sure that you teach that the human soul is not surrendered and ready to cooperate with God just because a person has accepted Christ. Only the spirit gets linked to its Creator at the time of the new birth. Teach some of the original meanings of the words *binding* and *loosing* (basic meanings can be found in the glossary on page 303 of this book).

Convince your hearers of biblical reasoning for your teaching about these life-changing principles. Use Scripture to back up your statements, but use other reference book quotes sparingly unless you have a group of people who are exceptionally interested in backup information. Refer to the different prayers in the different books of the Keys of the Kingdom Trilogy as means of practicing the principles. Assure them that the binding and loosing prayers that they pray, their frequency of prayer, and their studying of these principles are how they are making *application* of the Keys of the Kingdom message.

Use practical true stories of how these principles can apply to circumstances your audience can relate to. Tell this true story of how one lady wrote the LSM offices about praying and binding her own mind to the mind of Christ while she loosed her wrong attitudes and patterns of thinking. When she became nicer, her husband began to recognize his own bad attitudes and asked her to teach him how to pray the same way.

Research your message's focus thoroughly, using the Scriptures, commentaries, internet resources, and life stories. If you use someone else's story, always disguise the person and the situation unless you have explicit permission from that person so share his or her story. Sometimes I create a composite story from certain things I've seen in several peoples' lives.

Make a rough outline of the points you want to make. Decide on the actual sequence you will use with the points. Be sure to always include reasons (more than once) for why the subject of your message will benefit the listeners. Try to tell them what this new principle will "look like" in their lives if they will try it. Explain the life-change principles involved in the particular teaching session you are doing; i.e., how to stop recycling old wrong patterns of thinking or how to stop having wrong attitudes towards others.

Style is how you present the content of your message. A style can be very formal; e.g., how you would teach a conservative, early morning service in a very fundamental church. You might use an informal style if you share at a campground meeting. Most presentations fall somewhere between these two extremes, being determined by your message's subject, your audience, the occasion, and the setting. Your style would also vary greatly if you were teaching leadership in a church, if you were teaching teenagers in a youth home setting, or if you were teaching a home Bible study of friends and neighbors. When you are speaking to a specific group, be sure to consider how to tailor your message for your audience: such as just men, women, teens, a jail study, or businessmen. Don't use pie-baking examples with businessmen, don't use men's issues with teenage girls, don't use business jargon in a jail study, etc.

Another factor in determining style is what kind of a person you are. Are you extremely outgoing, are you more serious, are you funny, or are you intense? Remember that even though you have a distinct type of style, you can blend in small doses of other styles for variety. For example, if you are a very intense person, you can work at little spots of humor that feel comfortable to you. The key words here are "comfortable to you."

If you are not comfortable with what you do, you will make your audience uncomfortable. Be yourself in whatever style you represent, be real, and don't be afraid to be transparent. Thoughtful use of your own personal openness helps build trust with your audience and helps them relate to you. Don't ever be afraid to be real about what has made you the person you are, but never bury your audience with the "gory details" of how you survived to get there.

I am a dynamic mixture of Scottish, Irish, German, and Cherokee Indian heritages—and I think everyone in my family all received more than their fair share of those nationalities' warrior genes. I describe my relatives by saying that everyone in my family is a Chief—a lance-packing, war-bonneted, turf-oriented, territorial Chief—we have no Indians, just Chiefs. It is amazing how many men and women will come up to me after the meeting and say, "I knew exactly what you were talking about. Everything you said described my family's dynamics. I didn't know anybody else grew up like that." They were right with me because they related to me.

Structure is the third point in preparing your message. Structure should always consist of an introduction, a body, and a conclusion. The introduction should include an attention getter—a dramatic story that no one knows, a humorous story, an unusual quote, or an unknown statistic. Just be sure that the one you choose relates to your subject. Your introduction should also tell the people what you intend to teach them, and what you expect them to understand when you are finished.

The body of your message should progress through a basic outline of your subject, with each point building upon the point before it. Every point should be related to the focus of your message. To progress smoothly from point to point, you must learn how to make effective transitions. Try to be creative with your transitions so that you don't use the same one over and over, just because it feels smooth to you. This can become very boring, even irritating to your listeners. The purpose of a transition is to lead your listener from one idea to another without giving them whiplash. You can use certain words or short phrases such as: "And that point leads us to … " "Now, in addition to what I've just said, we have to expect that … " and "Which finally brings us to … "

You can also ask your audience a question such as, "How many of you … ?" Or you can say, "Do you remember what I said about …" to set up a reinforcement of an earlier statement that will now take on a new twist with your next point. I have a beloved overhead transparency I call my Donkey Picture that I often use to make a final statement on one point. Then I tease the audience about relating to the donkey while I segue into a new point.

Many people come up to me and say, "I wish I could do what you do, but I never have anything funny happen to me." I tell them that the funny stories I tell were not funny when they happened. You have to learn to see the humor in your experiences. You have to learn to see things from a perspective that will teach and preach a concept to others. Doing that helps you keep your soul from building any memorials to your being embarrassed or being hurt.

Everyone has examples or real-life stories that can illustrate a point far more effectively than just concepts and research. One day I was teaching a seminar class and my slip slid down all the way to the floor. The audience gasped, covered their mouths to keep from laughing, and waited to see what I would do. I kicked the slip to one side, cocked one eyebrow, and said, "And furthermore, you stay loosed!" Sometimes things happen and you just have to go with whatever you can think of.

One of my staff members called out from the back, "Can't wait to hear how you're going to preach that!" A key to using stories, or surviving accidents, is to be sure to use them to make a point that illustrates, explains, or reinforces what you are teaching.

Several of the funny life stories that I tell on myself can be told from a funny point of *view* or a compassionate point of view, depending on whether I tell the whole story or certain parts of the story that fit different points. One of the hardest things I have had to do while learning the best ways to teach was to realize that I do not have to tell the "whole story" every time in order to include a specific point I want to make. I can make a special point with just part of the story that fits the emphasis I am making. For example: the story I tell about the "bug spray/hair spray" fiasco the morning of my trip to give my parents an anniversary party some 200 miles away. Here are the points I usually follow:

1. Humor about how I ruined a "good hair day" with bug spray in a hair spray bottle.

2. Humor about my car's name (Shadow) and why I named all my cars, praying for Shadow who had abnormally high

mileage, and car problems in hot weather on an Interstate Hwy in July.

3. Arriving at the anniversary party late and finding that I had major surprise in my duffel bag.

4. Surviving the semi-dressy party while looking like a demented dandelion in a greasy T-shirt and white Bermuda shorts.

5. Reminding God frequently that I really wanted to talk to Him when the party was over, because I had bound my will to His will and my mind to Christ's mind early that same day.

6. Telling of God's response to me later than night about how He had trusted me enough to make me a living sermon in front of a room of people who were unreachable by normal means of the Gospel (His words!).

7. Then telling them the story of "Blessing," the beautiful car He gave me to replace Shadow.

Sometimes I tell the whole story as a finale to a teaching to underscore the truth that we don't always know what God is doing in our difficult circumstances. Other times when I am teaching about life change, I can incorporate just point 6. Other times when I am teaching about being flexible, I can incorporate points 1-3. Perhaps I want to teach about how we sometimes need to surrender something dear to us to the Lord to create room to receive something much better and I use point 7.

When you use jokes or funny stories, *always personalize them in some way to relate to your subject matter*. Don't tell a golf joke, and then launch into a teaching on soul ties. That is, unless your golf joke is about golfers who have soul ties. A dramatic quotation from a well-known source can add punch to a teaching—but only if it reinforces the points you want to make. Don't tell stories and jokes that have nothing to do with your teaching, regardless of how funny they are.

I often teach up to seven or eight sessions during a weekend seminar at a church. To keep my notes organized for seven or eight specific yet progressive subjects, I keep the notes on 3x5 cards. I have been working with the same basic message, the Keys of the Kingdom Prayer Principles and surrendering to God's will, for some 15 years.

I know the material inside and out, but I think of too many different paths to follow at every juncture my message comes to.

Once while teaching without notes at a church in Oklahoma, I noticed the pastor (in the front row) kept shutting one eye and pointing an imaginary gun at the podium. Then he would pretend to shoot the gun. Finally, I said, "Pastor, what are you doing?"

He replied, "I'm just shooting those rabbits you keep chasing down those rabbit trails." I've come to realize that my use of 3x5 cards is very helpful for me to stay focused and on track. I don't chase near as many rabbits now as I used to.

Sometimes I will pick out a certain person in a section and ask them to keep an eye on the people in their section because I think they're a little rowdy and we don't want any trouble breaking out. While this would not be appropriate in every setting, if it seems like you can have a little fun with the people, it will bring some of the outer edges of your audience into a connection with you. Most audiences will cheerfully play the role you have assigned to them.

During the funniest moments of my story about my demented dandelion hair and the anniversary party, some people will be laughing incredibly hard and loud. I usually point out one of them and say, "You are having entirely too much fun over my distressing moments in the story!" You, of course, will need to pick your own points and your own moments, but never hesitate to make real connections with the people in your audience.

Applications

Applications that help people relate personally to what you are teaching are very necessary. Good applications help the people grasp concepts that may be too abstract for their daily experiences. Following are some applications that our teaching team has used as well as some exciting new ideas we have learned from some of our Teacher Certification students.

While teaching about soul ties, Patricia slowly unwound a coil of soft rope and looped one end of it around her neck as she told us of some difficult times she had experienced with other people. These people were still seeming to influence her thoughts and actions, she said (see chapters on Soul Ties in *Breaking the Power* and *Producing the Promise*). Everyone's eyes were fastened on that rope, especially when she began unwinding several more feet of the rope to loop it around first one and then another of two students' necks in the front row, asking them to agree with her that something was wrong with some other people at the school!

As she presented the concepts of soul ties and how they "bind" us to other people, she began to move beyond the two "roped" students, gently tugging at them until they felt forced to get up from their seats and follow her. This was an extremely dramatic representation of the power of a soul tie to pull someone into the actions and behaviors of another person.

Another student spoke of becoming homeless after having a seizure, which caused her temporary brain damage. She said she was living on the streets when some well-meaning Christians gave her several cans of food—soup, tuna, fruit, and other good things to eat. She said she remained hungry, however, even though she embraced the canned food she had been given. *No one thought to give her a can opener!* This spoke so clearly to me. If we do not give people the Keys of the Kingdom to open up the "canned" spiritual food they may be receiving, they can try to embrace the teachings with all of their being and still be starving for spiritual nourishment.

Another application of this is that canned food can be likened to the hidden understanding within some verses of the Bible. These verses can be read faithfully, just like reading the label on a can of tuna. But the "meat" within a verse (the principles of life change) must be opened up and eaten (received and acted upon by faith) before it can bring life change. If the soul is fearful of acting upon a new concept by faith, it can run all sorts of sub-programs in the mind and the emotions to keep the person from opening up a new concept to act upon it.

Another student held a tall candle, lit it, and then explained that the candle wax was like our body. The soul was like the wick running through the wax. The flame on top of the candle was the light of our born-again spirits that would shine for others to see. She said, "This works just fine when the body, soul, and spirit are lined up in the right manner. But when you turn that order upside down and place the light in your spirit beneath the needs of the soul and the body," she then turned the candle upside down, "the light goes out." Upside down, the flame was quickly snuffed out with melting wax.

Another student told us about having been adopted as a child from a Middle Eastern country. All she knew was that her parents had ridden into a war-torn town on horseback and tossed her into the arms of a startled woman standing on the street. She had always felt that she had come to terms with being adopted, but she wanted to tell us a story of another adoption. Then she began to tell us about how a stray cat showed up at her apartment—a very pregnant mother cat. She felt so bad for this seemingly homeless mother-to-be that she hid the cat in her no-pets-allowed apartment. She said that she wanted us to know that the binding and loosing prayers worked in some very unusual situations.

She kept telling herself that as soon as the kittens were born, she would find them a good home and a home for the mama cat, too. The blessed event occurred, and she now had three orange kittens and one black kitten hidden in her closet as well as the mother cat. The apartment manager found out about the kitty maternity ward within a short time, and told her to get rid of the cats. After much tearful pleading and an additional deposit, she managed to get a 30-day extension of grace for the cats, but when that was up the cats had to go, or she had to go.

Finally the kittens were old enough to be adopted out to good homes. But everyone she asked said, "No, thank you. I don't want a cat." The kitty eviction notice was only about ten days away, and she was beginning to get worried. She began binding the kittens to God's will and purposes for their lives. Within three days, she had good homes lined up for the three orange kittens. However, no one seemed to want the black kitten, and she felt that it was because Halloween was only days away. So she redoubled her prayers of faith and bound the black kitten to a good home while she loosed all superstitious thoughts and wrong agreements off it. The last night before the deadline was up, someone came and offered the mama cat and black kitten a home.

This was a very sweet story about unusual binding and loosing prayers and I was touched. But then she said, "God spoke to me as I collapsed in tears of joy that the kittens and the mama cat all went to good homes. He said, '*You have been so very concerned about these little kittens not having homes. Do you not think that I was concerned for you when you were tiny and suddenly no longer had a home? Your parents rode into that village and threw you into the arms of that woman, praying to me for safety and a good home for you, and then galloped away because they were being pursued by military enemies. If I would answer your prayers for homes for those kittens, can't you see how much more I was concerned about your parents' prayers for a safe home for you? Can't you see how much I have loved you and cared for you all this time?*'"

As she softly closed with her expressions of love and gratitude for such a great God and how He helped her to understand her parents' love for her even though she had never seen them since they gave her up, we all began to cry. Our God is indeed a great and mighty God, and He loves us all. Even the kittens.

Always prepare, prepare, and be prepared. But don't ever rely solely upon your preparation. Paul said:

"*And I (passed into a state of) weakness and was in fear (dread) and great trembling [after I had come] among you. And my language and my message were not set forth in persuasive (enticing and plausible) words of wisdom, but they were in demonstration of the Holy Spirit and power [that is, a proof by the Spirit and power of God, operating on me and stirring the minds of my hearers the most holy emotions and thus persuading them]*" (1 Corinthians 2:3-4, *Amplified Bible*).

Conclusions and Commitments

If you are new to teaching, before you teach any group, try to get some idea of how much material you will need to stay within your time limit. All too often, new teachers have no sense of timing as they are progressing through the points they want to make and suddenly find themselves out of time without having given their conclusion and challenge to the audience.

Your conclusion should always include a summary of your main points, a tying up of any loose ends, and a dynamite closing story or creative proposal ("What if … ?" or, "Have you ever wondered how you might … ?"). Following your conclusion, you need to urge your audience to stop and think about applying what you have taught. Being aware of your audience helps you recognize when lights are going on in their heads, which is always a good time to allow them to reflect on the point they have just heard. Perhaps walk out from behind a pulpit, stand up from a chair, or sit down to signify that you are changing your emphasis from teaching to something new perhaps to challenge them.

Convince them that just agreeing with the principles they've just heard *is not* the same as taking action on them or being obedient to them. Be direct and don't beat around the bush—be convinced that you are giving out life-changing truths that they need and will want to use as soon as you explain how to them.

Be sensitive to where your audience is at the moment, and don't rush. You can tell when they are ready to move on; they will begin to raise their heads, look around, cough, and readjust their sitting posture. Never, never, never close off a teaching without making some attempt at getting the people to admit they would like to change if they could. Then reinforce the application of the principle you are teaching them so they can. Get them to agree to pray after you. Then pray the binding and loosing prayers emphasizing the subject you have just taught.

Practice, Practice, Practice

No matter how worried you might be about leaving out important points and making good transitions, never read your teaching. Practice, practice, practice your message out loud until you become comfortable with the flow of your ideas. After you have taught your message, don't beat yourself up if you have left out an important point or two. You will teach the same session differently every time. Just focus on getting your main message across as comfortably as you can. If the Holy Spirit is trying to get through your careful preparation, let Him. He often edits me to make room for His inspiration to drop into my message. I love that kind of inspiration! The teacher speaks it and hears it for the first time right along with the audience.

Always watch the facial expressions of your listeners, which indicate they do or do not understand what you are saying. When you teach, your eyes involve your listeners in your presentation. No matter how large your audience may be, each listener wants to feel that you are talking to him or her. I often look at the section farthest from me when speaking to large groups; then I point at them and say something like, "Good for you! You got that, didn't you? Could some of you come up and sit over here in this section? I think this group needs your help!" I do that while pointing vaguely in the direction of other sections.

Because I have already established a humor bond with the people, and I say these things in a smiling, laughing way, it always invokes laughter from the audience. The added benefit is that the group in the back has just been drawn into my teaching and feels the connection I have made with them. By speaking to and looking at your audience as individuals, you can convince them that you are sincere and interested in them, that you care whether or not they accept your message. When you develop the ability to gauge the audience's reactions and adjust your presentation accordingly, you will teach more effectively.

If you want to use visual aids, costumes, or props, do so sparingly. I have seen good teachings get lost in the clutter of extra "stuff." Also, practice with the props and visuals before you speak. Don't ever wait until you are in front of an audience to see whether or not the prop will work for you. Overhead transparencies and simple PowerPoint slides are a good way to illustrate points, but use them sparingly. Make sure that the information on each overhead or slide is to the point and can easily be read by all in the back of the room. When using such aids, be sure to keep eye contact with audience members as much as possible. Do not let your visual aids take precedence over your connection with the people.

The one visual that you can use for an extended period of time while teaching this message is the X-Ray of the Unsurrendered Soul Chart. When you are teaching from this chart, its layout allows you to cover the basics of the entire Keys of the Kingdom message. Begin with discussing the Original Causes Which Cannot Be Changed, starting from the bottom of the chart and teaching up to the top, concluding with strongholds.

When you are using the X-Ray of the Unsurrendered Soul Chart to demonstrate how to pray for yourself or someone else, pray it from the top down. Begin with the binding prayers, and then continue with loosing the stronghold patterns of thinking. Then loose wrong patterns of thinking about using wrong behaviors to subdue, pacify, and dull the pain and anxiety that are connected to the symptoms coming up out of the original sources. Loose the layers or facades of the self-interest, the self-reliance, and the self-focus. The whole point of loosing these things is so that God has an access given to Him voluntarily that He might heal the unhealed hurts, meet the unmet needs, and resolve the unresolved issues. Always remember that you cannot loose unmet needs, unhealed hurts, and unresolved issues. They actually exist; they are facts. You cannot loose a fact.

If someone becomes difficult, remember that the true teacher is like a bridge for men and women to get to the ways of God. All good teachers see difficult moments as teaching moments. When someone challenges you in your teaching, use that for a teaching moment. Go back over your points to restate your information. This is why you absolutely need to know your subject by having walked it out in your own life. You will be able to explain your experience with the point someone is questioning.

Always try to answer difficult questions carefully, but briefly. Don't ever let your soul get flustered, because that may well be the enemy's intention behind pushing the person to challenge you. If you have prayed the binding and loosing prayer for teaching, then you will have His spiritual strength helping you keep your soul calmed down. Sometimes, you simply need to stop and pray out loud, binding everyone's will to the will of God and binding everyone's mind to the mind of Christ. Then proceed.

Of course, you must always be prepared for the unexpected even when you do everything right. Teachers who have taught for any length of time know that there is going to be that time where there's a cable missing or the slide projector is jammed or the overhead projector has blown a lamp. A true teacher just carries on, using humor about the technical snafu to build rapport with the audience. I promise you that the people will sympathize with you, as technical problems are everyone else's worst nightmare, too.

Pray Some More

Be sure you pray and pray, right up until the time you step behind your podium. Sometimes you need to keep praying in your spirit even once you are there. Especially pray as you use participants out of the audience to help you in skits (which most people seem to love), because you need to be prepared for surprises. I do a skit to show how unforgiveness ties you emotionally to the other person, using a rope to tie people's legs together as in a three-legged race. Then I offer the unforgiving one some ridiculously extravagant prizes if he or she will run to some place or establishment I've already scoped out. I tell this person to bring back a bottle of Coke, a menu, or a flower from some bush within a certain number of minutes.

I chose two men recently, having already briefed and set up one man who was to be the unforgiving one. He was supposed to be continually grumbling about how he could not forgive the other guy for what he had done. Having done this skit with other audiences with a good response in the people's understanding, I was looking forward to doing it again this time.

When Linda Cady, my traveling assistant on this trip, tied one of each of their legs together, I looked expectantly at "Pete" to start grumbling. He just smiled at me. I cued him with a hint to grumble and he just smiled at me. I suggested that perhaps he was struggling with some bad feelings. He shook his head, smiled, and said, "No, I'm okay." I said, "Are you sure?" He said, "Yes, I'm sure." I tried everything to get him to grumble so that Linda could wrap another length of rope around him and the other man each time he restated his unforgiveness. The audience was howling because they knew that I could not get Pete to do what I wanted him to. So, I gave up and said, "Okay, Ross, you have just suddenly developed some really strong unforgiveness for Pete."

Ross quickly picked up on the change right away and began to grumble and mumble about what Pete had done to him. Linda quickly wound the rope around and around the two of them. When they were completely tied up, I said, "Now, Ross, I'm going to offer all these prizes to you if you can run down the street to that convenience store and bring a cold Coke back to the pastor. Even though you are all bound up with unforgiveness, a nice deed like that might help you out."

Ross was very quick as he said, "Sure, but first I want to forgive Pete so I don't have to be in all this bondage. I'll be able to get down there and back quickly if I don't have to drag him with me. I forgive you, Pete!" Linda quickly unwound the rope and Ross jumped off the stage and ran for the door of the church. The audience howled with laughter even more, but they had definitely understood the intent of what we were doing.

Later Pete came up to me and earnestly said, "I was just trying to be real. I never get upset with other people, and so I thought I should act like that." I hugged him and thanked him for being real. I didn't even try to explain the concept of acting or role-playing to him. One other time I chose someone to play the unforgiving person who was such a ham, we couldn't get her to stop complaining and grumbling. Every time I would try to tell her that if she would just forgive, she could run to a Wendy's nearby and get the Coke for the pastor, she would take off on another tirade. Linda had wound so much of the rope around the two women by now, I didn't know if we'd ever get them free.

Finally I said, "If you would just forgive this woman, you could go free and win the prizes." She stopped and just stared at me. I repeated that and sort of hinted that she should do it, and she stared at me. Finally I said, "Work with me, Carolyn, work with me!"

Carolyn said, "Oh, I thought you wanted me to portray denial." Again, the audience got the gist of the skit and understood about the bondage of unforgiveness, but I thought I would never get them to settle down and stop laughing. Just be prepared, be flexible, and be ready for God to also show up and show out when you least expect it. The people might forget your name when you're gone, but they will never forget the hilarious outcome of your teaching skit.

Now Teach

Never try to determine how well your teaching is going by looking at just the first two rows. Check out the ones in the very back row. Do you have their attention? If the building is not filled to capacity, watch the ones who choose to sit on the less-occupied rows. Are they staying with you? Actually watch all of the people, catching eyes, speaking right to individuals. Always remember to make and keep eye contact with your audience.

Explain what the life-change principles you are teaching would look like in your students' lives if they implemented them. Offer these questions and explanations: "Wouldn't you like to be able to walk past a group of people you used to be intimidated by, feeling God's love and compassion towards them? Wouldn't you like to be able to have full knowledge that you are not who they say you are—you are who God says you are? He says that you are the apple of His eye, you are His Son's bride, and you are a new creature. You can when you finally believe that binding your will to the will of God puts the two of you—that's you and almighty God—together wherever you are walking. When you loose all the layers over your unmet needs and unhealed hurts, God will be healing your wounds so that others' negative comments won't even touch you. You'll be so aware of Him, you won't feel their darts."

Explain how the life change could impact their families. Set up different family scenarios, such as rebellious teenagers fighting with their parents. Teach them how to pray for their own souls, for their reactions to the teens, and then for God's will to be done in their teenagers' lives. Teach them that the key issue is to get everyone's wills bound to the will of God, so that you are all looking to one Master Will, not each individual will. Teach them while that while they may have never learned the best parenting skills, God is the best parent ever and He is more than willing to share His experience with them.

Persuade them of good reasons to apply the main truth of your teaching, i.e. to be more positive, to be more Christ-like, to be more helpful, to be more aligned with God's will, to have harmony in their homes, to reduce tension in their marriages, etc. Good teaching always attempts to convince the student that there is something in the principles being taught that can change his or her life in a beneficial way.

Don't ever be afraid to say this after blurting out something you did not mean to say, "That is not what I wanted to say. That was what my soul wanted to say. Soul, I bind you to the will of God. You are not in control here." If only one person shows up at your teaching, have a friendly sharing time with them. Tell them you came to teach, they came to learn, and what could be more special than God preparing this moment for one-on-one sharing.

Starting Your Own Study Group

If you want to start a home Bible study with the principles of the Keys of the Kingdom, begin to speak to several of your friends and others who have been reading the book. Ask your local Christian bookstore if you could put up a notice of such a meeting. If your church allows such things, ask if you can put a notice of the study in your church bulletin.

Bind the wills and minds of the people (the ones God would want to come, not necessarily the ones you want to come) to His will and the mind of Christ. Loose the enemy's assignments from the people who would benefit from this study group. Loose the stronghold thinking in their minds that would prevent them from coming and receiving new ways to pray their souls into submission so that they might be free permanently.

Make it a requirement that everyone have at least a copy of *Shattering Your Strongholds* or *Breaking the Power*, whichever book you are studying. Please do not reproduce the workbooks, as they are copyrighted. But you can always read the questions in your workbook to the group, let them copy them down, and then create their own handwritten manual/journal if they are unable to get personal copies of the workbooks.

Be careful that you do not allow the group to turn into just a sharing and testimony time. Sharing and testimonies are important, but when they are allowed to take up the teaching time, this robs others of learning opportunities. Establish a time, say 45 minutes of teaching with 30 minutes of discussion. These don't have to be separate times; they can be mixed. Do not worry about completing a set amount of material every week, as you will find that people are very interested in going deeper in some places, and not as interested in others. This all depends upon where they are in the Lord. If you can, let the group's particular needs and interests set a time frame for some of the deeper areas. This could mean, of course, that you may have to move on while some would prefer to stay on certain issues past a reasonable length of time.

Always open with prayer and then go right into a good hour of teaching and discussion. Then you could go into the second phase, a more relaxed time where people could be encouraged to pray for one another, out loud preferably. This is like role-playing, but is actually using the prayer principles for real needs and concerns. Remind everyone that one of the most beautiful parts of these prayer principles is that you don't have to know the details, you don't have to hear all of the story, you don't have to be in the position of "passing on" spiritual gossip about someone else's personal life. We only have the "right" to expose and relate our own innermost secrets, never to repeat another individual's private issues.

Then have some informal time of sharing. The leader should close in prayer, perhaps reinforcing an aspect of the teaching or discussion of that particular meeting.

God is always looking for right and godly agreement on earth in our prayers. He is looking for prayers that agree that His will, already set in heaven, is the answer to every need on earth. We do not know everything that has contributed to the situations we find ourselves in or we see others in, for only God knows what is really happening and why. The Keys of the Kingdom are our means of bringing things here on earth into alignment with God's already established will in heaven. This is a powerful agreement partnership that God has established. We don't need to try to improve on perfection with our ideas of telling God what we think should be done and how!

Teach those in the group that if someone's marriage is in trouble, you should bind the wife's and the husband's wills to the will of God, both of their minds to the mind of Christ, and so on. Loose wrong patterns of thinking from each of their souls. Loose the effects and influences of wrong agreements from each of them. If another person is involved in the problem, pray the same prayers for that person. Ask the Holy Spirit to minister truth and healing to each of them. Do not allow sharing of "her" drinking, "his" infidelity, or "their" fighting. Teach those in the group that if a child is on drugs or drinking, or if a relative is indulging in dangerous activity, they do not have to share these facts. By agreeing with each other in prayer and binding those persons' wills to the will of God, wonderful things can begin to happen. By agreeing with each other in prayer and loosing wrong patterns of thinking from their souls, wonderful things can begin to happen. Without knowing one detail, you can loose the effects and influences of wrong agreements from each of them.

Ask the Holy Spirit to minister truth and healing to their unmet needs, unhealed hurts, and unresolved issues that have been so hidden and protected by the rationalizing and justifying of their stronghold thinking. I believe it is a good idea for all teachers of the first book of the trilogy, *Shattering Your Strongholds*, to also read *Breaking the Power*, the second book. This will give teachers added insight to help them guide their classes through some of the deeper areas of discussion that will arise out of the first book's teaching.

Teach that wrong behaviors come out of our developing wrong patterns of thinking and wrong reactions to old memories, old hurts, and grudges all protected by strongholds. Teach that we have all learned how to compensate and cope with our unmet needs, unhealed hurts, and unresolved issues in very unhealthy ways. These coping mechanisms and these needs and hurts were not washed away at our new spiritual birth. If anything, our souls (used to having to deal with all of this however they could) became fearful and hostile and just dug themselves in deeper to protect our secret hurts and unmet needs. These Keys of the Kingdom prayer principles are very effective in tearing down our souls' strongholds as well as their self-defense mechanisms so that God might begin to heal us.

Always stress to your class that God will not dismantle your strongholds and your self-defense mechanisms. He knows you have built them because you saw them as your only means of self-defense. If He were to smash through them to get to that part of you that desperately needs healing, it would just be one more violation of your already wounded soul. He is asking you to take down all of your inner self-defense mechanisms and voluntarily allow Him access to fix everything within you that has been broken and abused. He won't destroy your self-protection mechanisms to heal you, however wrong and personally disabling they are. True intimacy with Him is always voluntary, never forced. These suggested guidelines can be tailored to your own group's needs.

appendix two

Teaching Kids About the Keys

Written together with the teachings of Carla Clark
(Level II Eagle Teacher)

When teaching children about abstract concepts such as unmet needs, the unsurrendered soul, and the born-again spirit, you need to be very flexible. You are never sure what will pop out of their minds and mouths in response to what captures their interest, and sometimes great teaching opportunities arise when you least expect them. Always be prepared to slow down and pursue questions and answers with the kids when they light up in certain parts of your teaching.

These teachings are basically geared to groups, such as Sunday School, Vacation Bible School, and neighborhood Bible studies. They can be easily adjusted to teachings for individual children as well. With minor changes, they can even be read to children as stories.

Always have the children pray the following prayers (for their appropriate age) before and after your teaching. These prayers are taken from our laminated prayer charts for kids and young teens, 5"x8" charts on hot colored paper (and hole-punched to fit a standard three-hole binder).

Younger Kids

Jesus, you said you were giving me THE KEYS of the KINGDOM (Matthew 16:19). These are kind of like my keys to my house, but much better. One key is to BIND (hold tight and hang on to). TO BIND can also be like hugging. The other key is to LOOSE (tear off and smash). TO LOOSE can also be like erasing when I make a mistake on a school paper.

I BIND myself to you, God, just like I'm putting on a big seat belt. I know I'm safe and I know that you love me. I LOOSE scary thoughts about what might happen to me, and I feel BRAVER because I'm closer to you.

I BIND myself to the truth, just like I'm putting on fresh new clothes that everyone else thinks are really cool. I LOOSE everything from myself that is not true—just like taking off dirty stinky clothes that have gunk and grease and gross stuff on them. I feel BETTER now!

I BIND my own "want-to's" to you, Father God, so that I will always "want to" do the best things you have for me. I sometimes think about doing things that I shouldn't. So I LOOSE all of my wrong "want-to" thoughts that are not safe or good. I want what you say is BEST!

I BIND my thoughts to your mind, Jesus. I LOOSE all of the yucky thoughts that keep making me feel bad. I LOOSE the wrong thoughts that make me think I don't know what to do. I LOOSE wrong thoughts that bad things are going to happen to me or my family.

I BIND my feelings to the Holy Spirit. The Bible says He is the Comforter! I really need some comfort, Holy Spirit. I LOOSE all of the hurt feelings I have inside of me right now because other kids have said mean things to me. Help me know why they act so mean so I can try to say something to make them feel better.

I BIND myself to you, Jesus, and I ask you to help me tear down any walls I have built up to try to protect myself. I LOOSE and tear down all the walls that keep you from living inside every part of me. Nothing I have ever tried to do has ever made up for my needs, healed my hurts, or answered my questions. I believe you can, though. So please do and I thank you, Jesus.

I BIND the "want to's" of my Mommy and my Daddy to your plans for them, Father God. I BIND my Mommy's thoughts and my Daddy's thoughts to your thoughts, Jesus. Help them to feel better. I BIND my Mommy's feelings and my Daddy's feelings to the Holy Spirit. I know they both could use some comfort. I LOOSE scary thoughts and worry from them. Please keep them well and safe today.

I BIND the "want to's" of all of my relatives, my friends, and my teachers to you, Father God, just like Super Glue. I BIND their thoughts to your thoughts, Jesus. Help them to feel all right and not be mad or sick. I BIND their feelings to the Holy Spirit. They all really need some comfort. I LOOSE any scary thoughts and worry from them. Please keep them all safe and please keep my pets safe today, too.

Please help _____ to stop smoking.
Please help _____ to stop drinking.
Please help _____ to stop doing drugs.
Please help _____ to stop getting mad.
Please help _____ to stop crying.
Please help _____ to get well.

Please help the kids all over the world to have food and someone to love them and a safe place to live. Please help people everywhere to stop fighting and get along. Thank you, Jesus, for helping me today. I love you! Amen.

Older Kids

Jesus, you have given me THE KEYS of the KINGDOM (Matthew 16:19). Thank you! These are like keys to the biggest mansion ever, only much better. One key is to BIND which means to stick to something like Super Glue! The other key is to LOOSE which means to smash and cut away, or to erase.

When I pray with these two keys, I know I can be in your will, God. I BIND myself to YOU, just like putting on the safety bar before riding the biggest roller coaster! My life feels like that sometimes, but I know you love me. I LOOSE all scary up and down thoughts from myself, and I feel STRONGER!

I BIND myself to the truth, which is like knowing all the right answers on the hardest final test at school! I LOOSE all ideas from myself that are not true, which is like brushing and scrubbing the morning fur off my teeth!

I BIND my will (my want-to) to you, Lord, so that I want to do what is right. Sometimes I think about doing things that I shouldn't. I LOOSE any wrong desires out of my soul that are not part of your plans for my life.

I BIND my whole brain to your mind, Jesus. I LOOSE (tear off) all of the ugly thoughts that keep making me feel that I'll never have a great life. I LOOSE the wrong thoughts that make me feel like I don't know what to do. I LOOSE wrong thoughts that bad things are going to happen!

I BIND my feelings to the Holy Spirit. I really need some comfort, Holy Spirit. I LOOSE all of the hurt feelings and the angry feelings that are inside me because other people have said things that are not true—really bad stuff—about me and to me. I know you can tell me how to help them.

I BIND myself to you, Jesus, and I ask you to help me tear down any walls of self-protection or self-defense that I have built up to try to protect myself. I LOOSE and tear down all the stronghold walls that keep you from living inside every part of me. I know I can't meet my own needs, heal my own hurts, and answer my own questions. But YOU CAN and I believe you will. Thank you, Jesus.

I BIND my Mom's and my Dad's wills to your plans for their lives, Lord. I BIND their thoughts to your thoughts, Jesus. Please help us to understand each other and get along better. I BIND my Mom's feelings and my Dad's feelings to the Holy Spirit. I know they both could use some comfort. I LOOSE stressful thoughts and worry from them. Please keep them well and safe today.

I BIND the wills of all my relatives, my friends, and my teachers to your will, Lord. I BIND their thoughts to your thoughts, Jesus. I BIND their feelings to the Holy Spirit. I LOOSE wrong expectations and wrong desires from them. Please keep them safe today.

Please help _____ to stop smoking.
Please help _____ to stop drinking.
Please help _____ to stop doing drugs.
Please help _____ to stop getting mad.
Please help _____ to stop crying.
Please help _____ to get well.

Please help our leaders to do right, and please protect our country. Help the hurting people in the world to get food and a safe place to live. Thank you, Jesus, for showing me how to pray right prayers that agree with your will. I love you! Amen.

Getting Into the Secret Place With God

Purpose: To give kids "steps" to remember how to pray the binding prayers.

Materials Needed: A large umbrella like a golf umbrella that you can write on with a permanent felt tip marker. If your umbrella does not have enough panels for all of the prayer steps below, make signs that list the prayer steps and pin them on the umbrella. Photocopy two pictures of an umbrella (one for front view and one for a back view) on a drawing paper. Let the children color their own umbrella panels and print the prayer steps in them to take home with them.

(TEACHER first reads Psalm 91 to the children, drawing their attention to the reference to the Secret Place. Then the TEACHER reads Matthew 16:19 and tells the children that this will show them how to get to that Secret Place. If the children are under six years of age, keep it very simple. Use the *Message Bible* or the *Living Bible* version.)

TEACHER: Do any of you have a "secret place" that only you and a few other people know about? If someone wanted to get into your secret place with you, they would have to know you pretty well. If they didn't, they wouldn't even know where your "secret place" was. They would have to know you really well for you to invite them into your secret place.

The Secret Place in Psalm 91 is not a specific place like your bedroom or your back yard. It is a place that you can carry with you wherever you go, and God is always ready to meet you there. Getting into the Secret Place depends on your knowing your Father God really well. How do you get to really know someone? You spend time with them, listen to them, talk with them, and sometimes share your feelings with them.

God wants more than anything to have a close friendship with each of you in His Secret Place. The Secret Place is a wonderful place full of God's love. You don't have to worry about anything because God is in control and He will take care of you in the Secret Place. So, how many of you would like to discover how you can have a really close friendship with God and actually live in His Secret Place?

TEACHER: (Pulls out her big umbrella, which has drawings and words in each panel or signs pinned to each panel, and says:) I have made a very special umbrella to help you have a great friendship with God. Each one of these pictures (or signs) tells you a step you can take to get into the Secret Place.

When you pray and bind yourself to the right things in your prayers like you did when we started, it's like getting a special pass into the Secret Place. When you pray these prayers you actually put yourself into God's safety harness while you walk into the Secret Place of His love and protection. Let's talk about each picture (or sign) on the umbrella. This one says you need to:

Bind your minds to the Mind of Christ—Did you know that you can have the mind of Christ in your own minds? Isn't that great? Jesus always thinks good thoughts, and He never thinks bad or scary thoughts. When you pray and say that you bind your mind to the mind of Christ, you are saying that you want to think like He does instead of your own thoughts or the devil's thoughts. This means:

> You will be able to see yourself like He does,
> You will be able to see others like He does, and
> You will be able to see your problems like He does!

You can't just do that by yourself, you know. We all see things around us and we think that is just the way things are. That is not always true. Have any of you ever been lost for a few minutes and thought that you might never find your mommy and daddy again— but you did? God knew where you were all the time and He helped them find you. You need to think like Jesus thinks so that you will know He is taking care of you. Let's look at this next picture (sign) now. You need to:

Bind your will to the will of God—Each one of you has a will, which is really like the muscle in your soul. Your wills are what get you to actually go ahead and do things—whether it is a good decision or a bad decision. If you decide that you want to draw a pretty picture, your will keeps you drawing until you have it just the way you want. If you decide you want to get a good grade on a test at school, your will keeps you reading and studying so you can get the good grade you want. If you decide you want to do something that you know you are not supposed to do, your will is what pushes you to do it even though you will probably get into trouble.

God also has a will, and He has specific plans for you that are good plans. Jeremiah 29:11 (*NKJV*) tells you that God has said: "*I know the thoughts that I think toward you, says the LORD, thoughts of peace and not of evil, to give you a future and a hope."* His will is what keeps everything in the world happening until everything gets where He wants it to be. When you are praying this part of your prayer, you are asking God to help make sure your will is in line with His will and His plans for your lives. Now let's pray the next picture (or sign). You should:

Bind Your feet to the Paths of Righteousness—Every day you walk along different paths and meet other kids and people on these paths. If you are not careful, the other kids you meet and the things you do can actually get in the way of the close friendship that Jesus wants to have with you. When you pray and bind your feet to the paths that God wants you to walk, He will walk right with you. No matter where our feet take us, God wants us to hear His voice above all the other voices that we hear in our day. We hear these voices in our homes, on TV, at school, on the playground, in our neighborhoods, etc.

When we listen hard for His voice, He can guide us in every decision we have to make when others are talking to us. As we listen to Him, it's amazing how close we get to Him. Our friendship with Him just grows and grows the more we listen for His voice and obey what He says.

As we walk the different paths each day, no matter what path we take, we have an opportunity to act like Jesus Christ would when we run into other kids and people. He really loves it when we try to act like Him in all we say and do. We should always want others to see that we act like Jesus would in everything we do and say. You need to remember that when you are tempted to walk somewhere you shouldn't. Maybe Mommy, Daddy, and your teacher don't always know where you are thinking about walking, but God does. When you bind your feet to His paths, He will keep reminding you where you should walk. Let's look at another picture (or sign). You should:

Bind yourself to God's Word—Reading God's Word is the only way you can ever really get to know Him and be good friends with Him.

You should read from the Bible every day, because His Word makes you strong. His Word can heal you when you feel sick. His Word can help you stop being upset when you don't get your way. As you read or somebody reads it to you, you can be snugged up tight to His words by binding yourself to God's Word. Let's pray another picture (or sign). You should:

Bind yourself to the power of the Blood of Jesus—The blood of Jesus is the part of the Secret Place that heals you, washes you, fixes you, and puts you back together when you get broken. Have any of you ever broken something and you were in trouble? Didn't you really wish that you knew how to put it back together just like it was perfect again? That is what the blood of Jesus can do to your body, to your soul, and what He has done to your spirit if you have asked Him to be your Savior. When you pray and bind yourself to the power of His blood so you will be safe, you are covered with a blanket of His love and His blood. This is good. Let's pray another picture (or sign). You should:

Bind Yourself to the Truth—The Holy Spirit is God's gift to help you be able to tell God's truth from some of the lies that your SOUL MAN wants to believe. If you don't let the Holy Spirit guide you every day in everything you do, you will not be able to do and say everything the best way. You will end up doing things that your SOUL MAN wants you to do. You will keep getting tricked by your own ideas, your own thoughts, and your own demands to have your way. You should always bind yourself to the truth of God's Word because it will remind you not to tell something that isn't true. Let's pray another picture (or sign). You should:

Bind yourself to God's Timing—When you pray and bind yourself to God's timing, you can live in the Secret Place without any worry about getting what you want when you want it, because God's time is never late. You never have to get upset because something doesn't happen when you want it to. You never have to worry when things seem to be going too slow for you. God's time is always the best time. It helps you wait and be patient when things take longer than you thought they would. Let's pray another picture (or sign). You should:

Bind yourself to the Work of the Cross—The Cross of Calvary, where Jesus died to take away our sins, is really our Season Pass into the Secret Place. You have to believe that Jesus died for you and shed His blood on the Cross for you, or you can't even get into the Secret Place at all. You need to bind yourself to the work of the Cross in your lives so that you stop only thinking about what you want. God loved you so much that He sent Jesus to die for you to make a way for you to get into friendship with Him. Jesus actually paid the admission price for you to be able to get into the Secret Place with your Father God.

Boys and girls, in the weeks ahead, you are going to talk more about being close to God. You are going to show Jesus how you love Him by how you act with others and how you obey and respect your parents. You are going to find out how to get into the Secret Place even if you are having a bad day. Let's pray the binding and loosing prayers together now before you all go home. (Have kids pray the age appropriate prayer one more time after the TEACHER.)

Soul Surrender for Kids

Purpose: Teaching basics of soul surrender to children. Children will learn the basics of the soul and its self-centered characteristics as well as how to make it behave by using the binding and loosing prayers.

People Needed: Teacher and two helpers, SPIRIT MAN and SOUL MAN.

Materials Needed: A blue costume (any kind) for SPIRIT MAN and a yellow costume (any kind) for SOUL MAN.

SPIRIT MAN (dressed in blue) enters singing:
I am SPIRIT MAN and I have a soul
I live in a body and one thing I know

Jesus Christ is my Best Friend
He loves me and loves me with no end
He came down to earth to set men free
From all their needs and all their misery
He makes me happy and so very free
Thank you, Jesus, for always loving me!

TEACHER: Boys and girls, did you know that you had a SPIRIT MAN? He's just one part of you, though, because you are made up of three parts—just like your face is made up of three parts—your eyes, your nose, and your mouth. You have a body—which everyone can see—and you have a spirit that only God can see—and you have a soul that thinks it can see everything. But it just thinks so; it really can't!

Today we're going to have some fun learning about our SPIRIT MAN and our SOUL MAN. You have a SPIRIT MAN and a SOUL MAN living inside of you.

When we accept Jesus into our hearts, SPIRIT MAN gets very excited because he's always been like an orphan with no way to get to his Spiritual Father up in heaven. When SPIRIT MAN finally gets hooked up with his best friend, Jesus, he's really happy. (SPIRIT MAN starts singing and dancing around). SPIRIT MAN knows that Jesus came to set him free from being a spiritual orphan by making a bridge for him to get to his Spiritual Father, God.

This SPIRIT MAN loves Jesus and he listens to Jesus all the time. (TEACHER pauses as SPIRIT MAN cups his ear to hear, and then laughs and claps his hands). SPIRIT MAN is happiest when we're worshipping Jesus and praying and reading our Bibles because when we do all these things, we're really, really getting to know Jesus. We're getting closer and closer to our Spiritual Father in heaven.

Our SPIRIT MAN wants us to know Jesus better than anyone else because he knows that Jesus has all the answers to all of our questions. He knows that Jesus loves us like no one else in the whole world can. Jesus loves us even more than our mommies and our daddies. But, wait ... we also have SOUL MAN living inside us.

(SOUL MAN comes in, dressed in yellow, singing rap style.)

I am SOUL MAN and I want you to know
I'm here to protect you wherever you go.
With my mind, my will, and my emotions, too
I'll make good excuses to get you through.
I can build walls to hide behind and lies to confuse.
I can get what you want and see you never lose.
Trust me, listen to me, just wait and see.
All you have to do is think Me, Me, Me

(Then SOUL MAN walks around looking proud and bossy.)

TEACHER: Our SOUL MAN is made up of three things:

1. Our mind where he tries to control how we think (Yellow SOUL MAN points to head), and

2. Our will where he tries to control how we make our choices (Yellow SOUL MAN holds out arms and makes muscles), and

3. Our emotions where we feel sad, mad, or glad (Yellow SOUL MAN makes a sad face, and puts hands over heart).

Our SOUL MAN thinks it's his job to make sure that nobody can take any of our rights from us! He thinks he's helping us when he makes us want to get even if somebody hurts us. He's always trying to get other people to do what he wants, pushing them around, too. (Yellow SOUL MAN jumps into Karate stance — perhaps even shouting and throwing a kick).

But, you know what, SOUL MAN really can't do these any of these things. He just gets us into trouble when he tries. We know the only one who can protect us and defend us, and get us what we need. Who is HE? (asking the children)

JESUS!!!

So even as a little boy or girl, you can know that SOUL MAN can't help you handle your own fears, hurts, and worries. But you can take them to God in prayer and trust Him to:

1. Protect you
2. Heal your hurts

3. Meet your needs, and
4. Answer your questions.

Our SPIRIT MAN knows that Jesus and Father God are the only ones who can do this. (SPIRIT MAN nods his head, vigorously!) But SOUL MAN doesn't know this at all! So, we need to make SOUL MAN get it right and get lined up with our SPIRIT MAN. (SPIRIT MAN walks over and tries to wrap his arms around SOUL MAN— SOUL MAN pushes him away.) Only when SOUL MAN is willing to line up with SPIRIT MAN can he learn to hear from God and walk in God's love, too.

Did you know that Jesus is always talking with you? He sure is. Why don't we always hear Him? Because our SOUL MAN doesn't want to listen to Him. SOUL MAN gets our minds busy with all kinds of stuff, he gets our wills all stubborn, and he gets our emotions all fussy so we can't hear Jesus. He gets us wound up until we feel just like a circus full of busy, stubborn, out-of-control animals. When that happens, we just can't hear from Jesus very well.

SOUL MAN knows how to get us out of being lined up with Jesus and then we stop being obedient. When you learn how SOUL MAN does this, you'll be able to stop him! But the best part is that you'll be able to keep him in his place. When he is out of his place, we can't hear from Jesus, and we don't want to do what God has asked us to do. When SOUL MAN is in his place, then both SPIRIT MAN and SOUL MAN have a direct hook-up with God and things get really good!

When SOUL MAN is out of his place, he starts running all over the place trying to take charge! You know, like when you get your feelings hurt, SOUL MAN immediately starts getting pushy. He wants to push others out of the way and he wants to get even with them. But when you know that this is what SOUL MAN is going to do, you can ignore him and run straight to Jesus with the prayers we just prayed.

When you bind your mind to the mind of Christ, you can let Jesus love on you and help you. This is much better than hoping that SOUL MAN will be able to bail you out of your trouble. (Yellow SOUL MAN pouts and looks upset).

(TEACHER turns to yellow SOUL MAN and says:) SOUL MAN, get ready. I'm going to ask you some really important questions that need really honest answers. Are you ready? (Yellow SOUL MAN frowns and slowly nods his head.)What do you do when you don't get your way? What do you do when somebody hurts you? What do you do when things don't go the way you want them to? Do you cry, whine, complain, sulk, feel sorry for yourself, throw a fit, blame someone else, and go off by yourself to pout? (SOUL MAN vigorously nods head yes, or says "Yes" to every question.)

Well, that's SOUL MAN for you. These are the things he does best—crying, whining, complaining, pouting, feeling sorry for himself, throwing a fit, blaming someone else, and sulking. These are the tricks that he thinks will help us get our way, and he always fights to keep us from being blamed for things. SOUL MAN, can you give us a few examples of how you think when things are not going your way?

SOUL MAN says:

- Well, people should do what I want and everything would be OK.
- I say, "You don't always have to obey Mommy and Daddy right now. You're right in the middle of your favorite TV program."
- I don't think I should have to share my toys with anyone else unless I want to. They are my toys and besides, someone else might break them.
- Oh, yes, and junk food makes me feel better. So, if I'm feeling sad or mad, I'll just go to the kitchen and get something sweet to eat.
- If people really aren't paying attention to me, I just throw a fit until they do what I want them to again.

TEACHER: Wow, SOUL MAN, these are some pretty incredible things you say you think you should do. These sound an awful lot like excuses for acting wrong to me. You're pretty good, SOUL MAN, at coming up with excuses for acting wrong, aren't you? Just like a baby cries when it wants something, SOUL MAN cries and tries to get back in control. (SOUL MAN looks upset with TEACHER.)

So, what do we do to get SOUL MAN lined up with Jesus? We BIND him to the will of God, to the mind of Jesus Christ, and to the healing of the Holy Spirit. Oh, I'm sure SOUL MAN will try to kick up a fuss about that, but it really is for his own good. Because we know he will get so upset, let's LOOSE some of the things he tries to use to get his own way. Let's LOOSE his bad thoughts and his bad attitudes, and let's loose his selfish ideas. Now, let's BIND him to the Father, Son, and Holy Spirit so that he will get healed and helped and he won't get us into trouble anymore.

Pray the binding and loosing prayer together now, after me. (Pray the Younger Kids prayer or the Older Kids prayer according to the age group, having them repeat the words after you.)

Unmet Needs, Unhealed Hurts, and Unanswered Questions

Skit's Purpose: To show children how they get unmet needs, unhealed hurts, and unanswered questions in their SOUL MAN. To show how these three things keep hurting inside of their SOUL MAN.

People Needed: Teacher and one helper, SOUL MAN.

Materials Needed: Three white felt or cloth bags (about 10 inches square) that have a slit (about 3-4 inches wide) in them. One bag should have UNMET NEEDS written on it, one should have UNHEALED HURTS, and one should have UNANSWERED QUESTIONS written on it—use wide-tip felt marker so it can be seen clearly. You could actually use grocery bags if you had to. Have a long raggedy strip of black fabric (approximately 48" long and 2" wide) poked inside each of the bags, with the end just barely showing through the slit (so that it is easy to get hold of). You will also need three one-foot squares of red felt or cloth (approximately 12 inches square). You will also need pictures of bricks and pins to pin them onto SOUL MAN.

TEACHER: Let's look at how SOUL MAN gets so good at making excuses. Even when you are pretty little, like some of you are, you can have something called an **unmet need**. An unmet need is something good that should have happened to you but it didn't.

(Teacher pins the white bag that says UNMET NEEDS onto SOUL MAN's costume. The words UNMET NEEDS are written on the white in as large of letters as possible).

(SOUL MAN begins to slowly pull the black fabric strip out through the slit in the bag marked UNMET NEEDS as TEACHER begins talking about the feelings, thoughts and behaviors that grow out of these unmet needs.)

TEACHER: I want to ask you, SOUL MAN, how would you try to deal with the following unmet needs?

Judy has a mommy and daddy who are just really busy doing things and working—never having time to spend with her. They don't seem to care how she thinks and feels. Judy doesn't get all the love and hugs and help that she needs from both of her parents, and it makes her feel bad.

What would you tell Judy to do, SOUL MAN?

SOUL MAN: I would tell her to find some kind of mischief to get into so people would notice her. She should figure out some way to get Mom and Dad to pay attention to her, even if it might get her into real trouble. At least they would be paying attention to her for awhile.

(SOUL MAN continues to slowly pull the piece of black fabric out of the white bag.)

TEACHER: Now let's talk about Roger.

Roger grew up in a home where everyone was always going somewhere or doing something. Everybody was busy, busy, busy. The family would go to soccer games, football games, movies, and all kind of places with each other. But no one ever talked about what they were feeling inside. No one really felt close to the other people in the family.

What would you do, SOUL MAN, if you were in Roger under these circumstances?

SOUL MAN: Well, at first, I would probably really like all the things we did together. But if no one ever seemed to want to hear if I was feeling bad, my feelings would be hurt. After awhile, I guess I would realize that the other family members weren't interested in me. So I would stop caring about them, and sometimes tell them I didn't want to go with them. I'd tell them I would rather play my video games or get on my computer.

(SOUL MAN continues to slowly pull the piece of black fabric out of the white bag.)

TEACHER: Wow, SOUL MAN, you're starting to get a lot of ugly black stuff coming out of you. This stinking thinking and the things you do to try to make yourself not feel so bad are not all that pretty. Let's take a look at another source of pain in our lives. This one is called **Unhealed Hurts.**

(Teacher walks over and pins another white bag on SOUL MAN. The words, UNHEALED HURTS, are written on the white bag in as large of letters as possible).

(SOUL MAN begins to slowly pull the black fabric out through the hole in the white felt bag marked UNHEALED HURTS as the TEACHER begins to talk about the feelings, thoughts, and behaviors that grow out of unhealed hurts.)

TEACHER: An unhealed hurt is something really bad that happens to you that should never have happened. Because we live in a world of sin with lots of other hurting people, we get hurt and we even hurt others.

So, SOUL MAN, what would you do if people said hurtful things to you over and over like: "You're so dumb; you're just a baby; can't you do anything right? I hate you! What's wrong with you? You're stupid. You're ugly. You talk weird."

SOUL MAN: If it was my parents saying these hurtful things, I wouldn't say anything. I would sit there and take it. But if it was kids my own age or smaller than me, I'd hit them upside their head. That would make them sorry. But after a while, I would kind of start to believe all the stuff they were saying to me, and I would start acting just like they said.

(SOUL MAN continues to slowly pull the piece of black fabric out of the white bag marked unhealed hurts.)

TEACHER: And what about the stuff on television? Some children watch a lot of bad things on TV or read books that are really scary. SOUL MAN, how would you deal with that?

SOUL MAN: At first I would get really scared. In fact, even now I don't like to be home alone or go out in the dark. I don't really believe any of that stuff because it is just all made up. But for some reason, I'm just not as sure about myself anymore, and I won't let people leave me by myself.

TEACHER: SOUL MAN, what about when some children have seen someone get really hurt and they weren't able to do anything to help them. Has that ever happened to you, SOUL MAN?

SOUL MAN: Yeah, once I saw one of my friends get hurt really bad when they were skateboarding on a road that their parents said not to go near. But I told them it would be OK, as long as they were careful. Now I feel kind of guilty because I should have done something to stop them. I know I'm going to get blamed and they are going to hate me now. Man, I hate that!

(SOUL MAN looks really distressed as he continues to slowly pull the piece of black fabric out of the white pouch marked UNHEALED HURTS.)

TEACHER: One more thing that can cause you a lot of pain is called **UNANSWERED QUESTIONS (or Unresolved Issues)**. These are tough questions that we keep asking about why awful things have happened, and no one is able to give us a good answer. These are the tough questions that we keep asking ourselves about why we did something that turned out really bad.

(TEACHER walks over and pins another white bag on SOUL MAN. The word UNANSWERED QUESTIONS are written on the white bag in as large of letters as possible).

(SOUL MAN begins to slowly pull the black fabric out through the hole in the bag marked Unanswered Questions as the TEACHER begins talking about the feelings, thoughts, and behaviors that grow out of these unanswered questions.)

TEACHER: So, SOUL MAN, have you ever had any questions like this?

1. Where was God or where were my parents when this awful thing happened?
2. How come this happened to me?
3. Why don't they love me?
4. How come nobody likes me?
5. Why don't they ever come and visit me?

SOUL MAN: Sure. I have lots of questions like that. I try not to think about them, but they just never go away. I'm getting pretty upset right now. Can we stop this?

(SOUL MAN begins to pull the piece of black fabric out of the white bag with a great deal of nervousness.)

TEACHER: Wow, SOUL MAN, you sure have a lot of yucky black stuff hanging out all over you. You look awful. How can you stand having all that stinking thinking and wrong attitudes and bad behaviors in you?

SOUL MAN: As soon as you quit bugging me, I'll just stuff these things back inside where no one can see them. They usually stay there pretty good. It's only when I get nervous and start pulling them out sometimes that they show. I'm pretty good at keeping them out of sight. I'll just put up some more of these walls to protect myself from getting hurt more, and pretty soon they will be hidden forever. At least I think they will. When things get really bad enough, I just make some vows like this:

(SOUL MAN begins to stick on drawn pictures of bricks over each hurt, need or unanswered question as he says the following. You can have these following lines printed on the back of the brick pictures.)

1. I'm never going to tell anyone anything again.
2. No one is ever going to hurt me like that again!
3. No one is ever going to put me down like that again!
4. No one is ever going to see me cry or be scared like that!

TEACHER: Well, SOUL MAN, that might work for you for a short while, but it won't last very long. You will just keep having to do it over and over and over, you know. I want to tell you something, because I know something you don't know about this. When you put all those walls up, you are not really getting rid of that ugly stuff. You're just putting it back behind the walls where it is still festering and hurting and getting worse. Worse yet, those walls are keeping Jesus out of where He needs to be! How can you ever really get to know and trust Jesus if you have all these walls over you, SOUL MAN?

SOUL MAN: I don't know the answer to that. Who cares?

TEACHER: The devil cares; that's who! He loves it when you stuff all that junk inside you because he sniffs it out and feeds on it. (TEACHER, make sniffing and snorting noises towards SOUL MAN like the devil is trying to sniff out stuff.)

TEACHER: Hey, SOUL MAN, I know how to really get rid of this stuff. Would you like for me to show you?

(SOUL MAN looks very unsure.)

TEACHER: First you have to tear some of these walls down. You might think that is scary, but you will feel so much better if you do, because then God can really take care of you and really protect you. And guess what—He does a much better job of this than you ever could. Here, let me help you while the kids get ready to pray.

(TEACHER begins to pull off the brick pictures taped over the UNMET NEEDS, UNHEALED HURTS, AND UNRESOLVED ISSUES as he/she says:) I LOOSE these walls, and bricks, and stones that you have been trying to protect yourself with. Come on, kids, let's pray the binding and loosing prayers again. Pray after me:

(Have kids pray one of the Kid's Prayers at the front of this chapter.)

As TEACHER finishes praying, he/she walks over to SOUL MAN and pulls the black strips of fabric completely out of the white bags. The TEACHER then takes one of the three squares of red cloth and pokes part of the center of it into the slit of the pouch, spreading the rest of it out to cover the words UNMET NEEDS, UNHEALED HURTS, or UNANSWERED QUESTIONS.

TEACHER: That's the blood of Jesus, SOUL MAN. See now how the blood of Jesus has covered over and wiped away the needs, healed the hurts, and answered the questions? Isn't that better than pulling out and stuffing back and pulling out and stuffing back that ugly, black stuff that kept coming out of your pain and fear? I think so, too. Thank you, Jesus.

(SOUL MAN wipes away a few tears and smiles as he takes the TEACHER's hand).

Mind of Christ

Purpose: This teaching will convey the principle of the children being able to line their minds and thoughts up to the mind and thoughts of Jesus Christ.

Materials Needed: Two hats—one dark and one light (or white), a large bowl, a plastic baseball bat, a large drawing tablet or poster board and colored markers (particularly a black one), safety pins, pen, and 3x5 cards.

TEACHER: When we bind our minds to the mind of Christ, we are asking Jesus to help us think like He thinks. Do you know why we want to do that? Because Jesus only thinks good thoughts about others and about life. He never thinks bad thoughts. He never worries. He is never afraid. He is never confused. He never gets angry and frustrated when things don't go His way.

Jesus just loves everybody all the time, and He is very patient and kind. Jesus also loves to have fun and be happy. He wants us to have fun and be happy too, even when people and things around us aren't very happy. Can you be loving even when you have friends around you who aren't being very loving? Yes, you can, but it is not easy to do. Why? Because we all have something inside us called a soul.

The soul is made up of our minds, our wills, and our emotions. Our mind is like a big bowl in our heads that holds all of our thoughts. (TEACHER holds big bowl) Just listen to some of these thoughts in here (already written on 3x5 cards): "I don't want to go to school." "I don't like him." "I'm not going to do what Mommy wants me to do." "I'm afraid of the dark." My, my, we have some dark thoughts in here, today, don't we? I'm glad this isn't my mind, because I would feel bad if those were in my mind.

Our will is like the muscle in our soul, and it is what we use to help us make good decisions and even bad decisions. Our will can be pretty pushy some times. If it could talk and we could hear it, our wills would probably say something like this (TEACHER starts pounding on his/her hand with the plastic bat, even waving it in the air):

"Nobody is going to stop me from doing what I want! I will go to the mall! I will eat that cake! I am not going to clean up my room. Nobody is going to make me do what I don't want to do. If I have to bonk you (shakes bat at audience) to get you out of the way, then I'll just bonk you!"

(TEACHER picks up drawing tablet and begins to draw happy faces in green, pauses and then draws sad faces in blue, pauses again and then draws red frowny/cranky faces, and finally draws purple angry faces. These faces can overlap each other, until there are so many faces that it looks all messy. Then he/she begins to point to colored face that fits while saying:) Our emotions are the part of our soul where our feelings come from — happy feelings, sad feelings, cranky and crabby feelings, and even angry feelings.

Our emotions and our thoughts go together (TEACHER puts drawing tablet and markers in bowl with thoughts). Most of our emotions, or feelings, come from how we are thinking. If we think thoughts like, "If they don't do this my way, I'm going to throw a fit," then how do you think we will feel when things don't go our way? If we think thoughts like, "Everybody hates me, nobody loves me," then we will feel very sad, won't we? If we think thoughts like, "Jesus loves me and I am going to ask Him to give me a fun day, Mommy and Daddy a fun day, and my friends a fun day," then you will probably think happy thoughts, won't you?

If you think about how everyone else seems to get more than you do, then you will find that cranky feelings start coming up from the inside of your soul. But, guess what? These feelings only come up out of your emotions when your soul starts thinking certain thoughts. Let me show you what I mean.

Illustration: See these two hats? This dark one represents the SOUL MAN on the inside of all of us. When we are born as little babies, we all are born with a soul but it really doesn't show at first. However, our souls, even when we're just little bitty babies, did not know how to think and act like Jesus would like them to. We were born trying to get things to be the way we wanted and trying to get other people to treat us the way we wanted them to.

We call this the "unsurrendered soul" because it hasn't learned how to think and act like God wants it to yet. It hasn't learned how to surrender to God yet. To surrender means to "give in." Has anybody ever made faces at you and tried to make you laugh, but you were not about to "give in" to them? When our soul surrenders to God, then we "give in" to Him and begin to want His way of thinking and acting.

This white hat stands for the "mind of Christ." The mind of Christ is always pure and good. The mind of Christ is filled with loving, obedient, and kind thoughts. (TEACHER peers into white hat and says): Yes, I see lots of loving thoughts in here, kind thoughts, patient thoughts. Oh, this is good. We want this. When we pray and bind our minds to the mind of Christ, it's like we are putting on Christ's way of thinking. (TEACHER puts on the white hat).

That's much better! Now I can think kind thoughts and good thoughts really easy. And I don't have any sad or grumpy thoughts at all right now. (TEACHER takes off the white hat.)

Let's take a look at what some of our bad thoughts look like. (Teachers picks up pen, 3x5 cards, and safety pins.) What are some bad thoughts? Can you tell me some? How about:

1. I won't eat my vegetables!
2. I don't like her because she is always mean to me.
3. I hate having to go to bed.
4. I'm going to get even with him.
5. I don't want anybody sitting with me.
6. I want my way or I'm going to throw a fit!

I've already written some of those thoughts down on these cards and now I am going to pin them onto our unsurrendered SOUL MAN's hat (dark). (Then TEACHER puts the SOUL MAN's hat on his/her head.) Ewwww, this doesn't make me feel very good. In fact, I feel sad and bad and cranky all at once. Ewwwwwwww! I don't feel so good. (TEACHER goes through several negative emotional expressions on his/her face.)

(Then TEACHER picks up the Mind of Christ hat and holds it).

The mind of Christ is loving, kind, obedient, respectful, and patient. We should all want to think like Jesus thinks. Now I'm going to take each one of these unsurrendered SOUL MAN's thoughts on my head and rewrite them so they sound more like the thoughts of the mind of Christ.

Here are some examples:

1. I am not going to eat my vegetables. I NEED TO TAKE CARE OF MY BODY SO THAT GOD HAS A GOOD PLACE TO LIVE.
2. I don't like her because she is always so mean to me. GOD WANTS ME TO LOVE THE WAY HE LOVES ME, EVEN WHEN I FEEL MEAN.
3. I want my way or I'm going to throw a fit. GOD TELLS ME TO TREAT OTHERS LIKE I WANT TO TREATED. SO, I'M GOING TO TRY.
4. I don't want anybody sitting with me. JESUS TELLS ME BE KIND, SO I WILL LET HER SIT HERE WITH ME.

(TEACHER has already printed the Mind of Christ thoughts on new cards. He/she pins each of these right thoughts onto the white hat.)

(TEACHER asks for a volunteer to come forward and read one of the SOUL MAN thoughts—and then TEACHER puts the SOUL MAN hat on the volunteer. He/she encourages everybody to all say, "Ewwwwwwww!" Then TEACHER hands him/her the Mind of Christ hat, and tells him/her to read the good thought and then put the Mind of Christ hat on over the SOUL MAN hat.)

TEACHER: Now, look! Now he/she has on the Mind of Christ hat, and because it's on top, His thoughts rule!

(TEACHER then calls up a volunteer and repeat the process above. Do one or two more times until children seem to get the idea.)

TEACHER: Now, boys and girls, every time you have a SOUL MAN thought this next week, what are you going to think about doing? You are going to pray and bind your mind to the mind of Christ and see Christ's white hat coming down from Heaven onto your head. Then all you have to do is pray and bind your will to God's will and put the white hat on!

Let's all pray the binding and loosing prayers together. Pray them after me: (TEACHER has children pray after him/her.)

Soul Surrender and the Rest of God

TEACHER: Do you know when your body is the most peaceful? When you are asleep! Your body is at rest, and your soul should be, too. It doesn't always rest when we sleep, because it can be too upset. When you know you have to go somewhere or do something that you don't want to the next day, you can have a hard time getting SOUL MAN to take a nap!

When we were really little, our mommies used to put us down for a nap. How many of you still like naps today? Most grownups love to get a chance to take a nap during their days, but not many get to. When you're young, you don't always enjoy resting and napping because you have so much you want to explore and get into. But did you that know our bodies have to have rest or they will get sick? That's why our parents make sure we get to bed at night and get plenty of sleep. What happens when you don't get enough rest? Come on— tell the truth. You get cranky!

Today we're going to talk about the "rest of God." Did you know that God wants us to rest in Him, too? His kind of rest is different. Instead of our bodies lying down for a nap, He wants us to put our SOUL MAN down for a nap several times during the day. Who can tell me what parts of you make up your SOUL MAN? (TEACHER helps the kids remember to say mind, will, and emotions)

God wants our SPIRIT MAN to be alert and listening to Him all the time, but our SOUL MAN doesn't always like it when SPIRIT MAN listens to God. This is because SOUL MAN doesn't want to miss out on anything going on in the world. We need to teach our SOUL MAN that when SPIRIT MAN is listening to God, SOUL MAN has to step aside and give up control.

When SPIRIT MAN listens to God, who is in control? God! When SOUL MAN listens to SPIRIT MAN, who is in control? God! You see, we really want God to be in complete control of us all the time, no matter what we are doing, who we are with, or where we are. We need to want what God wants before we ever think about what we want. But our SOUL MAN doesn't really like that.

Remember how I said that we get cranky when we don't get enough sleep? Well, SOUL MAN gets really cranky when he doesn't get enough rest in God. He needs to have lots of naps in God so that he learns how to listen to God and obey God.

Let me show you what it means for SOUL MAN to take a nap. He doesn't really fall asleep like we do. But he learns to lean on Jesus. (TEACHER asks for a child to come up and demonstrate how they can fall backwards into his/her arms. TEACHER asks the child to stand up with his/her arms folded and stand with his/her back to the TEACHER. On the count of three, TEACHER asks the child to fall backwards into his/her arms.)

This is what Father God wants us to do when our SOUL MAN gets cranky. He wants us to call out to Him and say, "Papa God, I need to rest." Like a flash, He shows up and we can just lean back into His arms. We need to ask Him to put His arms around us; we need to tell Him that we need Him to put His arms around us.

I remember pushing (my little boy or girl or niece or nephew, etc.) in their swings. I would stand behind them and push them as soon as they started to slow down. They kept saying, "Push me higher, please. Push me higher." So I would catch them in mid-air as they came swinging back towards me, by wrapping my arms around the swing and their bodies. Then I would pull them backwards as high as I could and let them fly forward. As soon as they started to slow down again, I'd catch them and pull them backwards and start all over again. I call that the God Catcher's swing.

The Bible tells us that God delights in taking care of us. Psalm 95:3-5 (*NKJV*) tells us: "*For the LORD is the great God, and the great King above all gods. In His hand are the deep places of the earth; the heights of the hills are His also. The sea is His, for He made it; and His hands formed the dry land.*" Wow, He is so powerful, He made the hills, He made the sea, and He made all of the dry land. Don't you think that if God made and holds the entire world and the heavens in His hands that He has some pretty strong hands and arms? I can't think of any place that I would rather be than in God's loving arms. When He wraps His loving arms around me I feel safe and secure. No matter where I am or what I'm doing, I can always know that my Papa God is in control and He will take care of me.

God's love is like that. He's with us all the time because the Bible says that God's love is shed abroad in our hearts (Romans 5:5). That means that His love is everywhere! So no matter what we're involved in, God's love and His strong arms are right there to "catch us," protect us, guide us, and help us. We have to ask Him to do it, just like my children (niece, nephew, neighbor, etc.) asked me to catch them.

We're going to act out some stories for you today (or TEACHER can just read them like a story if he/she doesn't have any helpers). When we get to the point where you can tell that SOUL MAN is trying to take over, I want you to yell, "SOUL MAN, you need a nap!"

Let's just practice that now. Everybody yell it out together, "SOUL MAN, you need a nap!" Great. As soon as you shout that out, I want you to think of SOUL MAN just falling backwards into Papa God's loving arms and letting Papa God tell him to chill out. Then He will show SOUL MAN how God's love should be passed out everywhere in the situation.

Now remember, only yell it out when you can tell that SOUL MAN is trying to take over, and not wanting to listen to SPIRIT MAN and God.

STORY 1: Two little girls are in Julie's room playing with her dolls. They are both having a great time, when suddenly Julie decides that she wants the doll that Barbara has. So Julie says, "Can I please play with that doll for awhile?" Barbara says, "No!" Julie says, "You do know this is my room and these are all my dolls. So give me my doll."

STORY 2: Two little boys are running to the swing sets on the playground and there's only one swing left. They both arrive at the same time, and Tommy gets into the swing. Donald says, "When can I swing?" "You can take your turn when I'm through," Tommy answers. Donald asks, "How long will that be?" Tommy shouts, "Get out of here. I got it first."

STORY 3: Gary and his teacher are working together in the classroom on a worksheet that Gary finds very hard to do. He keeps

299

making mistakes. The teacher is being very patient, but Gary gets very upset because he wants to do it just right. Gary says, "I can't do this. It's too hard for me." The teacher says, "Gary, I know you can do this and I'll help you." Gary cries, "You're not fair to make me do this."

STORY 4: Mommy asks Johnny to eat his carrots. Johnny doesn't like carrots, and he says so. His mother says that he needs the good vitamins in the carrots, and asks him if he doesn't want to grow up big and strong. Johnny doubles over and moans that his tummy is too full and he doesn't feel very good. Then he asks, "What's for dessert?"

STORY 5: Two little boys are playing on the playground having a great time when a third boy comes up and asks if he can play with them. He is friends with both of the boys. They have a great time until the new boy begins to play more with one of the boys and the other boy begins to feel left out. The boy feeling left out says, "Hey, you go home. We were having fun until you came along. He's my friend."

Conclusion: The main purpose of this lesson is that the children grow to understand that their soul is the part of them that will always try to control things and others so they can have things their way. But their born-again spirits will always want to listen to and yield to God. The only way our soul can learn to yield to God is if we learn how to know when we are out of the "rest of God" because our soul is trying to take over.

In teaching children about these principles, explain to them that they have certain symptoms of being sick in their souls. Pin or tape some "soul flu symptom" balloons on their clothes, some on the front that they can see and some on the back of them that they cannot see. Write symptoms on them, such as *cranky, angry, upset, sad, argumentative.*

These ideas, teachings, and skits are all for you to use in teaching children about their souls and how they can pray the binding and loosing prayers and get their souls to surrender to God. I pray that you will find them helpful and that you will use them. So many people have said to me for so long, "Why don't you get these principles in a format where we can teach them to children before they get so many strongholds built? It would be easier to keep them from building them, wouldn't it?"

Yes, it would. So, go get it started in your sphere of influence, in your home, in your Vacation Bible Schools, in your church's children's Sunday schools. Just do it!

Glossary

For terms used in *The Unsurrendered Soul*

Bind – Undergird, heal, hold, persuade, steady, cause fragmented pieces to come back into one whole, put oneself under obligation, and cling to. Binding prayers stabilize you, steady you, give you a spiritual safety harness, and give you a spiritual seat belt when you pray them. (Read more about the key of binding, along with original Hebrew and Greek meanings in *Shattering Your Strongholds*, *Breaking the Power*, and *Producing the Promise*.)

Body – Our flesh, bone, sinew, and organs that relate to the world and the environment around us through our fives senses: taste, touch, smell, sight, and hearing.

Emotions – The part of our souls that has the ability to feel joy, anger, sadness, happiness, fear, and other feelings.

Keys of the Kingdom – In Matthew 16:19, Jesus said, *"I will give to you the keys of the kingdom of heaven; whatever you bind on earth will be bound in heaven; whatever you loose on earth will be loosed in heaven."* Praying with these keys—binding and loosing—is our means of bringing things on earth into alignment with God's already established will in heaven. These prayers are only permanently effective when we bind and loose that which is God's will, not our own wills.

Layers – The soul first creates and then lays down layers of certain façades and false personality traits to protect and hide its unmet needs, unhealed hurts, and unresolved issues. This layering is like the bottom line of the soul's self-defense system. These layers are self-protective devices, self-reliance, self-understanding, self-defense systems, self-image, and more. They are intended to cover over and hide the pain and neediness, just like a new hardwood floor might be laid down to cover over and hide a rotten, mildewed sub-flooring over a basement filled with toxic waste. The new floor might look good, but the toxic emissions from the waste in the basement would keep coming up through the floorboards every day to poison that person's life.

Loose – Untie, break up, destroy, dissolve, melt, put off, wreck, crack to sunder by separation of the parts, shatter into minute fragments, disrupt, lacerate, convulse with spasms, break forth, burst, rend, and tear up. Loosing prayers shatter strongholds, smash and slash deception, allow you to perform self-surgery on your own soul, and are very effective at spiritual warfare. (Read more about the key of loosing and its various original Greek meanings in *Shattering Your Strongholds, Breaking the Power*, and *Producing the Promise*.)

Mind – That part of our soul that has the ability to think, to form ideas, and to rationalize.

Right agreement – God has established agreement as an immutable law. Whenever you are in right agreement with God or with another person according to His Word, God's power is always released into your situation. (Read more about the power of agreement in *Producing the Promise*.)

Salvation of the soul – The process of ongoing surrender (the renewing of the mind, surrendering of the will, and healing of the emotion) that we all must go through in order to walk in God's will. In Philippians 2:12, Paul told the Philippian Christians, *"Continue to work out your salvation with fear and trembling."*

Salvation of the spirit – That incredible transaction of heaven that is made when an individual believes that Jesus Christ was crucified to shed His blood in a final sacrifice for sin—once and for all—whereby Jesus Christ forgives this person's sins and gives him or her a new life to live. Jesus Christ took our sins upon Himself and placed His righteousness upon us that we might be justified in the eyes of a Holy God.

Soul – That part of our three-part being that is made up of our minds, our wills, and our emotions.

Soul power – The incredible power within the human soul that has remained dormant, for the most part, since Adam and Eve were sent out of the Garden of Eden after sinning. Eastern religion and new age cults all attempt to release that power of the soul through meditation to release "the force" within. Whenever man manages to tap into the power of the soul, it is always used fro the wrong reason. Cult leaders use soul power to prey upon those with unmet needs and unhealed hurts, convincing them that they have the "power" to help them. Soul power can be very overwhelming, as in the soul power that David Koresh of Waco, Texas, and Jim Jones of Guyana, South America learned to tap into to lead people to follow them—even into mass suicides. Or soul power can be more subtle, as in intimidation through staring, temptation through flirtatious looks, and such. Soul power being directed at another person can be thwarted through binding and loosing prayers. (See chapters on Soul Ties and Soul Power in *Breaking the Power, Producing the Promise,* and *Keys to Understanding Soul Ties, Soul Power, and Soulish Prayers.*)

Soul ties – Whenever a person enters into a wrong agreement with someone that appears to offer a personal benefit to each person, there is a connection made between their souls. This causes a form of co-dependency between the ones making the wrong agreements. In a soul tie, one soul is always stronger than the other soul, even if it starts out as a minor difference. The longer the soul tie exists, the more power the dominant soul is able to assert over the other. Soul ties are generally involved in acts of extreme influence, control, and manipulation. Soul ties can be severed and broken through right prayer. (See chapters on Soul Ties and Soul Power in *Breaking the Power, Producing the Promise,* and *Keys to Understanding Soul Ties, Soul Power, and Soulish Prayers.*)

Spirit – Our spirits were orphans when we were born into this world because of the severing of the spirit-to-Spirit connection that Adam and Eve lost with the Father in the Garden of Eden when they sinned. This is why the Bible said that we must be "born again," so that our spirits can be connected to the Spirit of their Creator. The born-again human spirit is no longer an orphan then, but is connected to its spiritual Father.

Stronghold – The logic, reasoning, arguments, rationalization, justification, and denial that our souls use to defend their positions and beliefs, right or wrong. Strongholds in the mind are created whenever we try to make excuses for why we have disobeyed God. One example of a stronghold and its consequences is found in Ephesians 4:26-27, especially in the *Amplified Bible* version. Ephesians 4:26 tells us to never let the sun go down on our anger. God knew we would get angry as long as our soul remains unsurrendered to Him, but He has commanded us to deal with our anger, release it, and forgive before one day is over. Ephesians 4:27 tells us that if we don't, we have just given the devil room, opportunity, and a foothold in our lives.

Tripartite being – Man's makeup of body, soul, and spirit.

Unhealed hurts – One of the three sources of all the pain and struggles within our souls. Unhealed hurts are birthed whenever we lose something good that we had received and needed in order to be whole. For example, if we had always felt secure and were unexpectedly violated and traumatized, we would lose all sense of security. We would have an unhealed hurt that only God could heal to make us whole. (Read more about Unhealed Hurts in chapters in *Breaking the Power.*)

Unmet needs – One of the three sources of all the pain and struggles within our souls. Unmet needs are birthed when we don't get all we need to be whole. For example, if we did not get the love we needed in order to be whole, we may grow up with a drive to keep seeking love, even in the wrong places. We would have an unmet need for love that no human, no possession, and no amount of fame could ever meet. Only God can meet that need and make us whole. (Read more about Unmet Needs in chapters in *Breaking the Power*.)

Unresolved issues – This source of pain and struggle within our souls is birthed when we do not know how to productively process our unmet needs and unhealed hurts, and they become issues and questions that drive us to find out why bad things happened to us. Only God can ever resolve these kinds of issues, answer these kinds of questions, and make us whole. (Read more about Unresolved Issues in chapters in *Breaking the Power*.)

Will – That part of our souls that has the ability to enforce decisions, provide the drive to keep pressing on, and to bully other people.

Wrong agreements – When wrong agreements are made between two people, the enemy shows up with his power. When wrong atreements are made corporately (by groups of people) because of strong reactions to injustices and persecution and then are passed on from generation to generation, territorial spirits have a right to set up powerful domains over such areas and feed off those wrong agreements. Example: The Prince of Persia was a territorial spirit with a domain over Babylon where the Israelites were in captivity. It had a right to be there because the Israelites were constantly grumbling and making wrong agreements about God and how He had let them down. (Read more about the power of wrong agreements in *Producing the Promise*, and *Keys to Understanding Soul Ties, Soul Power, and Soulish Prayers*.)

Wrong behaviors – When long-term reactions coming up out of the three original sources (see unhealed, unmet, and unresolved above) of all of our struggles and pain manage to get past our souls' layers of self-defense, they manifest themselves in mental, emotional, and even physical symptoms of distress. Examples: pain, fear, insecurity, distrust, neediness, etc. When these symptoms are being driven up into our consciousness with great force, the soul begins to seek behaviors that will take the edge off, pacify, and decrease the fear and pain. The soul does not distinguish between wrong and right behaviors to act out. It seeks only to drive the person to act out whatever brought relief at some point and time in that person's life.

For further information on speaking engagements, seminars, Teachers' Training schools, radio and television interviews, U.S. and international itineraries, teaching tapes and CDs, videos, DVDs, Long-Distance Teachers' Training by DVD, and monthly e-newsletters, please contact:

Liberty Savard Ministries, Inc.
(a non-profit organization)
P.O. Box 41260
Sacramento, CA 95841-0260

Office phone: 916-721-7770
Facsimile: 916-721-8889

E-mail: liberty@libertysavard.com
Web site: www.libertysavard.com

THE KEYS OF THE KINGDOM TRILOGY
by Liberty Savard

Shattering Your Strongholds
Shattering Your Strongholds Workkbook
Derribe sus Murallas
(*Shattering Your Strongholds* – Spanish)
Breaking the Power
Breaking the Power Workbook
Producing the Promise

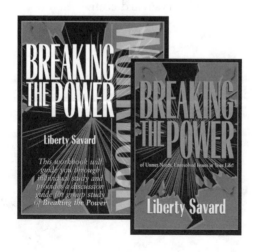

ALSO AVAILABLE FROM BRIDGE-LOGOS

KEYS TO UNDERSTANDING "Minibook Series"

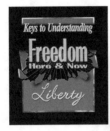 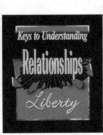 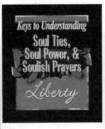 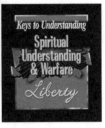

Keys to Understanding Freedom Here and now
Keys to Understanding Relationships
Keys to Understanding Soul Ties, Soul Power and Soulish Prayers
Keys to Understanding Spiritual Understanding and Warfare

Fear Not America
Apples of Gold in Baskets of Silver

And Liberty's latest ...
BEYOND Shattered Strongholds